G. J. PINWELL: 'Shadow and Substance'
[*Wayside Posies*]

ILLUSTRATORS
OF THE
EIGHTEEN SIXTIES

An Illustrated Survey of the Work of 58 British Artists

Forrest Reid

DOVER PUBLICATIONS, INC., NEW YORK

Published in Canada by General Publishing Company, Ltd., 30 Lesmill Road, Don Mills, Toronto, Ontario.
Published in the United Kingdom by Constable and Company, Ltd., 10 Orange Street, London WC 2.

This Dover edition, first published in 1975, is an unabridged republication of the work originally published under the title *Illustrators of the Sixties* by Faber & Gwyer Limited, London, in 1928. The present edition is published by special arrangement with Faber and Faber Ltd., London.

International Standard Book Number: 0-486-23121-6
Library of Congress Catalog Card Number: 74-12539

Manufactured in the United States of America
Dover Publications, Inc.
180 Varick Street
New York, N. Y. 10014

NOTE

I WISH to express my gratitude to those who have helped me in the preparation of this book. For nearly all the illustrations I am indebted to the generosity of Mr. Harold Hartley and Mr. J. N. Hart, who placed their collections at my disposal, lending me either the original blocks, from which electros have been made, or proofs of the engravings. Apart from this, they have given me many valuable suggestions springing from their expert knowledge of the subject. Mr. Gilbert Dalziel and Mr. T. Balston also have taken the kindest interest in the book. Mr. Hart read the manuscript and Mr. Balston the proofs. Likewise, my thanks are due to Mr. Michael Sadleir, Mr. Richard de la Mare, Mr. J. N. Bryson, Sir John Murray, Mr. A. W. Browne, Messrs. Ward, Lock and Co., Messrs. F. Warne and Co., Messrs. William Blackwood and Sons, Messrs. Macmillan and Co., The Religious Tract Society, and The Society for Promoting Christian Knowledge, who have all in one way or another come to my assistance.

CONTENTS

LIST OF ILLUSTRATIONS

The numbers given in this list are the numbers of the pages facing which the illustrations appear. In a few instances two or more illustrations will be found to face the same page.

[ix]

[xi]

[xii]

[1] Sandys was dissatisfied with this block. 'The Sailor's Bride' that appeared in *Once a Week*, 1861, was cut by Swain.

CHAPTER I

PROLEGOMENA

HAVING grouped the following notes and divagations under the general title of *Illustrators of the Sixties*, I must explain that the word ' Sixties ' has been used here to describe a movement rather than a decade. Even Gleeson White's admirable monograph[1]—though its design, as a kind of huge annotated catalogue, made a strict time limit necessary— prolongs the decade to a period of fifteen years, from 1855 to 1870. But many of our illustrators did not cease to make designs in 1870, and some of them began to make them before 1855, therefore, in a book which was undertaken less as an essay in art-criticism and in bibliography than as the chronicle of a hobby, it seemed best to follow the impulse of the collector, while always remembering that the collection itself is a collection of the wood engravings of the sixties.

And it remains true, though the work of Charles Keene, Arthur Hughes, du Maurier, Tenniel, William Small and others was prolonged over several decades, that the vast majority of the finest and most character- istic drawings were produced between 1860 and 1870. This was the really great period, during which the output of first-rate work was remarkable. It would have been more remarkable still had not drawing on wood been regarded by several of our artists only as an interesting experiment, and by others as a method of keeping the pot boiling when the more serious work of painting failed to do so. This is why we have so few designs by Rossetti, by Burne-Jones, by Holman Hunt, by Ford Madox Brown, by Whistler, by Watts, by Pettie, by Orchardson, by Sandys. Nevertheless they all did make designs, often wonderful designs, Whistler, as usual, in his own manner, and Sandys more orthodoxly, achieving perfection. Millais and Fred Walker, on the other hand, found time for a good deal of illustration, and Pinwell, that strangely attractive and uncertain genius, was even more prolific. It was Pinwell's ambition to be a great painter, but the master- piece over which he had pondered so long was never finished. He died when he was thirty-three, and of that group of artists with which we are

---

[1] *English Illustration: The Sixties.* By Gleeson White. Constable, 1897. Third im- pression, 1906.

[1]

concerned his was not the only tragically brief career. Though he lived on till 1905, we lose sight of Simeon Solomon when he is thirty-two; Paul Gray was twenty when he died, Matthew Lawless twenty-seven, Morten thirty, Fred Walker thirty-five, Houghton thirty-nine.

A school of illustrators—in many cases the drawings they made were afterwards expanded into large paintings in oil or water colour. To-day their methods and ideals have fallen into temporary disrepute. In spite of the fact that most of the masterpieces of the world are illustrations—if not of literature at any rate of life—illustration has come to be regarded as a dubious mixture of art and something that is not art. Probably the lectures and writings of Whistler did more than anything else to create this prejudice, though if one desired to choose a picture completely expressive of that spirit of poetic naturalism which was essentially the spirit of the sixties one could find no better example than Whistler's ' Piano '. In ' The Piano ' he does exactly what Pinwell was always trying to do, if only occasionally with success: as a drawing on wood, engraved by Dalziel or Swain in *A Round of Days* or *Wayside Posies*, it would be entirely in place, entirely typical of the school that immediately followed the Pre-Raphaelites. And ' The Little White Girl ', that too is an illustration, for Swinburne's poem *Before the Mirror*:

Face fallen and white throat lifted,
    With sleepless eye
She sees old loves that drifted,
    She knew not why,
Old loves and faded fears
Float down a stream that hears
    The flowing of all men's tears beneath the sky.

It is true that the words were written after the picture had been painted, but so, in many cases, were the words for our wood engravings, the drawings being submitted to the writer, who found or tried to find his inspiration in them.

The fact that a picture may be devoid of aesthetic value and yet, because of some story or sentiment in it, give pleasure to those indifferent to form and colour, means nothing. If the sentiment is false or cheap it is bad, that is all. Take Ghirlandajo's famous portrait of the bottle-nosed old man and his grandson:—does not much of its charm lie in the relation of trust and affection that obviously exists between the old man and the child; lie, that is to say, in its sentiment? It is certainly there, the dreaded quality, yet, being the expression of an emotion that is true and fine, it becomes a part of the picture's beauty; in other words, possesses a definitely aesthetic value.

[2]

WHISTLER: ' The Trial Sermon '
[*Good Words*, 1862]

To oppose this point of view Whistler misrepresents it. ' My picture of a " Harmony in Grey and Gold " ', he writes in *The Gentle Art of Making Enemies,* ' is an illustration of my meaning—a snow scene with a single black figure and a lighted tavern. I care nothing for the past, present or future of the black figure, placed there because the black was wanted at that spot. All that I know is that my combination of grey and gold is the basis of the picture. Now this is precisely what my friends cannot grasp. They say, " Why not call it ' Trotty Veck ', and sell it for a round harmony of golden guineas ? " naively acknowledging that without baptism there is no market. But even commercially this stocking of your shop with the goods of another would be indecent—custom alone has made it dignified. Not even the popularity of Dickens should be invoked to lend an adventitious aid to art of another kind from his. I should hold it a vulgar and meretricious trick to excite people about Trotty Veck when, if they really could care for pictorial art at all, they would know that the picture should have its own merit, and not depend upon dramatic or legendary or local interest. As music is the poetry of sound, so is painting the poetry of sight, and the subject matter has nothing to do with harmony of sound or of colour.'

All this, however, is beside the point, particularly the last statement, for if a picture be not devoid of any intellectual, spiritual, and emotional content, its subject *must* contribute to the appeal it makes. It is true we may have Manet's picture of a dish of peaches, in which we are mysteriously soothed and gratified by what is nothing more than a rhythm of tone and pattern; but is that to deny the value of the profound imaginative penetration that has gone to the making of Rembrandt's later portraits (which are portraits of the soul as much as of the body), or to suggest that it is the function of art to present life that is not 'still' as if it were? This penetration, this gift of imaginative sympathy, is an essential part of the artist's equipment, of his genius, and without it that genius would be so much the poorer. As a matter of fact, though in theory Whistler seems to be trying to divorce art from life, in practice, in his finest things, the theory is forgotten. He exhibits the portrait of his mother in the Royal Academy as an ' Arrangement in Grey and Black ', but that does not prevent it from being the portrait of his mother, nor deprive it of that spiritual emotion from which all great art must spring, and lacking which it would really have been merely an arrangement in grey and black, leaving us as cold as the cleverness that had invented it.

CHAPTER II

ON COLLECTING, COLLECTIONS, AND SELECTIONS

O NE must make a start somewhere, and it is customary to regard the publication of Allingham's *Music Master* in 1855 as marking the beginning of the revival of the art of English illustration. The illustrators of *The Music Master* are Arthur Hughes, Rossetti, and Millais, but, though the Pre-Raphaelites did much to influence, and prepare the way for, the later men, the artistic movement associated with the sixties is by no means a Pre-Raphaelite one. Turning over any collection of drawings of that period one cannot fail to be struck by their variety: nobody will mistake a Charles Keene or a Houghton for a Millais or a Sandys. On the other hand, in spite of a marked individuality of method and vision, many of the artists did exercise a mutual influence upon one another; and of course echoes from the earlier schools of design reached on into the sixties— the first drawings of Fred Walker are reminiscent of John Gilbert and even of William Harvey.

Hall's *Book of British Ballads*, for which Tenniel made a few designs, dates back to 1842; *Undine*, illustrated entirely by him, to 1846, and *Aesop's Fables* to 1848. Their dates probably will not deter the collector from adding them to his shelves, and the *Aesop* is in fact one of the rarer and more expensive volumes, costing from a pound to thirty shillings. This, it is true, is not a great deal in excess of the published price, but then most of the books of our period can be acquired for a few shillings each, though their intrinsic value may far exceed that of the *Aesop*. Prices, indeed, here as elsewhere, are no guide to the real value of a book. Commercially, the *Aesop's Fables* has benefited from Tenniel's association with *Alice's Adventures in Wonderland*—that is all. Nor does the cheapness of other books imply that they are plentiful, or, in good condition, easy to find; it is simply the result of caprice, of the strange fact that collecting wood engravings of the sixties has never become fashionable. If *Wayside Posies*, *Touches of Nature*, Jean Ingelow's *Poems*, and Millais's *Parables* are rare to-day, it is even partly because they have *not* been sought after, and therefore fail to interest booksellers, who relegate them to damp lumber-rooms where they lie forgotten, or to sixpenny stalls where they are purchased by the artless for the sake of their reading matter. Another cause of the steadily diminishing supply lies in that lamentable method of binding which consisted in fastening the plates into the cover with a solution of gutta-percha. After a few years the solution perished and all the pages became loose. It is true, the gutta-percha method was only employed with the more elaborately printed volumes, but in books like Millais's *Parables*, Charles Keene's *Our People*, Houghton's *Home Thoughts and Home Scenes*, Birket Foster's *Pictures of English Landscape*, the pages are really thin boards, and the only satisfactory way of securing them would have been to attach them to linen strips which *could* have been sewn. In *Dalziel's Bible Gallery* and one or two other volumes this actually has been done, but such exceptions are few, and in most cases the collector before completing his bargain had better make sure none of the plates is missing, for even though the binding may look perfectly fresh the original possessor, once the contents became loose, is just as likely as not to have extracted his favourites.

A further destructive agent is the nursery artist. This little pest was ever ready with his brushes and his box of water-colours. When he has adorned only a single design in a rare book it is tempting to try to remove his handiwork, but personally I have found such efforts unavailing, and it is better to make up one's mind never to buy an imperfect book no matter how many years one may have been searching vainly for a sound copy.

To set over against these unfortunate results of neglect we have the happy one that our hunting-ground at present is open to all. The rarer Cruikshanks, Gilrays, and Rowlandsons are treasured under lock and key and sold at high prices, but here are things aesthetically much more desirable yet within the reach of everybody—things, too, whose whereabouts is not to be discovered by a mere question, but which the hunter must track down for himself. Those volumes that have acquired a sale-room value are few: the Tenniel I have just mentioned is one of them, Allingham's *Music Master* is another, Thornbury's *Legendary Ballads* a third, and yet none of these is actually among the very scarcest of our books. I searched for many years for a copy of George MacDonald's *Dealings with the Fairies*, illustrated by Arthur Hughes, and advertised for it more than once without getting a reply; but in the end, in a shop in Eastbourne, dumped on the floor among a heap of Sunday school prizes, I came upon a perfect copy which cost me ninepence. In the same heap was *Lilliput Levée*, with Millais's and Pinwell's illustrations.

I am taking it for granted that the collector wants the first editions. If, like Gleeson White, he is indifferent to editions when the state of the prints is satisfactory, his task will be so much the easier. But the desire for ' firsts ', I think, can here for once be defended on rational grounds, since nearly invariably (there are exceptions which I shall note) the earliest printings from the blocks are the best, and certainly some of the late printings are markedly inferior. Now and again, indeed, in a very late issue they are hardly recognizable. I have before me *A Picture Book* published by Routledge in 1879, in which the designs, for the most part by William Small, have, through too frequent service, lost every quality they once possessed.

It might be as well here to mention a few other books for which the collector may expect to be asked a comparatively high price. Tennyson's *Poems* (Moxon, 1857) (the reprint is cheap enough); *Dalziel's Arabian Nights*, either in the parts or in the first two-volume edition of 1865; *Dalziel's Bible Gallery* (1881); the first issues of *Orley Farm* and other novels of Trollope, illustrated by Millais; the first issues of *Our Mutual Friend* and *Edwin Drood*; *Tom Brown's Schooldays* (1869). The novels of Trollope and Dickens in the original parts, with the wrappers and advertisements, are of course extremely expensive, and when we come to the tales of Lewis Carroll we encroach on the preserves of millionaires and their agents. Moreover, the desire for a first edition of *Alice's Adventures in Wonderland* can hardly be defended from our present point of view, since its distinguishing feature lies in the defective printing of the illustrations. It was because of this defective printing that the edition was withdrawn from sale: it is for a series of printer's failures that one pays one's three hundred pounds, or whatever the market price may be.[1] Reduced to an average, I should say that my own collection of books of the sixties cost from half a crown to three shillings a volume.

The bound volumes of magazines cost less, and, though these must have been issued in vastly larger editions, it is to be remembered that here the number lost through scrapping—particularly during the last years of the war—has been proportionately greater. It is still easy to collect complete sets of *The Cornhill, Good Words*, and *The Sunday Magazine*; not quite so easy to collect a set of *Once a Week, London Society, Cassell's Magazine, The Leisure Hour*, and *The Quiver*. *The Argosy, The Churchman's Family Magazine, Saint Paul's Magazine*, and *Good Words for the Young* are becoming distinctly rare; while *Dark Blue* and *The Shilling Magazine* will only be discovered by a stroke of luck. The last two publications, however (both very short-lived), contain little of interest with the exception of a couple of masterpieces—Ford Madox Brown's design for Gabriel Rossetti's *Down Stream*, and Sandys's more famous drawing for Christina's *Amor Mundi*.

[1] Mr. Balston tells me that this edition was sent to the U.S.A. where, with a cancel title, it became the first American edition.

[8]

F. SANDYS: ' The Sailor's Bride '
[Unpublished]

The magazines present a difficult problem. They are essential to a collection that pretends to any degree of completeness, but on the other hand they take up a great deal of room, and it is extremely tedious to have to turn over several hundred pages for the sake of perhaps a dozen, perhaps only two or three, drawings. To those whose shelf room is limited the temptation to extract the prints worth extracting becomes almost irresistible, and so far as the collector himself is concerned this course is undoubtedly the more satisfactory. Not only will he be able to classify his drawings, but the drawings themselves will look much better when mounted separately on white boards than when wedged between unattractive slabs of letterpress. The margin of the board supplies at once a foil to the tint of the paper and a frame, showing the whole picture to the best advantage. Yet, to mutilate a volume of *The Cornhill* or *Good Words* is an act of vandalism, to say nothing of the really rare magazines. In the case of a magazine like *Good Words for the Young* it is to be hoped that nobody will think of doing so, any more than of cutting up a volume of *Punch*. After all, the original setting has an interest of its own, and as time passes this interest increases. For this reason I prefer sets issued in the publisher's cloth binding to those re-bound in the more durable half-calf. Most interesting of all, of course, are the original monthly issues, which offer a gold mine of publishers' advertisements, as a rule infinitely more thrilling than the contents of the magazine proper.

Suppose, however, what seems most unlikely, that the collector decides *not* to burrow into the dusty catacombs of extinct periodicals, he may still bring together a fairly representative selection of their contents by means of the following publications. These contain selections made at the time (for the most part by the proprietors of the magazines themselves), and though they include only a fraction of the work actually produced that fraction possesses the advantage of particularly careful printing and good paper.

The first of such selections was *The Cornhill Gallery*, published in 1864 by Smith, Elder, and Co., and reprinted in 1865. It is a handsome folio, with the designs printed on boards on one side only and without letterpress, the titles of the drawings and the names of the artists being given in an index. All the designs are taken from *The Cornhill Magazine*, and the engravers are Dalziel, Linton, and Swain. A quotation from the preface will show how seriously the 'art side' of their magazines was regarded in those days by editors and publishers:

'In offering *The Cornhill Gallery* to the notice of the Public, the Publishers have been influenced by two considerations:

'1. A desire to render an act of justice to the eminent artists of whose talents they have availed themselves in the illustration of *The Cornhill Magazine*, by exhibiting, with the aid of the finest printing, the real quality of those illustrations, as Works of Art. The impressions of the Pictures which have appeared in the various numbers of *The Cornhill Magazine* were unavoidably subject to the disadvantage of being printed from electrotype casts taken from the Wood-blocks, and with the great speed necessary to insure the punctual publication of a Periodical Work which enjoys the favour of a very large circulation. *The Wood-blocks themselves have now been printed from for the first time*, in the production of *The Cornhill Gallery*; and the Publishers trust that, with the very careful and skilful aid of the Brothers Dalziel, the Pictures are now produced in a style which will place them in their proper rank as Works of Art.'

The Cornhill Gallery was published 'at the almost nominal price of one guinea ', and contained one hundred engravings, of which twenty-eight are by Millais, illustrating *Framley Parsonage* and *The Small House at Allington*; twenty-seven by Fred Walker, illustrating *Philip*, *Denis Duval*, and some shorter tales; twenty-five by Frederick Leighton, all but one, a picture of ' The Great God Pan ', illustrating *Romola*; two by Sandys; three by du Maurier; one by Noel Paton; and the remaining thirteen, of little interest, by Thackeray and G. A. Sala.

Two years later Strahan published a similar work, except that a smooth yellowish paper was employed instead of the boards of *The Cornhill Gallery*, and that this time all the drawings were by Millais. Of the eighty wood-engravings contained in *Millais's Illustrations* (Strahan, 1866) twenty-five are from *Once a Week*, thirteen from *Good Words*, sixteen from *Orley Farm*, and the remainder from Tennyson's *Poems*, *Lays of the Holy Land*, *The Home Affections*, *Papers for Thoughtful Girls*, and Willmott's *Poets of the Nineteenth Century*, with, as a bonus, three hitherto unpublished designs—one for the title-page, and the others entitled respectively *Watching* and *Pick-a-back*. I am assuming that the publisher's description of *Pick-a-back* as an unpublished drawing is correct, though in *Studies for Stories* (1866), a work issued anonymously by Jean Ingelow, I find this very drawing, illustrating a tale called *The Stolen Treasure*. The date—1866—is the same as that of *Millais's Illustrations*.

To be perfectly frank, for the bibliographical notes given in these pages I can claim no more than that I have tried to make them as accurate as possible. Often one is working more or less in the dark. The title-pages of the books themselves give little or no information. Sometimes they are undated, and almost invariably the editions are unrecorded. Catalogues cannot be relied on, for it was a common practice to issue a book in the autumn of one year and date it with the date of the year following. Gleeson

White, who was a pioneer in the field, in his invaluable *English Illustration: the Sixties* gives much useful information, but as for the dates suggested light-heartedly by the Brothers Dalziel in their own account of their work, these are so unreliable that the collector would be wiser to ignore them altogether. In an appendix to their *Record* they furnish a bibliography of the books published under their supervision and also of those in which they assisted, but a single instance will suffice to show how little this side of their subject interested them. They give the date of J. D. Watson's first drawings in *Good Words* as 1865 (this, to begin with, is an error), and add that on the strength of these drawings they commissioned him to make a hundred designs for an edition of *The Pilgrim's Progress*. Their bibliography gives the date of this particular edition of *The Pilgrim's Progress* as 1863: the actual date of it is 1861.

The third of our magazine selections is *Touches of Nature* (Strahan, 1867). Gleeson White gives the date as 1866, but I have never come across a copy with an earlier imprint than 1867, which is that, moreover, of the copy in the British Museum. Probably, however, the book, post-dated, was actually issued in time for the Christmas trade of 1866. With the exception of the exquisite vignette by J. Pettie on the title-page, which is taken from *Wordsworth's Poems for the Young*, all the illustrations are from Strahan's magazines, *Good Words*, *The Sunday Magazine*, and *The Argosy*. Of the ninety-eight full-page drawings three are by Sandys, eleven by Fred Walker,[1] four by Millais, five by Houghton, eight by Pinwell, three by Lawless, three by Pettie, three by North, two by du Maurier, seven by J. D. Watson, four by Tenniel, thirteen by Robert Barnes, two by H. H. Armstead, four by William Small, two by Paul Gray, two by T. Graham, two by J. Mahoney, two by Edward Hughes, six by R. P. Leitch, three by J. Wolf, and one each by Holman Hunt, Charles Keene, T. Morten, F. J. Shields, T. Dalziel, M. E. Edwards, Marcus Stone, Orchardson, and W. J. Linton. It is a collection of the greatest variety and interest, though the page of letterpress that faces each drawing might well have been omitted.

With *Pictures of Society* (Sampson Low, 1866) we descend the scale perceptibly. Here, amid a few designs of first-rate importance, there are many that are frankly bad. In this case the pictures have been selected from the files of James Hogg's magazines, *London Society*, and *The Churchman's Family Magazine*, and amongst them will be found Sandys's famous 'Waiting Time'—re-named 'Lancashire's Lesson'. The book, a small quarto, is almost as much an anthology of literature as of art, but the literature is

---

[1] In the index ten drawings are given to Walker and three to du Maurier, but 'Bad News', on page 68, given to du Maurier, is really Walker's, being one of the *Oswald Cray* drawings.

[13]

uniformly feeble, in spite of the fact that ' a great many well-known pens have been employed to supplement the talent already at the Editor's disposal '. Curiously enough, with the exceptions of Sandys and Matthew Lawless, the artists who prove the most interesting are not those to whom naturally we first turn. Neither Millais nor Fred Walker is at his best, and du Maurier has suffered terribly at the hands of Harral the engraver. But J. D. Watson *is* at his best, and for five of his designs alone—' Blankton Weir ', ' Too Late ', ' Prayer ', ' Evenings Long Ago ', and ' Thinking of Heaven '—the book would be worth possessing. The Walter Cranes must have required some ' living down ' on that artist's part, but there are two excellent Mortens, ' Waiting by the River ' and ' In the Belfry ', and an unusually good Charles Green, ' Suspense '. The ninety-five engravings have in fact been brought together without discrimination. The editor and publishers assure us that they are the best, but sufficient light is thrown on this statement when we find that ' the best ' does not include the work of Charles Keene, and does include that of such draughtsmen as Keyl and Godwin. Of the drawings of the more important artists, three are by Millais, eleven by J. D. Watson, two by Lawless, four by A. W. Cooper, three by du Maurier, six by George Thomas, two by Walter Crane, nine by M. E. Edwards, five by Morten, and one each by C. H. Bennett, C. W. Cope, Pickersgill, W. P. Burton, T. Dalziel, J. C. Horsley, Fred Walker, Sandys, E. J. Poynter, Marcus Stone, and Charles Green. *Pictures of Society* is one of the scarcer books of the period, and, though its contents are so uneven, masterpieces like Sandys's ' Waiting Time ' and Lawless's ' Silent Chamber ' more than compensate for a good deal of hack work.

Idyllic Pictures (Cassell, Petter, and Galpin, 1867) follows closely on the lines of *Pictures of Society*, but it is more tastefully produced, and if it contains nothing to equal ' The Waiting Time ', or perhaps even ' The Silent Chamber ', the general level is higher than in the earlier volume. The drawings this time have all been chosen from *The Quiver*, and we find many of them, under new titles, masquerading as illustrations for poems with which they have nothing whatever to do. *Idyllic Pictures* is an even rarer book than *Pictures of Society*. It contains only fifty wood engravings, but they are exceptionally interesting, all the artists doing themselves justice and occasionally more than justice. Since for some inexplicable reason their names are not given in the index, and the drawings themselves are not always even initialed, a list may be found useful.

' Cousin Lucy '. Paul Gray (his finest drawing).

' Night and Morning '. R. Barnes.

' Echoings from Faded Flowers '. Pinwell.

' A Reverie'. Paul Gray.

WHISTLER: 'Count Burkhardt'

[*Once a Week,* 1862]

'By the Dead'. Paul Gray.
'Out of the Deep'. C. J. Staniland.
'Between the Cliffs'. William Small (a masterpiece).
'Truer Lights'. M. E. E(dwards).
'Jeannie's Blue E'e'. H. Cameron.
'My Ariel'. Small.
'The Sailor's Valentine'. Pinwell.
'A Lullaby'. M. E. E.
'Morning'. M. E. E.
'Under the Lamp'. Barnes.
'October'. F. Sandys.
'Margaret's Birthday'. M. E. E.
'Izaak Walton'. T. Morten.
'The Angel's Song'. Pinwell.
'The Fisher Lads'. Staniland.
'Hassan'. Morten.
'A Retrospect'. Small.
'Wee Rosie Mary'. Houghton.
'On the Wings of the Wind'. Small.
'On the Shore'. M. E. E.
'Over the Hills'. Small.
'No Hope?'. Barnes.

'Babble'. Small.
'A Message from the Sea'. Staniland.
'Seeing Granny'. M. E. E.
'The Organ Man'. Pinwell.
'The Aged'. Cameron.
'Unrequited'. M. E. E.
'An Old Story'. Small.
'The Hostage'. George Thomas.
'Mary's Wedding Day'. Paul Gray.
'My Sister'. M. E. E.
'The Empty Cage'. M. E. E.
'The Captain'. Houghton.
'Going Away'. M. E. E.
'On the River'. M. E. E.
'Recollections'. M. E. E.
'Straight On!'. Pinwell.
'Church Bells'. Small.
'Shadows on the Stream'. M. E. E.
'St. Martin'. Houghton.
'Wounded'. John Lawson.
'Sowing and Reaping'. Houghton.
'The Holy Light'. Paul Gray.
'The Betrayed City'. Staniland.
'Beauty in Winter'. R. P. Leitch.

Thornbury's *Legendary Ballads* (1876) is a book indispensable to the collector, for here, printed on excellent paper and with every care, are eighty-two of the famous *Once a Week* designs. Had a further engraving been substituted for each of Thornbury's poems, there would have been nothing comparable to this volume among the English art books of the last century. But one must not look a gift-horse in the mouth, and the poet's preface is disarmingly modest. It is also something of a curiosity, not so much because of the passage in which his old schoolfellow E. J. Poynter receives special praise for a design executed by Sandys, as because of an ingenuous allusion to ' a pleasant collaboration ' between the artists and the author. ' In this case,' the latter thinks, ' there has been a mutual sympathy.' One would like to know how the artists themselves described the particular ' sympathy ' which dragged their work out of its proper context and tacked on to it absurd titles and quotations—what Whistler, for instance, thought of his marvellous drawing for *The Relief Fund in Lancashire* being offered unblushingly as an illustration for *Oh, should I know him if he came?*, or Sandys of his powerful ' Helen and Cassandra ' figuring as ' Ceres Seeking for Proserpine '? Of course a good many of Thornbury's verses did appear in *Once a Week*, and in such cases the illustration was actually made for the text, or vice versa; but to use Sandys's superb 'Harold Harfagr' to illustrate some wretched doggerel about *The Labours of Thor*, and Lawson's 'Theseus and Ariadne' to illustrate a Norse ballad, is surely to stretch sympathy rather far. The eighty-two drawings in *Legendary Ballads* represent only a tithe of the first-rate work in *Once a Week* (of the matchless designs of Charles Keene, for instance, we have only a single example); still we are very glad to have them. M. J. Lawless heads the list with twenty drawings. There are ten by J. Lawson, nine by Sandys, eight by Pinwell, seven by Morten, five by Small, four by Whistler, three by Tenniel, three by Eltze, two by Fred Walker, and one each by Skelton, Charles Green, Houghton, Fairfield, du Maurier, E. H. Corbould, Charles Keene, T. R. Macquoid, J. D. Watson, Townley Green, and A. Riou.

On the 4th of December 1869 there appeared the first number of *The Graphic*. With *The Graphic* is associated the rise of a new school of artists; nevertheless many of the older men worked for it, and in 1876, the year of the *Legendary Ballads*, was issued *The Graphic Portfolio*, 'a selection from the Admired Engravings which have appeared in *The Graphic*, and a description of the art of wood engraving'. It is a cumbrous volume, and without doubt the new spirit prevails in it. The majority of *The Graphic* illustrations were topical in nature, though the serial story was illustrated week by week and there were occasional pictures the subjects of which were not drawn from passing events. Of the *Graphic Portfolio's* fifty designs the greater number are by artists whose work is permanently associated with the sixties. The place of honour is given to George Thomas's 'Portrait of Queen Victoria', drawn from life. Luke Fildes supplies 'Houseless and Hungry', a singularly powerful drawing admirably engraved, also an illustration for Charles Reade's story *The Wandering Heir*, which had appeared in *The Graphic Christmas Number* for 1872, and two other drawings, 'Under Fire' and 'One Touch of Nature', from sketches supplied by Sydney Hall. Houghton is represented by a couple of scenes from his *Graphic America*; Pinwell has only one drawing, and it is not characteristic; but William Small has three West of Ireland sketches, and three others, 'After the Last Fence', 'The Old Coaching Days Revived', and a brilliantly decorative 'November Fog in London'. Of the two du Maurier's 'The March Past' is in his *Punch* manner, a charming thing, remarkable for its rich velvety blacks and the fine realization of texture in the children's clothing. 'The Rival Grandpas and Grandmas', an out-of-doors group, has even greater beauty, showing his work when it was still influenced by the Pre-Raphaelite ideal. The light on the leaves of the creeper on the wall of the old house is exquisitely suggested, and the grouping is most graceful. 'In the drawings of Mr. Small's school', says a publisher's note, 'the engraver has himself in great

[18]

measure to create the texture of the illustration.   Here, on the contrary, the
cutting of the wood is almost mechanical, the drawing having been made with
simple pen and ink lines, which form a complete guide to the engraver.'
' St. Valentine's Day ' shows M. E. Edwards at her best; ' Dolly Varden ',
by the same artist, is less interesting.   Charles Green has four capital drawings; F. W. Lawson two; Hubert Herkomer four; and Helen Patterson
two, including an excellent illustration for Victor Hugo's romance *Ninety-
Three.*

Two or three other books remain to be noted, for though published
later they are connected with our period.   *English Society at Home* (1880) is a
folio volume containing sixty-three of George du Maurier's *Punch* designs
printed on India paper.   The selection must have been made by the artist
himself, nevertheless it is disappointing.   The aesthetic value of the drawings obviously has been only a secondary consideration, for the early and
by far the most beautiful work is not represented at all.   The point of view
governing the book is very much that governing Henry James's essay
on du Maurier, in which the importance of dialogue and situation is so
stressed that one seems to be reading an appreciation of a novelist of manners
rather than a black and white artist.   And no doubt the observer of character,
the story-teller latent in du Maurier, *was* what appealed most to Henry
James, but one is a little surprised to find the artist himself adopting a similar
standard of values.   *A Legend of Camelot* (1898) contains some of his fantastic *Punch* drawings, yet here again, with the exception of the five pictures
of the *Legend*, we find few of our favourites.

A far more important book than either of these is *Our People* (Bradbury,
Agnew, 1881), in which we get four hundred and four of Charles Keene's
immortal *Punch* drawings, and, by a curious mistake, a picture of Corbould's.
(It will be found on page 131, entitled ' Compliments of the Season '.)   The
grouping of two or three designs on a single page does not show them to the
best advantage, but since so many of the earliest were ruined on their first
appearance in *Punch* by hasty printing—the sheets having been folded
before the ink was dry—we are rejoiced to get them properly produced
even if they do look a little crowded.   *Our People* is among the collector's
really precious books: the wood engravings in it cover a period of many
years—from the fifties till the date of publication—and represent more or
less adequately at least one side of the artist's genius.

CHAPTER III

SOME PRECURSORS

JOHN GILBERT; BIRKET FOSTER; TENNIEL

CHIEF among the men of the sixties who may be described as precursors, since they were working before that date and remained un-
influenced either by the Pre-Raphaelites or the school of naturalistic
artists that succeeded them, are John Gilbert, Birket Foster, and Tenniel.

I. JOHN GILBERT[1] (1817-1897)

John Gilbert was the most prolific black and white artist of his time.
He drew for *Punch* in its early days (the design for the fourth cover—1843—
is his); he drew for *The London Journal*; his work appeared in most of the
illustrated books of the fifties; when *Old Moore's Almanac* was planned by
Ingram, Gilbert was to illustrate it; and for *The Illustrated London News*
alone he is reputed to have made some thirty thousand drawings. This
probably is an exaggeration, but he undoubtedly possessed a marvellous
facility, and it is said would make a full-page drawing on the block while
the messenger waited. According to Harrison Weir, on one occasion
two-thirds of all the drawings which appeared in that week's *London News*
were Gilbert's, and when in a particular hurry he would even unscrew the
squares of which the wood-block was composed and send the parts piecemeal
to the engraver, actually not seeing the whole until it was cut. Such tales,
it must be confessed, arouse only a qualified admiration: art, after all, is
not a feat of legerdemain: but to a publisher who had been held up for
weeks by Rossetti's methods it is easy to understand how meritorious the
dispatch and punctuality of Gilbert must have appeared. The Dalziels,
in their *Record*, give an example of it.

'Our first personal interview was to ask him to make two drawings,
a title page and frontispiece to *Praise and Principle*. He took a small rule
out of his pocket, measured the size of the two wood blocks, and said, " The

---

[1] I have thought it best to write the artists' names as they actually appear in the books
and magazines of the period—that is to say without the honorary titles which, from Sir John
Gilbert on, many of them subsequently received.

J. GILBERT: 'The Suit of Armour'
[*Once a Week*, 1866]

price will be thirty-five shillings each, but I could not possibly give them to you to-morrow; but the next morning you may rely on having them." The drawings were duly sent, and with them an account for the sum named; also a letter to say he had made a mistake in the price, and that all future drawings of the same size and character would be two guineas each. . . . We have no remembrance of him ever being a day behind the time he promised to send in his work.' [1]

Taking everything into consideration, it is remarkable on what a high level that work is maintained, for it was work done against time, work done frankly for money. Gilbert had perhaps rather a weakness for money; nor do I mean money in the abstract, money represented by the figures in his bank book, but the actual golden coins we now see so seldom. These had a fascination for him, and even when he was busiest a little pile of them placed judiciously on the table beside him was always sufficient to make him change his mind had he refused a job. Publishers and engravers were aware of this idiosyncrasy, and the messenger who brought the commission brought also the golden sovereigns. The artist would look at them, grunt, and tell the boy to go out and play cricket on the heath. When he returned after an hour or two the completed drawing would be ready for him to take away.

Gilbert was a thrifty man and accumulated a considerable fortune which he knew very well how to take care of. When it was proposed to call little Gilbert Dalziel after him, and he was asked to be godfather, he was for a minute or two delighted, but presently it was observed that he looked less pleased. A vision of the silver spoon, or still more expensive silver mug it is customary to bestow on such occasions had risen before him, and the clearer it grew the less he liked it. In the end he turned his back on it and on his prospective godson. The latter might have his name, but as to anything else—no, no; he could not possibly accept the responsibility. He was very sorry, but the responsibility of a godparent was too great, it was quite impossible.

Gilbert did not draw from life, but one need hardly attribute the lack of variety in his figures to this, since many artists who did draw from life were almost as constant to a few types. Rare indeed is it to find an artist, once his style is formed, bringing such completely new people into existence as Pinwell did in his illustrations for *Fated to be Free*. Among the early volumes Gilbert illustrated, *The Salamandrine*, a poem by Charles Mackay (1853), need not detain us. ' It reveals ', says Gleeson White, ' —as any of the rest must equally—the powerful mastery of his art and its limitations.' But this, surely, is to do much less than justice to the *Longfellow* of three

[1] *The Brothers Dalziel. A Record of Fifty Years Work*, 1840-1890. (Methuen, 1901.)

years later. The forty-six drawings for *The Salamandrine* are insipid as the
poem itself: the *Longfellow* contains among its many designs some exquisite
work, while taken even as a specimen of engraving it is incomparably
superior: indeed, in none of their later books did the Dalziels ever surpass
the cutting of some of these blocks. It is not in the figure subjects that the
chief beauty will be found, but in the tiny landscapes and the drawings of
still life—such things as ' Sea-Weed ', ' The Day is Done ', ' The Old Clock
on the Stairs ', ' The Evening Star ', ' Flowers ', and the ' Drinking Song '.
The evening scenes in particular have a lovely quality of tone: line remains
line, yet the drawings have a miraculous softness. In succeeding years the
Longfellow was re-issued several times with additional poems and designs,
till in the final edition the drawings actually number one hundred and
seventy-four.

It is unnecessary to enumerate, much less describe, all the books illustrated either wholly or in part by Gilbert. He has some fine things in
Eliza Cook's Poems (Routledge, 1861), especially those on pages 23 and 253.
Gleeson White gives the date of this volume as 1856, but the Dalziel albums
now in the British Museum show that the proofs were first pulled in 1860:
and the title-page bears the date of the following year.

Though it is engraved on steel, because of its singular beauty I cannot
refrain from mentioning a design of a girl reading in an old terraced garden
which Gilbert made for a frontispiece to Julia Kavanagh's *Adèle* [1862],
published in Hurst and Blackett's ' Standard Library ', before passing on to
what usually is regarded as his masterpiece, the *Shakespeare*. This huge
work was published by Routledge in parts, from 1856 to 1858, and for it
Gilbert made about eight hundred drawings. The planning of it was not
left in his hands, however, and we find him writing to the Dalziels that
' large cuts are wanted, *fewer* and *larger* '. In this he was perfectly right:
it is exactly the impression we receive to-day on turning the pages. And in
spite of the fine designs for the frontispieces to the different plays—several
of which, rather oddly, remind us of Tenniel—the book as a whole fails to
reach the level of the *Longfellow*. It is partly no doubt because of its
arrangement, the drawings being embedded, to their great disadvantage, in
a large page printed in double columns; but this is not the only reason.
Very likely there are as many good things in the *Shakespeare* as in the
Longfellow, but in proportion to the total number there are certainly not so
many; and when we come across a vignette like the vignette at the beginning
of *Hamlet*, which is distinctly in the *Longfellow* manner, it arrests us instantly
by its beauty. Lastly, there is the subject. Shakespeare seems impossible to
illustrate, in the true meaning of the word, and Gilbert has not illustrated
him. So far from throwing a light on the text, these drawings cast a shadow:

they stand, in fact, in much the same relation to it as do Lamb's *Tales*; they miss everything, or nearly everything that matters. And of course just where Shakespeare is most magical the artist fails most completely. It is not to be wondered at: all other artists—including E. A. Abbey—who have attempted the same task, have failed. As an attempt, indeed, Gilbert's is among the best. The perfectly illustrated books are things like *At the Back of the North Wind*, or *Alice's Adventures in Wonderland*, and for the very reason that there is no great gulf between the imagination and power of expression of Arthur Hughes and George MacDonald, or Tenniel and Lewis Carroll. But between Shakespeare and those who have attempted to illustrate him the gulf exists. As for Gilbert, he may have understood and appreciated the dramatic quality of his author, but that he was completely insensitive to the poetic quality we have only to turn to his drawings of the peasants in *A Midsummer Night's Dream* to see. What have these degraded half-witted clowns to do with Shakespeare's rustics, whose very simplicity is a kind of poetry? The melodrama Gilbert could at least echo in his own medium; he could draw a Shylock or a Richard III, or even a Lear; he could draw a scene of murder or of madness; the grotesque, too, he could often grasp (he draws Bottom with an ass's head, for instance, nearly as well as Linley Sambourne, that master of animal grotesque, could have drawn him); but even of grotesque he only understood the prose; it is utterly impossible that his Caliban should ever have spoken as Shakespeare makes the real Caliban speak:

> Be not afeard ; the isle is full of noises,
> Sounds and sweet airs, that give delight and hurt not.
> Sometimes a thousand twangling instruments
> Will hum about mine ears ; and sometimes voices,
> That if I then had waked after long sleep
> Will make me sleep again.

II. BIRKET FOSTER (1825-1899)

Birket Foster came of a Quaker family. ' We first knew him ', say the Dalziels, ' as a little boy with a round jacket and turn-down collar. . . . Later he came to be apprenticed to Ebenezer Landells to learn the art of wood engraving; but in this he made literally no progress, and Landells considering that as a landscape draughtsman he might be more likely to take a foremost position, the youth's attention was turned to this branch of art with the most satisfactory results.'

Like Gilbert, who was eight years his senior, Birket Foster worked for the *London News*, and very soon began to make drawings for the illustrated books of the day. He made a great many, but their variety is not sufficient to demand a detailed account. They are often charming, in Foster's somewhat finikin way, but they are so little experimental as to suggest that the artist, having once invented a formula, was ever after too timid to depart from it. In any true sense of the word he was not an illustrator at all. He had no imagination, and apparently took little account of the imaginations of others. Whatever poet he may be illustrating—whether it be Edgar Poe, Wordsworth, Milton, or the amazingly geographical James Montgomery— he gives us precisely the same delicate little Birket Foster idyll. If the poem should be *Ulalume* or *The Sleeper* he may introduce an owl and a cypress, but that is as far as his sympathy carries him. In fact, the whole of Foster can be found in a single volume, *Pictures of English Landscape* (Routledge, 1863). In this book he is absolutely at his best; the drawings are broader, looser, bolder than his work is apt to be; the *Beauties of English Landscape*, published many years later, is not comparable with it. *Pictures of English Landscape* is one of the collector's indispensable books. The plates in the first edition are nearly always a little foxed, but in 1881 the Dalziels brought out a special edition with the pictures printed on India paper. The Dalziels were always doing things like this. In a very real sense they are the onlie begetters of much of the finest work of their day, the publishers whose names we read on title pages often being no more than the distributors they employed. It is to Dalziel Brothers we owe Millais's *Parables*, *A Round of Days*, *Wayside Posies*, Houghton's *Arabian Nights*, Pinwell's *Goldsmith*, and the famous *Bible Gallery*; and it was not their fault that we have not, among other works, a *Don Quixote* illustrated by Charles Keene, and a *Life of Joseph* illustrated by Sandys.

Here is the story of *English Landscape*. Birket Foster received from the Dalziels a commission to make a series of fifty full-page drawings, the most perfect he could do. There were also to be fifty vignettes, and the price arranged was £350. But Foster was becoming enormously popular as a water-colour artist, and he found painting water-colours to be a good deal more lucrative than making black and white drawings. Four years later the fifty large pictures have been reduced to thirty, while the vignettes have disappeared altogether. It was, I suppose, to make the book larger and more saleable that some kind of text was now thought desirable, and through the intervention of Millais Tennyson was invited to write the poetry for Foster's drawings. On his refusal, Tom Taylor was appealed to, and this time the appeal succeeded. Tom agreed to write the poems, and it is rather amusing to find the verses and not the pictures figuring in subsequent correspondence as the illustrations. ' I send you two samples ', Tom Taylor writes, ' of the kind of illustration I should supply to the drawings. The price I would

Birket Foster: 'Donkeys on the Heath'

[*Pictures of English Landscape*]

suggest for thirty poems is £100. This is putting the work at *Once a Week* terms. . . . If my terms or my verses do not suit you, I should suggest your application to the Rev. J. W. Barnes of Dorchester.' By Tom Taylor, in fact, the Muse is revealed in an embarrassingly homely light, so that she turns out to be of a much more accommodating nature than any of us who are not poets could possibly have imagined. When she had inspired Tom Taylor precisely thirty times the *Pictures of English Landscape* was complete. And the odd thing is that the verses seem to be just as good as verses usually are.

It is hard to choose among these admirable drawings, but if I had to select one only, it would be the second picture, ' Donkeys on the Heath '. The landscape here is quite free from that crowding of detail, and also from the too obvious prettiness, which spoil so much of Foster's work. As to the engraving, Foster himself has written on the margin of the proof, ' I could not better this if I tried.' ' The Mill ', too, shows what his drawing gained by a broader handling:—' The Mill ', and ' The Farmyard ', ' The Country Inn ', ' The Old Cottage ', ' The Lock ', ' At the Cottage Door ', and ' At Sunset ' are all charming designs; but the ' Winter Piece ', and the two sea pieces at the end are less successful. The former, in spite of the grey frosty light that fills it, is too pretty, too much arranged, to be convincing. Many a carelessly drawn *Punch* picture by John Leech has more of the true feeling of an English winter landscape in it—but then Leech was a ' dab ' at winter skies and fields, and could suggest the weather with an uncompromising realism which would have shocked Birket Foster.

A word as to the first edition of *Pictures of English Landscape*. There is a copy in the Kensington Borough Library, undated on the title page, but which, in the manuscript catalogue, is dated 1862, the year of the preface. After comparing the two issues page by page, however, I am inclined to believe that this copy is not of an earlier but of a later impression than the 1863 edition. The publisher's imprint reads:

London: George Routledge and Sons.
Broadway, Ludgate Hill.
New York: 416, Broome Street.

The imprint on the 1863 edition is:

London:
Routledge, Warne, and Routledge.
New York: 56, Walker Street.

MDCCCLXIII

[25]

III. JOHN TENNIEL (1820-1914)

The work of John Tenniel, whom I place third on our list of precursors, never exercised the slightest influence on his contemporaries, or at least on any of those whose names will subsequently appear in these pages. He is said by the Dalziels to have studied in Germany, and to have been 'strongly impressed with German Art'. Be that as it may, his style is his own, and, once formed, he never deviated from it. One may add that, though admirably adapted to his work as *Punch* cartoonist, for serious illustration, and above all for the illustration of tales of modern life, it was an unsympathetic and unsuitable style.

Tenniel drew in pencil on the wood, leaving Swain, his usual engraver, to interpret the delicate greys of the drawing as best he might. Sometimes he drew from photographs; to the end of his life he refused to draw from the living model. Lewis Carroll, in a letter to Miss Thompson on the subject, says, ' I want you to do my fairy drawings from *life*.[1] Mr. Tenniel is the only artist, who has drawn for me, who resolutely refused to use a model, and declared he no more needed one than I should need a multiplication-table to work a mathematical problem ! '—after which there is no more to be said; and it is not, of course, the absence of the living model that gives to Tenniel's line its coldness or to his drawings their hardness.

So we find his designs for *The Silver Cord*, a novel by Shirley Brooks, which ran as a serial through *Once a Week* during 1860 and 1861, with two or three exceptions, interesting rather than attractive. What the subject of that romance in ninety-seven chapters may be I have lacked courage to discover, but Tenniel seems to have seized on all its more stormy moments for the purposes of illustration. There is hardly a picture that does not confront us with wrath, horror, or despair. There is one, indeed, depicting a wasp-waisted, gaol-cropped Frenchman, who has been disarmed in a duel (apparently fought in a parlour), literally grinning with rage, and showing quite a dozen of his teeth as he glares at his opponent. Tenniel, who could put so much beauty into a horse's head, never found it easy to give beauty to his human figures. For female beauty especially, he relied entirely on regular features and unnaturally long eyelashes. The drawings for *The Silver Cord* were begun in 1860, and the same year saw the publication by Bentley of an earlier novel of Shirley Brooks's, *The Gordian Knot*. Tenniel's illustrations for this work are dated 1858. They are full-page plates, etched on steel, and whether it is due to the method of reproduction or not, certainly these pictures are far more satisfactory than the pictures for *The Silver*

[1] These drawings appear in Carroll's *Three Sunsets* (Macmillan, 1898), a posthumous volume of serious verse.

J. Tenniel: ' Malvolio '
[Unpublished]

Cord. They illustrate a tale of precisely the same character; but the drawing facing page 242, ' Duke's Grandfather ', is like an early Charles Keene, and the final drawing, ' The Iron Pit ', is an extraordinarily powerful and even terrible design. This book ranks distinctly higher among Tenniel's achievements than the *Lalla Rookh* (1861) for which he made sixty-nine drawings and which was at one time regarded as his masterpiece. *The Times* actually went so far as to declare *Lalla Rookh* to be ' the greatest illustrated achievement of any single hand '. It does contain several notable designs—those on pages 46 and 149 in particular—but *Lalla Rookh* was hardly the kind of poem likely to inspire Tenniel's best work, and did not in fact do so. Where his talent found its most lively expression was in what we may call grotesque comedy, or farce. We have only to turn to the very early volumes of *Punch*, while Leech was still doing the cartoons, to discover scores of instances of this. There, in initial letters, in head-pieces, tail-pieces and vignettes, in the *Illustrations to Shakespeare*, and other whimsical drawings, we find just the qualities which have made the designs for the two *Alices* famous. And except for the *Alices*, and *The Ingoldsby Legends* (Bentley, 1864), in which he collaborates with Cruikshank and Leech, Tenniel never got a text that suited him. He was essentially a humorous draughtsman: that is to say, taken by themselves, without any printed joke attached to them, his drawings are funny enough to make us laugh. Also he could draw animals with great skill and understanding. There is more charm in the picture of the black kitten at the end of *Through the Looking Glass* than in any of the pictures of Alice herself, pleasant little girl as she is. One has an idea that the black kitten actually sat for its portrait, but the portraits of Alice seem now and then slighfly out of drawing, the head just a shade too large for the trim little body.

Other books illustrated by our artist, two of which I have already mentioned in an earlier chapter, are *Undine* (1845), an uninteresting volume, showing hardly a touch of the later Tenniel; *Aesop's Fables* (1848), much better, though still obviously belonging to the pre-sixty period; and *The Mirage of Life* [1867], a very small book, but containing some excellent drawings. He also helped to illustrate Hall's *Book of British Ballads* (1842), *Poems and Pictures* (1846), *A Juvenile Verse and Picture Book* (1848)—all belonging to his prentice days; Tupper's *Proverbial Philosophy* (1854); a couple of drawings for *Childe Harold* (1855); Barry Cornwall's *Dramatic Scenes* (1857); Pollok's *Course of Time* (1857); *Bryant's Poems* (1857); Willmott's *Poets of the Nineteenth Century* (1857); *Poe's Poems* (1858); Blair's *Grave* (1858), containing a delightful surprise—namely, three or four drawings in his best *Alice* manner; *The Home Affections* (1858), Mrs. Gatty's *Parables from Nature* (1861); *Puck on Pegasus* (1861); *Passages from Modern English Poets*, illustrated by the Junior Etching Club [1862]; *English Sacred Poetry of the Olden Time* (1864); *Dalziel's Arabian Nights* (1865); Proctor's *Legends and Lyrics* (1866); the *Christmas Books* of Dickens (1869); while for Hurst and Blackett's 'Standard Library' he supplied steel engraved frontispieces to *Grandmother's Money, No Church*, and *A Noble Life*. About 1878 he made two or three fine drawings for an illustrated Shakespeare, one of which I reproduce here, but Mr. Hartley tells me he abandoned this project as too difficult. Proofs of a couple of these designs, engraved by Dalziel—one for *The Tempest* and one for *Twelfth Night*— will be found in vol. xxxvii of the Dalziel collection in the British Museum.

It is on his designs for the two *Alices*, however, that Tenniel's fame as an illustrator rests. Never was a text more completely grasped, expanded, and illuminated. Picture and text are indeed so entirely in harmony that one marvels and resents that any later artist should have attempted a re-illustration. The first issue of the first edition of *Alice's Adventures in Wonderland* was printed in Oxford in 1865. This is the extremely rare edition which was recalled because both author and publisher were dissatisfied with the printing of the pictures. The subsequent editions were printed by Richard Clay in London. It seems strange, considering how closely he was connected with the earlier book, that Tenniel, a few years later, should have refused to draw the pictures for *Through the Looking Glass*. But he pleaded occupation with other work, and it was only after strong persuasion that he yielded. *Through the Looking Glass*, with his designs, appeared in 1871, and we may take it he was responsible for the suppression of a chapter in the story in which a wasp appears to have figured in some legal capacity. 'A wasp in a wig is altogether beyond the appliances of art,' he writes to the author. 'Don't think me brutal, but I am bound to say that the "wasp" chapter doesn't interest me in the least, and I can't see my way to a picture. If you want to shorten the book, I can't help thinking—with all submission—that *there* is your opportunity.' What the 'wasp' chapter was about I suppose we shall now never know, but that the author looked after the artist as keenly as the artist looked after the author we gather from such instructions as, 'Don't give Alice so much crinoline'; 'The White Knight must not have whiskers; he must not be made to look old'; and again, from Tenniel, 'I think that when the jump occurs in the Railway scene you might very well make Alice lay hold of the Goat's beard as being the nearest object to her hand, instead of the old lady's hair'.

Lewis Carroll was never again to find such an illustrator. The choice of Harry Furniss for *Sylvie and Bruno* hardly strikes us as the happiest alternative he might have hit upon, though Furniss certainly took a lot of trouble over the drawings, and they pleased the author. A. B. Frost's designs for *Rhyme and Reason* are infinitely better, and Henry Holiday's for *The Hunting of the Snark* in their decorative beauty carry on the true Pre-Raphaelite tradition, bringing it into the world of grotesque. Nevertheless, neither Frost nor Holiday was inspired in the way Tenniel was inspired. They had not the same chance, it might be urged, and this is true. Still, the Tenniel designs remain supreme, and looking over the proofs in the Dalziel albums we see what pains he took with them. There are two entirely different versions of the picture of the King's Messenger (our old friend the Hatter) in prison, for instance. The first is good, but the second, which is the one used in the book, is better. And some of her admirers may not know that the incomparable Duchess is more or less a portrait of a real lady and a real duchess. The lady lived a good many years ago, and has the remarkable reputation of being the ugliest woman in history. She was the Duchess Margaret of Carinthia and Tyrol, and her portrait was painted by Quentin Matsys, the great Flemish master, in the fifteenth century. She is distinctly more simian than Alice's friend, and has an even longer upper lip; but there she is, head-dress and all, the latter hardly a whit exaggerated, in Quentin Matsys's picture. Where that picture was when Tenniel drew his Duchess from it I do not know, but comparatively recently it passed into the possession of Mr. Hugh Blaker, who bought it when it was put up for sale at Christie's a few years ago.[1]

Apart from *Punch* and *Once a Week*, Tenniel did very little work for periodicals. He has four drawings in *Good Words*, in 1862, 1863, and 1864, and a capital full-page (coloured), 'The Unexpected Guest', in the Christmas Number of *The Illustrated London News*, 1857, but, I think, very little else.

[1] Since these lines were written I understand attention has been drawn to the Duchess Margaret and also to Tenniel's design by the publication of Herr Feuchtwanger's romance, *The Ugly Duchess* (Secker, 1927).

CHAPTER IV

ALLINGHAM'S *MUSIC MASTER* AND THE MOXON *TENNYSON*

I

A T this point it might be as well to examine a couple of books usually regarded as marking the beginning of our period proper, and which do in fact introduce the Pre-Raphaelite group of artists, who had so much to do with the revival of wood engraving. The books are William Allingham's *Music Master* (Routledge, 1855) and Tennyson's *Poems* (Moxon, 1857), and, since the letters which passed between Allingham and Rossetti give us an excellent opportunity, it may be interesting to trace in some detail the history of *The Music Master*, always referred to by Rossetti as the *Day and Night Songs*.

Writing to Arthur Hughes on the 11th of July 1854, Allingham says that an edition of two thousand copies is to be published ' not later than 1st October, at Routledge & Co.'s risk. They will have the volume illustrated with not less than six full-page woodcuts, and will pay the artist who draws them three guineas for every such design, on his giving in the block.' The price seems small, especially when compared with what Moxon, a very little later, was prepared to pay for the designs for his *Tennyson*.

Rossetti first alludes to the *Music Master* on the 2nd of May 1854, when, in a letter to the poet, he says, ' I wish you would get those wood-blocks (at any rate two or three) sent by Routledge *at once*. . . . I have made a sketch for one.' From which we gather that at this time he purposed to make several drawings, and can only hope Allingham was sufficiently familiar with his habits not to build too much on early enthusiasm.

Sure enough, once the blocks have arrived, we find Arthur Hughes, his fellow-illustrator, experiencing the usual difficulty in discovering what Rossetti proposed to do, or indeed if he was going to do anything. ' I have been hunting him up ', he says, ' every day since getting your last, but have not succeeded in hunting him *down* yet, to know if he intends to design the children, or the Maids of Elfen-Mere, or both; ' and he adds this postscript, ' I open my letter to say that Rossetti just sends me word, but in great haste, that he believes he shall stick to the Maids of Elfen-Mere, but I expect from his letter he is somewhat uncertain.'

On September the 19th, 1854, Rossetti writes to tell Allingham that 'Hughes was here the other evening, and showed me several sketches and wood-blocks he has drawn—all of them excellent in many ways; but the blocks I think, especially the one of the man and girl at a stile, rather wanting in force for the engraver. He agreed with me, and I believe will do something to amend this.'

On October the 15th we find that Rossetti's own drawing is actually done. 'I have drawn the "Maids of Elfen-Mere" once on the wood, and find I have committed a stupid mistake in not drawing the actions reversed, so that, when printed, the figures will be left-handed. I am therefore going to trace and draw it again on another block, which I trust will soon be in Routledge's hands. I shall like, if I can find time, to do a second drawing from some other of the poems.' Upon which, more than a month later, we get Arthur Hughes's comments: 'I paid Rossetti a visit a fortnight since and found the drawing for the "Maids of Elfen-Mere" half done. The second time—for he made the maidens spinning left-handed—and foolishly, I think, began it afresh in consequence, for none but old women, I fancy, would have recognized the mistake.'

In November Rossetti is still uncertain about a second drawing, and is beginning to feel uneasy about the cutting of the first. 'I hope, above all, they mean to have the drawings well cut. For my part I should like to tell them that they had better in my own case give the price of the drawing as an extra bonus to the engraver, and that then they must let me see a proof as soon as cut—the thing to be cancelled altogether if not approved of by me. I expect this might partly impress upon them that some care was necessary, and that there was a reputation of some sort in some quarters that I had to take care of. Do you see any objection to my following this plan?'

On January the 23rd, 1855, the block is finished. 'I have tried to draw all the shadow in exact lines, to which, if the engraver will only adhere, I fancy it may have a good chance, but hardly otherwise, as there is a good deal of strong shade—dangerous especially to the faces, but I could find no other way.'

In the same letter we first hear of the *Tennyson*. 'The other day Moxon called on me, wanting me to do some of the blocks for the new Tennyson. The artists already engaged are Millais, Hunt, Landseer, Stanfield, Maclise, Creswick, Mulready, and Horsley. The right names would have been Millais, Hunt, Madox Brown, Hughes, a certain lady and myself. I have not begun even designing for them yet, but fancy I shall try the *Vision of Sin* and *Palace of Art*, etc.—those where one can allegorize on one's own

[31]

hook on the subject of the poem, without killing for oneself and everyone a distinct idea of the poet's. This, I fancy, is *always* the upshot of illustrated editions—Tennyson, Allingham, or any one—unless where the poetry is so absolutely narrative as in the old ballads, for instance.'

On March the 18th the proof of 'The Maids of Elfen-Mere' is in his hands. 'That wood-block! Dalziel has made such an incredible mull of it in the cutting that it cannot possibly appear. The fault, however, is no doubt in great measure mine—not of deficient care, for I took the very greatest, but of over-elaboration of parts, perplexing them for the engraver. However, some of the fault is his too, as he does not always follow my lines, but a rather stupid preconceived notion of his own about intended "severity" in the design, which has resulted in an engraving as hard as a nail, and yet flabby and vapid to the last degree. Before I sent in my drawing, however, to the engraver, I consulted a friend—Clayton, who has drawn much on wood—as to whether it were done in the right way for cutting, and he assured me it was not only adaptable but remarkably so. Clayton was of opinion that it was much more the thing for the purpose than the drawings made by Hughes, which, however, turns out a complete mistake, as Hughes's drawings, also cut by Dalziel, have come, with one exception, quite remarkably well. There are four of them are most beautiful designs.'

To this one must append the Dalziels' counter-protest. 'Rossetti made use of wash, pencil, coloured chalk, and pen and ink, producing a very nice effect, but the engraved reproduction of this many tinted drawing, reduced to the stern realities of black and white by printer's ink, failed to satisfy him. Indeed, Rossetti appears to have made up his mind that it would be a failure.'

The latter statement is quite true, but how much the design really suffered in the cutting we cannot now tell, for, until the process of photographing on to the wood was invented in the early sixties, any drawing once cut was lost for ever. That it suffered more than those of Arthur Hughes and Millais, with which Rossetti was perfectly satisfied, we may venture to doubt; Allingham, at all events, did not find it the monstrosity Rossetti described, and on returning the proof expressed a very strong desire that it should appear. Presently his persuasions begin to take effect. 'It would be possible', Rossetti admits, 'to improve it a good deal, I believe—not by adding shadows, which, though very advisable, would not be practicable; but by cutting out lines, by which means a human character might be partially substituted for the oyster and goldfish cast of features, and other desirable changes effected. On getting your letter I marked parts of the proof with white, and find something might probably be done. But first I should like to show the whitened proof to one or two friends, and take their opinion as to whether, even if the changes were properly made, the thing could possibly be allowed to come out. I cannot at present conceive of its being brought to any state in which my name could be put to it, much as I should like my name to appear in your book.'

It is difficult to believe we are reading of the very engraving that, when it did appear, was to fire the imagination of the young Burne-Jones, then a youth at Oxford, and lead him to write of it in *The Oxford and Cambridge Magazine* of 1856 with such enthusiasm. ' It is I think the most beautiful drawing for an illustration I have ever seen; the weirdness of the Maids of Elfen-Mere, the musical timed movement of their arms together as they sing, the face of the man above all, are such as only a great artist could conceive.' In fact, this design revealed to him, says Mr. Malcolm Bell, ' that there existed a strange enchanting world beyond the hum-drum of this daily life—a world of radiant, many-coloured lights, of dim mysterious shadows, of harmonies of form and line, wherein to enter is to walk among the blest—that far-off world of Art into which many a time since he has made his way and brought back visions of delight to show his fellow-men '.

Possibly the world of art is not so far off as this slightly purple passage would suggest—at any rate it ought not to be—but we certainly gain the assurance that Burne-Jones found the drawing beautiful. Rossetti's attitude, on the other hand, was quite sincere. From his own copy of *The Music Master* he immediately removed the offending drawing, and in writing to his mother of the book says, ' there are some illustrations by Hughes, one by Millais, and one which used to be by me till it became the exclusive work of Dalziel, who cut it.'

But it is high time to turn to the book itself, our account of it having developed into an account of the peculiarities of one of the illustrators, a result not unusual when one deals with anything in which Rossetti happened to have a share. *The Music Master* contains eight full-page designs, a vignette and a tail-piece, all, with the exceptions of one design by Millais and one by Rossetti, the work of Arthur Hughes. The little book is rare and important, though neither externally nor internally is it particularly attractive. The purple or green cloth binding, with its gilt design, is dull and tasteless; the poems are printed in a good type, but the page is too small and the whole appearance is undistinguished. The drawings by Hughes, in spite of the praise Rossetti gives them, have little of the charm of his later work. The frontispiece—' Crossing the Stile '—is perhaps the weakest. The maiden poised on the topmost bar of the stile is reminiscent of one of Dicky Doyle's young ladies, while the lanky youth who supports her must be at least seven feet high. The design of dancing elves for Allingham's best known poem is much more satisfactory, and this drawing has been particularly well engraved.

Up the airy mountain,
  Down the rushy glen,
We daren't go a-hunting
  For fear of little men ;
Wee folk, good folk,
  Trooping all together ;
Green jacket, red cap,
  And white owl's feather !

The little men are seen silhouetted against the sky, as, with joined hands and wild hair, they dance under a great full moon, their whirling shadows reflected in the water of the dark mountain lake.

' Lady Alice ', eloping with a theatrical lover, is feeble. That wrapping round her head, though blown out by the wind, is rigid and solid as the castle walls, and the attitude she has assumed while addressing a too placid dog is vaguely ' Anglo Saxon '. Such a subject does not suit Arthur Hughes ; the title poem, the *Music Master*, gives him a better opportunity, and the drawing of Milly listening through the open door to Gerald playing the piano is at least characteristic, the face of the musician having something of that dreamy innocence which, fifteen years later, we find in his drawings of the small heroes of George MacDonald's tales. ' Under the Abbey-Wall ' and ' The Boy's Grave ' are better still; their sentiment simple and true. The grave itself, in the latter drawing, is on an open hillside, and the three little girls gathered at it are more pensive than mournful. One of them is blowing the winged seeds from a dandelion stalk—clocks, as we used to call them—and the whole mood of the picture is quiet with the quiet of Millais's ' Autumn Leaves '. It is in this mood that its charm lies, for the drawing is uncertain and inclined to stiffness, though something about the girl with the dandelion does faintly recall an early Millais.

The drawing by Millais himself is entitled ' The Fireside Story '. Of the little group gathered round the hearth, the dog, one imagines, has suffered at the hands of the engraver, but after the more or less tentative Hughes designs it is easy here to perceive the work of a master draughtsman. Take that small boy, for instance, sitting on the floor, with his back turned, and one hand supporting his chin, the other clasping his knee: there is a living body inside his clothes, and the clothes themselves have the texture of cloth. Moreover, the relation between the different persons in the group is realized and expressed, they are not simply a number of figures placed in juxta-position. The smallest girl, sitting on the grandmother's knee, believes implicitly in the enchanting tale and is hanging on every word: her elder

D. G. Rossetti:
' The Maids of Elfen-Mere '
[*The Music Master*]

sisters and brothers, though interested, know that they are listening to what is only a story: the dog, seated between the two boys, is looking at something quite outside the charmed circle—he is not interested in the least, because nobody has mentioned his name. Of all the drawings in the book we recognize that this alone has been ' observed '.

Nevertheless, *the* drawing remains, the drawing about which we have heard so much, the drawing that was ruined by Dalziel, the atrocity, the horror that must be torn out before the book is presentable, the ' Maids of Elfen-Mere '.

> 'Twas when the spinning-room was here,
> There came Three Damsels clothed in white,
> With their spindles every night ;
> Two and one, and Three fair Maidens,
> Spinning to a pulsing cadence,
> Singing songs of Elfen-Mere ;
> Till the eleventh hour was toll'd,
> Then departed through the wold.
> > *Years ago, and years ago ;*
> > *And the tall reeds sigh as the wind doth blow.*
>
> Three white Lilies, calm and clear,
> And they were loved by every one ;
> Most of all, the Pastor's Son,
> Listening to their gentle singing,
> Felt his heart go from him. . . .

In the drawing, the Pastor's Son—a figure of extraordinary beauty, and among the most natural, the most human, Rossetti ever created—is not looking at the Maids. He is looking away from them, brooding perhaps on the trick by which he is to keep them beyond the appointed hour, and so destroy both them and himself. Through the window we catch a glimpse, not of the village of the poem but of a little Düreresque town, with its pointed roofs and the fateful clock tower.

What is strange, after all we have read, is to find that this drawing, as a mere example of the engraver's skill, seems at least equal to any of the other cuts and superior to some of them. The artist has treated the figures of the Maidens slightly archaically, but without stiffness; the Pastor's Son reveals a more modern manner. The difference is deliberate and subtle, for without reading a line of the text we should know that we are looking at the inhabitants of two worlds—that the boy belongs to this earth, while the Maids are only visitors here.

[35]

A glance through the Moxon *Tennyson* is sufficient to justify Rossetti's list of the ' right illustrators '—with the exception of ' a certain young lady ', who is of course Miss Siddal. To the loss of Miss Siddal's designs we can reconcile ourselves, and the marvel is that Rossetti, who had a keen sense of the ludicrous, should be so blinded by affection as not to perceive their yearning mawkishness. Feeble and exaggerated reflections of all that was weakest in his own manner, they at once reduce that manner to the absurd with a success no caricaturist could hope to emulate. Otherwise Rossetti's list seems to-day so natural, and even inevitable, that we find it difficult to understand what Moxon can have had in view when he made his own choice of artists. It was not economy, for with a single exception the artists were paid at a uniform rate. The exception, needless to say, was Rossetti himself, who, as Holman Hunt remarks with some asperity, insisted on receiving thirty guineas a drawing because everybody else had agreed to accept twenty-five. One could have understood Moxon's placing *all* the work in the hands of Maclise, Horsley, Creswick, etc., but surely it must have been obvious to him that a satisfactory artistic unity was not to be obtained by employing two diametrically opposed schools of illustrators. It may have been the author who favoured the earlier men, but one doubts this, though Rossetti says he loathed *his* particular designs, and one gathers that he was not particularly pleased with Holman Hunt's. Those of Millais struck the new note less emphatically and were perhaps more within the comprehension of the poet, whose *Princess*, three years later, was to be issued with twenty-six designs by Maclise.

In the Moxon edition the illustrations are divided fairly equally between the two schools; the older men supply twenty-four, the Pre-Raphaelites thirty. Of these thirty eighteen go to Millais, seven to Holman Hunt, and the remaining five to Rossetti. The Millais are the most varied in style, and also in excellence. Several of the outline drawings are not far removed from the school of Mulready and Maclise, while the ' Cleopatra ' on page 149 suggests J. R. Clayton. A wide gulf divides this not particularly happy dream of a fair woman from the incomparable ' Eve of St. Agnes ', which may not be the most interesting as a picture, but, as an illustration, an ideal illustration, is the most perfect thing in the book. First-rate also are ' Mariana ', ' The Sisters ', ' The Death of the Old Year ', ' Dora ', ' Day Dreams ', ' Edward Gray ', and ' The Lord of Burleigh '. ' The Death of the Old Year ' is in truth a masterpiece. It is an interior, with a vivid glimpse of landscape. Outside, ' full knee-deep lies the winter snow ', while within,

> Alone and warming his five wits,
> The white owl in the belfry sits.

J. E. MILLAIS: 'St. Agnes' Eve'
[*Tennyson's Poems*]

J. E. Millais: 'The Death of the Old Year'
[*Tennyson's Poems*]

This poem, *The Owl,* from which my quotation is taken, is not included in the volume, but that Millais's drawing was made for it and not for *The Old Year* I have no doubt at all, though I can bring no evidence to support the view but the picture itself.

Holman Hunt in two drawings for *Oriana* is at his best. The second especially has a gravity and a strength which make it singularly impressive. ' The Beggar Maid ', ' Godiva ', and the first drawing for *Recollections of the Arabian Nights* are also lovely things, but they have not the grandeur of this picture of the tomb of Oriana, and ' The Lady of Shalott ' owes too much to Rossetti to be really characteristic.

Rossetti's own design for the same poem shows the Lady dead in the boat, the swans floating on the river, Sir Lancelot leaning down to gaze into the still face that is lit by flickering candles and a waving torch flame. A strange exotic beauty fills the picture, sharper and more thrilling in its effect because of the very absence, or comparative absence, from it of that passionate languor which looms so largely in nearly all Rossetti's work, and which indeed is the note struck by his remaining drawings. His ' Mariana in the South ' is kneeling, not before the Virgin of Tennyson's poem, but before a carved figure of the crucified Christ, against whose feet her lips are crushed, while in her hands she grasps her lover's letter. His ' Sir Galahad ' is stooping over a vessel of holy water in the secret shrine, his white face fevered and restless, while the nuns are praying and ' the shrill bell rings '. But the design that was to arouse so much discussion and so many conflicting opinions was the ' Saint Cecilia ' of *The Palace of Art.* Tennyson himself gave up all attempt to discover what it had to do with his poem, and we have already quoted a letter of Rossetti's in which he expresses his view of illustration as a kind of ' allegorizing on one's own hook '. In this particular design he has put his theory into practice, the text on which he bases his elaborately subjective comment being a short descriptive stanza:

> Or in a clear-wall'd city on the sea,
>   Near gilded organ-pipes, her hair
> Wound with white roses, slept St. Cecily ;
>   An angel look'd at her.

The organ is there, and the sea with ships afloat on it, and the walled city, and St. Cecily:—and the angel too; but he is not Tennyson's angel. This splendid creature, with loose hair and flowered robe, who holds St. Cecily in his arms while he greedily kisses her, is not evil assuredly, like the angel in Beardsley's ' Mysterious Rose Garden ', but just as assuredly the form he has assumed has been chosen with the ultimate purpose of becoming St. Cecily's lover in the flesh. In fact, he already is her lover if that face of swooning ecstasy means anything. The whole picture breathes an atmosphere of sublime sensuality, which is marvellously accentuated by the indifference of the soldier in the foreground, who munches an apple, and might have been placed there to keep guard against intruders till the lover's meeting is accomplished. The sentry with the apple has given more trouble than anything else. That he is a creation of genius and of the utmost value in the design anybody with an eye can see; but this is not supposed to be enough. Has he been placed there for a symbolic purpose, and if so what does he symbolize? Mr. Laurence Housman will tell us that he is a ' masterly side-stroke at the sensuous philosophy of indifferentism on which life in that " lordly pleasure house " was based. . . . The illustrations of the Pre-Raphaelites were personal and intellectual readings of the poems to which they belonged, were not merely echoes in line of the words of the text. Often they were the successful summing up of the drift of an entire poem within the space of a single picture, as in Rossetti's illustration.' But the philosophy of *The Palace of Art* is the exact opposite of indifferentism; it is moral to the point of triteness. G. S. Layard, in *Tennyson and his Pre-Raphaelite Illustrators*,[1] offers another reading, ingenious enough to be the plot of a short story. It is based entirely on the frankly puzzling ' winglike somethings behind the head of the angel '. Rossetti, according to Layard, could not have drawn wings that are so unlike real wings by accident; therefore he must have drawn them intentionally. He *intended* us to see that they are not real wings; and if they are not real wings of course the angel is not a real angel, but a man masquerading as an angel for purposes far from angelical. In other words, Rossetti, bored by Tennyson's spirituality, could not resist the temptation to satirize it, which he did by turning the whole thing into a kind of Boccaccio tale.

Such a view is not likely to gain many supporters. It implies that Rossetti was willing to betray the confidence of both his poet and his publisher for the sake of a jest which he could never share with anybody, and which remained undiscovered until Mr. Layard pounced upon it. The drawing of ' St. Cecilia ' was made in Madox Brown's studio, and the elder artist's description of it is perhaps all we need. ' Rossetti has been here nearly a fortnight, coming about twelve, and working or not working at his drawing on wood for St. Cecilia. It is jolly quaint but very lovely.' At the end of the same year we find Rossetti himself sending a photograph of the drawing to Allingham. ' It is a horrid bad photograph,' he writes, ' but, as Dalziel has the settling of the thing since, it becomes of some interest.'

[1] *Tennyson and his Pre-Raphaelite Illustrators.* By George Somes Layard. (Elliot Stock, 1894.)

D. G. Rossetti:
' St. Cecilia—The Palace of Art '

[*Tennyson's Poems*]

Rossetti, in fact, was never to become reconciled to his engravers. 'These engravers! What ministers of wrath! Your drawing comes to them, like Agag, delicately, and is hewn in pieces before the Lord Harry. I took more pains with one block lately than I had done with anything for a long while. It came back to me on paper, the other day, with Dalziel performing his cannibal jig in the corner, and I have really felt like an invalid ever since. As yet, I fare best with W. J. Linton. He keeps stomach aches for you, but Dalziel deals in fevers and agues.'

Address to Dalziel Brothers

O woodman spare that block,
    O gash not anyhow !
It took ten days by clock,
    I'd fain protect it now.

Chorus—Wild laughter from Dalziels' Workshop.

To this again we may append a few words for the defence. 'It would be obviously out of place', write the Dalziel brothers, 'for us to comment upon the difference in treatment which we gave, and that of other engravers who were entrusted to operate upon some of the drawings [Rossetti] made for the *Tennyson*; we can only affirm that Mr. Rossetti expressed himself verbally and by letter as being well pleased with our work.' And though there is a softness in Linton's engraving of the ' Mariana ' and ' Sir Galahad ' designs which the Dalziel examples lack—something that may have come closer to the original drawings—I must confess that I prefer Dalziel's ' Lady of Shalott ' engraving to either of Linton's.

Because Rossetti was one of the collaborators, the Moxon *Tennyson* naturally has a history attached to it—a tragi-comedy—regarded at the time quite seriously, however, since it was supposed to have hastened the unfortunate publisher's end. Quite seriously W. M. Rossetti denies the truth of the rumour. 'I believe that poor Moxon suffered much,' he says, 'and soon afterwards died; but I do not lay any real blame upon my brother.' This artless statement is of the kind that proves embarrassing to both sides, but the apologist goes on: ' The trouble came in with the engraver and the publisher.' (We shall see in a minute that it came in earlier.) ' With some of the doings of the engraver—Dalziel, not Linton whom he found much more conformable to his notion—he was grievously disappointed. He probably exasperated Dalziel, and Dalziel certainly exasperated him. Blocks were reworked upon, and proofs sent back with rigour. The publisher, Mr. Moxon, was a still severer affliction. He called and he wrote. Rossetti was not always up to time, though he tried his best to be so. In other instances he was up to time, but his engraver was not up to his mark.'

That is the brother's version; we shall now hear Holman Hunt's. ' The publisher, Moxon, called upon me with many repinings that the book was so long delayed. I was steadily fulfilling my undertaking to do six illustrations and no other work, until they were completed. He revealed that his heart was sore about Rossetti, who having promised, had not sent any drawing, and now, when Moxon called, was " not at home ", and would not reply to letters.... As Rossetti was in pecuniary straits notwithstanding continual aid from his brother, his aunts, and Ruskin, it was difficult to account for this apparently determined neglect, so I took the first opportunity to see him. He allowed at once that he did not care to do any because all the best subjects had been taken by others. " You, for instance, have appropriated *The Lady of Shalott,* which was the one I cared for most of all." '

To which Hunt replied, ' " You know I made a drawing from this poem of ' The Breaking of the Web ' at least four years ago. My new drawing is now far advanced. I had determined also to illustrate the later incident in the poem, but that I will give up to you, and I'll relinquish any of the subjects that I've booked besides this, that you may have no cause for driving old Moxon to desperation."

' Gabriel then saw the publisher, and the matter was arranged, exacting however, it seems, a stipulation that his price should be five pounds more than any other designer was receiving. So often, however, did the poor expectant publisher get disappointed in the delivery of each block, that it was said when, soon after, Moxon quitted this world of worry and vexation, that the book had been the death of him.' [1]

We can see how seriously Moxon took his venture, and also how seriously it was taken by the Pre-Raphaelite artists. Even had they possessed his facility, theirs was not the method of John Gilbert, who rarely re-drew a line. There are letters from Millais to Dalziel which show the infinite pains he was prepared to take to secure the results he aimed at—pains he never would have taken in his later years. All of them made studies for their drawings exactly as they did for elaborate oil paintings. The difference between the two schools is the difference between art and journalism, and the result justified the labour; the only other illustration in the book that can hold its own for a moment with the Pre-Raphaelite designs is Mulready's drawing for *The Deserted House.*

Commenting on the Pre-Raphaelite pictures, Holman Hunt says, ' Mr. Joseph Pennell has stated that our drawings were based in style upon

[1] *Pre-Raphaelitism and the Pre-Raphaelite Brotherhood.* By W. Holman Hunt, 2 vols. (Macmillan, 1905.)

examples of those executed for books by Menzel in Germany. Whether Millais or Rossetti had seen Menzel's drawings I am unable to state, but Millais and I had not the time to go about to stray exhibitions, to booksellers' shops, or elsewhere, to find examples of unknown Continental work. . . . Rossetti certainly had more inclination to rout out new publications, but he never spoke to me of Menzel's achievements, and to this day, except for two water-colour drawings which were exhibited some years since by the Old Water-Colour Society, I have never seen a scrap of this artist's work!'

Tennyson, rather oddly, since after all they were *his* poems, took less interest in the matter than anybody else—so little indeed that he seems to have expressed no desire even to look at the drawings till they were, in some cases, already cut on the wood. To him, apparently, all were equally un-important. If the public wanted them they should have them, but the pic-tures that mattered were those his own art evoked.

At last, in 1857, the book was published, a small quarto, admirably printed upon admirable paper, nevertheless, sad to say, doomed to failure. It was published at a guinea and a half, and a large stock remained on hand. This stock presently was sold to Routledge, who now brought the volume out at a guinea. The difference in price seems slight, yet it worked wonders. The Routledge edition was a great success and was quickly bought up. Routledge now wished to bring out a new edition, but Tennyson, bored by pictures, demanded so much for his share that the scheme at once assumed a less inviting aspect. And here I leave it. The genuine first edition bears, of course, the imprint of Moxon, not Routledge, on the title page. It is an extremely interesting volume, even though the wide difference in spirit and in style between the two groups of illustrators makes it more valuable as a picture gallery than as an experiment in book decoration. Regarded from the latter point of view it is a failure—a delightful hotch-potch, as Rossetti from the beginning foresaw that it must be.

CHAPTER V

THE PRE-RAPHAELITE GROUP

ROSSETTI, HOLMAN HUNT, FORD MADOX BROWN, M. J. LAWLESS,
SANDYS, MILLAIS, ARTHUR HUGHES, E. J. POYNTER, BURNE-JONES,
SIMEON SOLOMON, H. H. ARMSTEAD

I.   DANTE GABRIEL ROSSETTI (1828-1882)

TWO years after the publication of the Moxon *Tennyson*, *Once a Week* was founded, the first number appearing on the 2nd of July 1859. The importance of this magazine would be hard to over-estimate. From the beginning, though Leech and Phiz drew for it, it was the journal of the younger men, of the new school.   Its first editor, Samuel Lucas, gathered round him a group of black and white artists more brilliant than any that had been seen before—or than, for that matter, has been seen since —a group including Charles Keene, Millais, Sandys, Whistler, Lawless, Fred Walker, du Maurier, Holman Hunt, Pinwell, Houghton, Tenniel, Poynter, William Small, J. D. Watson, Charles Green, and T. Morten. No wonder that the thirteen volumes comprising the First Series of *Once a Week* occupy a unique position in periodical literature.   With the four volumes of the New Series, started in 1866, though they contain some excellent work, the interest perceptibly declines.   With the Third Series, beginning in 1868, the magazine sinks rapidly from the commonplace to the deplorable.   A similar fate, after five yearly volumes, overtook *Good Words for the Young*, and since both these magazines were in their heyday firmly established favourites their sudden deterioration is the more remarkable.   It is so patent and so abrupt that it can only have been the result of a deliberate policy, but the reason dictating such a policy is impossible to fathom.

Once a Week was followed by *The Cornhill*, *Good Words*, and other excellent magazines, in most of which the drawings, though fewer in number, were printed on better paper than in the more brilliant pioneer journal. Rossetti made no designs for *Once a Week*: indeed his habit of procrastination (one cannot call it indolence, since he worked from morning till night) would have proved an insuperable difficulty. What is really hard to account for is his statement to Allingham, at the end of 1860, that he loathed *Once a Week*, 'illustrations and all'. Why should he loathe a magazine for which his friend George Meredith was writing both poetry and prose, which published contributions by his sister Christina and by Swinburne, which contained so many illustrations by Millais, which contained the matchless drawings of Charles Keene, and several masterpieces by Sandys, including the ' Rosamond ', a design after Rossetti's own heart, but revealing a technical mastery he himself never attained? Nor does it make his attitude less whimsical to find him adding in the same letter, ' I should like greatly to open a connection with *Once a Week*, though it is only once a century that I feel disposed to " illustrate ".' Whether he actually made an attempt to do so I cannot say, but at the end of the third number of the second volume (14th January 1860) will be found a poem entitled *A Border Song*, and signed with the initials D.G.R. From curiosity I have hunted through all the poetry in the first dozen volumes and cannot discover these initials occurring again. Most of the poets, particularly George Meredith, are represented fairly frequently, but D.G.R. remains the author of a single contribution. The evidence suggesting Rossetti's authorship is purely external. We know that his friend Swinburne contributed a few things in prose and verse; we know that another friend, George Meredith, was closely connected with the paper and could easily have placed the thing for him; we know that Rossetti was invariably short of ' tin ', as he called it; and, lastly, there are the initials. I hasten to add that only to the literary ghoul is the matter of the slightest interest, the *Border Song* in no way rising above the level of average magazine verse.

About this time Rossetti was asked by Chapman & Hall to illustrate *Aurora Leigh*, and refused the commission. He was also invited to contribute to Willmott's *Poets of the Nineteenth Century* and gave a kind of half promise. It is again Allingham who is his confidant. ' Dalziel—very good naturedly, *considering*—called here the other day to enlist me for an illustrated selection of Poets which he has the getting up of, it being edited by Revd. Willmott. That venerable parson had not, it seems, included Browning, for whose introduction I made an immediate stand, and said in that case I would illustrate him. I think it will probably be done, and I shall propose (I fancy as yet) *Count Gismond*—" Say, hast thou lied?"—which I designed some years ago.' Browning eventually *was* included, but the poems were not those of Rossetti's selection and he refused a drawing. 'What', he asks, ' could have been done with *Evelyn Hope*, or *Two on the Campagna*?' Henceforth he drops out of the movement entirely, except for four designs all made for his sister Christina's poems.

[45]

Goblin Market (1862) contains two of them—'Buy from us with a golden curl' and 'Golden head by golden head'. In the former, the quaint animal shapes of the goblins throw into vivid relief the beauty of the kneeling girl, who is cutting a golden lock from her hair. The second shows the two sisters asleep, while through the round window, under the moon and stars, we see the goblins carrying baskets of fruit on their heads. In a later illustrated edition of this poem, published by Macmillan in 1893, we find Mr. Laurence Housman accepting Rossetti's conception of the goblins. This delightful little book shows how admirably Mr. Housman carries on the Pre-Raphaelite tradition, without sacrificing his own individuality. He and Mr. Charles Ricketts are the true successors of the first little group of illustrators of the sixties, though their work reveals also a sense of decoration, the decoration of the page, which we do not find in the early books. Where the artist of the sixties thought only of the picture to be inserted, Mr. Housman and Mr. Ricketts—following Walter Crane and Burne-Jones —take also the book itself into consideration, designing initial letters and working out elaborate borders and title pages.

The Prince's Progress (1866) likewise contains two designs—'The long hours go and come and go'—a picture of a girl leaning from a window, waiting for her lover; and 'You should have wept her yesterday'—a picture of the Prince's arrival, too late.

These Rossetti designs are the work of a great artist though they are less perfect than many of the wood engravings of Sandys. Rossetti, unlike Sandys, was hampered by his medium, and achieved his effects in spite of it; perhaps, also, he tried to get too much into a single drawing; nevertheless, as in the drawings of Pinwell, even the faults one regards with a kind of affection.

Since the Rossetti illustrations are so interesting and so few, I may perhaps mention one or two further designs, which, though they do not legitimately come within our survey, have been used as illustrations. Such is the frontispiece to William Sharp's monograph on Rossetti himself; another, 'The Queen's Page', appears in Allingham's *Flower Pieces* (1888); a third, a frontispiece to the *Early Italian Poets*, was reproduced in the first number of *The English Illustrated Magazine*; and a special edition of his brother's poems in two volumes, edited by W. M. Rossetti (Ellis and Elvey, 1904), contains several more.

II. WILLIAM HOLMAN HUNT (1827-1910)

The illustrations of Holman Hunt, nearly as few in number as those of Rossetti, do not, to my mind at all events, reveal anything like the same

The black parts being too strictly adhere touches upon themselves little lines and spots to make them more transparent. the evenist of the woman's left hand wan't light and form. the man's left hand too organis some modefication in the line of the thumb. with these exceptions the cutting is very excellen

W. H. H.

HOLMAN HUNT: 'At Night'

[*Once a Week*, 1860]

[Showing the Artist's instructions to the Engraver]

intensity of vision. Hunt's work may be less exotic than Rossetti's, but it is at the same time less imaginative, less lyrical in quality. One feels how Rossetti must have brooded over his designs, distilling into them an intensely personal atmosphere; Hunt's work does not produce this impression. But it is always distinguished. His drawing for *Witches and Witchcraft* in the second volume of *Once a Week* (May 1860) is interesting not only in itself but because some of the earlier designs of J. D. Watson appear to have been modelled on it. ' At Night ' (vol. iii), a picture of a man watching by the deathbed of his wife, is a still finer thing. His only other contribution to *Once a Week* appears also in volume three (1860), and is an illustration to a poem entitled *Temujin*. The drawing is decorative and quaint, but viewed as an illustration unsuccessful. The real Temujin was a boy, and in this particular poem he is a boy ' who hath only fifteen summers seen ', but Hunt has drawn him as a stalwart, helmeted warrior of at least thirty. Nor has the problem of presenting him in full view, while at the same time hiding him under a heap of cotton which the Chinese soldiers in their search for him are thrusting through with spears, been very satisfactorily solved.

In the Christmas Number of *The Queen* (1861) Hunt has a poorly engraved and not very interesting ' Eve of Saint Agnes '; in *Good Words* (1862) he has ' Go and Come ', an excellent and characteristic drawing of two men reaping in the fields; and in the same magazine, sixteen years later, he has a charming study of a sleeping baby, ' Born at Jerusalem '.

To Willmott's *English Sacred Poetry* (1862) he contributes a frontis-piece, ' The Lent Jewels '; and to Mrs. Gatty's *Parables from Nature* (1861), ' The Light of Truth ', a very effective night piece, and ' Active and Passive ', a curiously arranged drawing of a sailor and a sexton in a graveyard. Better than these is the graceful design of ' Eliezer and Rebekah at the Well ', in *Dalziel's Bible Gallery* (1881), and the picture of a girl praying, in Isaac Watts's *Divine and Moral Songs*. A note tells us that all the engravings in the latter volume were ' executed by the Graphotype Engraving Process ', and the experiment is interesting as being one of the first attempts to employ a substitute for ' the lengthy and costly method of wood engraving '. There are several illustrated editions of Watts: this one was published by Nisbet, and is a thin quarto bound in cloth. There is no date on the title page, but Gleeson White gives it in his text as 1865, and in his index as 1866, while the Catalogue of the British Museum gives it as 1867. Probably this last date is correct, since an article *Concerning the Graphotype*, which appeared in *Once a Week* on the 16th of February 1867, tells us that the new process has only been ' before the English artistic world for a few months '. Its object, the article goes on to say, is to supersede the ' process of wood engraving as too troublesome and expensive for this rapid age '. But what is gained in time and money is more than sacrificed in quality, 'rapid ages' once more, it is to be feared, proving themselves inimical to everything except rapidity.

The vignettes for Macmillan's *Golden Treasury Series*, from designs by Holman Hunt, Millais, Arthur Hughes, etc., hardly come within the scope of the present chronicle, being, like the frontispieces to Hurst & Blackett's 'Standard Library' (also designed by the artists of our period), engraved on steel. In the latter series, the frontispiece to *Studies from Life* is Hunt's. It pictures an elderly woman in a bedroom, kneeling before a chest of drawers. An open Family Bible is propped on the drawer of carefully folded clothes she has pulled out, and her head is bowed in prayer or grief. The drawing is a miracle of minute detail, but, perhaps because of the smooth hard impersonal character it shares with all steel engravings, contains nothing by which one could identify the artist were his name not printed below it.

I fancy this completes the list of Hunt's designs, though one cannot be quite sure. In the case of those artists who, like du Maurier, worked habitually in black and white, one can indeed take it for granted that one's list is never complete. Could there be found to-day, for example, a complete collection of 'yellow-back' novels—'railway novels', as they were sometimes called? Yet such a collection would have to be examined. Not for Holman Hunts, it is true, but Charles Keene is said to have made designs for the covers of one or two of these novels, and indeed I seemed to see a suggestion of his hand in a design for a paper backed edition of *Old Mortality* published by A. and C. Black in 1861. Then there is the whole library of shilling and sixpenny toy-books—not the Crane and Caldecott toy-books, famous and duly catalogued—but others, illustrated by J. D. Watson, H. S. Marks, Harrison Weir, and I know not whom besides, many of which must have disappeared, leaving 'not a rack' behind. The early publications of the S.P.C.K.—things priced at a few pence—booklets, pamphlets, and what not—also have vanished: yet Millais is reputed to have made drawings for some of them, and Fred Walker and North certainly did.

III.   FORD MADOX BROWN (1821-1893)

So far as I know, Ford Madox Brown made only nine drawings on wood. The first of these appears in Willmott's *Poets of the Nineteenth Century* (1857), and illustrates Byron's *Prisoner of Chillon*. It is a beautiful but distinctly macabre design, the expression of grim amusement on the face of the saturnine grave-digger being masterly, while nothing could be more realistic than the dead body, which lies with its head dropping back into a black pit and its stiffened limbs outstretched. Yet, though the face of the

FORD MADOX BROWN: 'The Prisoner of Chillon'
[Willmott's *Poets of the Nineteenth Century*]

open-mouthed corpse conveys all the horror of death, and by no means recent death, it is wonderful how a delicate beauty shines through that visible corruption. Portions of the drawing suggest a certain mauling on the part of the engraver, but both in conception and execution it ranks among the masterpieces. For this design, the legend goes, the artist spent three days in a morgue, watching the gradual transformation taking place in one of the bodies there, making studies in colour and monochrome of the changing hues of decay. This is to take one's work in earnest, and there is no doubt that the drawing, like the drawings of Rossetti, leaves an ineffaceable impression on the mind.

The three designs in *Lyra Germanica* (1868) are good, but less interesting. Of the three for *Dalziel's Bible Gallery* the date is doubtful, for though the *Bible Gallery* did not appear till 1881 it was planned, and many of the drawings were executed, in the early sixties—Holman Hunt's, for example, are dated 1863. The *Bible Gallery* is the most sumptuous of all our books. It was issued in an edition of 1,000 copies, with the designs carefully printed on India paper. But the price—five guineas—proved too high; commercially the work was a failure, only some 200 copies being sold. The original idea, when the artists were commissioned to make their drawings, was to print the text also; but this plan was abandoned, and the huge folio contains the designs alone. And not even all the designs. Of the sixty-nine included, fourteen are by T. Dalziel, twelve by Poynter, nine by Leighton, six by Simeon Solomon, six by Pickersgill, three by G. F. Watts, two by Armitage, three by Ford Madox Brown, two by Armstead, two by Houghton, two by William Small, two by A. Murch, and one each by Burne-Jones, Holman Hunt, E. F. Brewtnall, E. G. Dalziel, Francis Walker, and Sandys. The remaining twenty-eight drawings did not appear till 1894, when, with the original sixty-nine, they were published by the S.P.C.K. in a volume called *Art Pictures from the Old Testament*. Of the twenty-eight new designs Simeon Solomon is responsible for fourteen, two are by Armstead, two by Pickersgill, four by Armitage, three by T. Dalziel, and one each by Francis Walker, Pinwell, and Dyce. The drawings, naturally, are not all of equal value, and there are a few which we feel should not be there. E. G. Dalziel's 'Five Kings', for example, is most emphatically an *Arabian Nights* picture, and Small's two contributions, drawn in wash, just as obviously belong to the *Graphic*.

Of the three designs by Madox Brown that of 'Elijah and the Widow's Son' is perhaps the best. Both the rugged old prophet who is carrying the boy down the stairs, and the mother who is kneeling below, with clasped hands, waiting to receive him, are excellent. The very slim and somewhat doll-like boy is less successful. All bound and wound in his grave clothes, but with a wreath round his fuzzy locks and a bunch of flowers in his hand, he gives the impression of being decked and adorned for some more festive occasion than this. Turning to the drawing of ' Joseph's Coat ', we find it filled with Pre-Raphaelite detail, but none of the figures is so good as the prophet and the mother of the previous picture, and the composition is less pleasing, being more crowded. The third drawing, ' The Death of Eglon ', is a fine piece of elaborate decoration, in which the dramatic element is not forgotten.

In *Once a Week* (Feb. 1869) appeared ' The Traveller ', an effective night piece, with a lighted inn, a lonely traveller on horseback, and a little group of rustics in the light of door and window. The drawing has an attractive atmosphere of romance, and was probably designed as an illustration though actually it is left to tell its own story.

Lastly, in 1871, we have the powerful drawing for Rossetti's ' Down Stream ', which appeared in that short-lived and rare magazine, *Dark Blue*. The drawing illustrates the opening stanza:

> Between Holmscote and Hurstcote
>   The river-reaches wind,
> The whispering trees accept the breeze,
>   The river's cool and kind :
> With love low-whispered 'twixt the shores,
>   With rippling laughters gay,
> With white arms bared to ply the oars,
>   On last year's first of May.

Rossetti himself most likely would have illustrated the fourth stanza, but Madox Brown's drawing really suggests the entire poem, its tragic ending being implicit in the half ugly and wholly animal abandon of the two figures adrift in the neglected boat.

Uneven as we may find them, all the drawings of Madox Brown are worthy of study. The beauty he puts into them is his own, and if it occasionally exists side by side with what we must regard as a failure in beauty, or even as a wilful departure from beauty, it is never obvious, and still less does it ever decline into prettiness.[1]

IV.   M. J. LAWLESS (1837-1864)

Matthew Lawless was an Irishman, the son of Barry Lawless, a Dublin solicitor, but he was educated in England. He died at the age of twenty-

---

[1] In addition to these nine wood engravings there is a much later illustration, reproduced by process, an extraordinary drawing of a girl in a hospital bed, which appears as a frontispiece to Mathilde Blind's *Dramas in Miniature* (Chatto and Windus, 1891).

M. J. LAWLESS: 'The Headmaster's Sister'
[*Once a Week*, 1860]

seven, with the great promise of his youth still unfulfilled. For Lawless had individuality, and, though he was faithful to the Pre-Raphaelite tradition, his drawings are stamped with a personal note that makes them as easy to identify as those of that very different artist, Charles Keene. Whether he would ever have developed into a great draughtsman it is impossible to say. At his death he had not yet done so; a certain laboriousness is traceable in most of his work up to the end, though the clumsiness of his first efforts is no longer there. But he is always interesting, always sincere, and the later designs do seem to show that eventually he would have abandoned the heaviness of line which is so marked a feature of his style.

We first meet with Lawless in volume one of *Once a Week* (December 1859). He was then a young man of twenty-two, and he supplied three illustrations for *Sentiment from the Shambles*—illustrations showing he had already developed a manner of his own, though it was not yet a particularly attractive manner. That squatness and coarseness which occasionally spoil even his later figures is very noticeable in the man in the foreground of the first picture. The second volume of *Once a Week* contains ten drawings by Lawless, but it would serve no purpose to go over these one by one. ' Florinda ' (p. 220) is an effective design, slightly suggestive of Millais, and was evidently a favourite with Lawless for he returned to it more than once. The drawing on page 352, ' Only for Something to Say ', shows how little his style was adapted to pictures of fashionable society. A much better thing is the river scene illustrating *The Headmaster's Sister* (p. 389); indeed the drawing of the boy here is singularly pleasing. The last drawing, ' The Lots upon the Raft ' (p. 620), I mention only because neither in the index nor in Gleeson White's catalogue is it given to Lawless, though it is his in every line. An unpleasant subject, however:—two men contemplating a sleeping youngster prior to murdering and eating him.

Volume iii has seven pictures, ' The Betrayed ' (p. 155) being a much finer version of the ' Florinda ' motif, and revealing a greater delicacy than the artist had hitherto attained. In vols. iv and v (1861) Lawless has ten drawings. In vol. iv the most interesting are those for the ballad of *Effie Gordon*, while vol. v contains the beautiful design, ' Twilight ', in which we see the sentimental verses of Walter Thornbury lifted into the world of poetry. In vol. vi (1862) he has only three drawings, but one of these is the admirable ' Dr. Johnson's Penance ': in vol. vii he has only one, illustrating Swinburne's story, *Dead Love*, a mediaeval tale, suggestive, in its erotic strangeness, of the more exotic poems and ballads.

In vol. viii (1863) there are five Lawlesses. Of these, an excellent hayfield scene (p. 712) is spoiled by an accident which appears to have happened to the engraving, leaving a curious flower-pot arrangement above the girl's head: but the grouping, the delicately outlined landscape, and the dog in the foreground are all particularly good. In this drawing, as in several others—the ' Honeydew ' of *London Society*, for instance, and ' Faint Heart Never Won Fair Ladye ', on page 98 of *Once a Week*, vol. ix—we seem to see Lawless reaching out to a new style—a style still retaining many of the old qualities, but in which the dark solid masses he first employed are giving way to a freer use of white and a daintier outline. The flowered coat of the man in the *Once a Week* drawing is singularly effective. In the pathetic ' Broken Toys ' we find him apparently returning to his earlier manner—unless, as indeed the monogram suggests, the drawing is one that has been held over. The last drawing of all, and by some considered his best, is the ' John of Padua ', which appeared in *Once a Week* on the 9th of January 1864. It is good, but not, I think, the best. The foreground and background seem slightly out of harmony, and the elaborate group of figures has not the beauty of pattern he now and then achieved in much simpler designs.

To *Good Words* for 1862 Lawless contributed ' Rung into Heaven ', among his finest things. This picture of three children in a belfry escapes sentimentality by a dangerously narrow margin, but that it does escape it is one of its triumphs. ' The Bands of Love ' of the same year is an almost equally notable drawing, and ' The Player and the Listeners ' (1864), a portrait of a man at a spinet, is full of a graceful distinction.

In *The Churchman's Family Magazine* for 1863 we find a masterpiece, ' One Dead ':—reprinted in *Pictures of Society* as ' The Silent Chamber '.

The large drawing, ' Beauty's Toilet ', made for *London Society* (1862), has been ruined by Dalziel, but in the same magazine, among one or two minor things, we find in 1863 the delightful old-world drawing, ' Honeydew ', and in vol. v (1864) another excellent design, ' Not for You '. ' Expectation ', a sketch of a seated lady in a landscape, is much more freely handled than is usual with Lawless. It did not appear in *London Society* till 1868, but was made six years previously, as the date in the corner shows. The ' Episode in the Italian War ', held over still longer, till 1870 in fact, is unimportant.

Between 1860 and 1861 Lawless made a few drawings for *Punch*. They are not signed, but the collector will have little difficulty in identifying them. Nevertheless, they are mentioned here only from a sense of duty. Lawless was not a humorous draughtsman, and his efforts to become one merely deprived his work of all artistic significance.

In 1861 there appeared the first of the only two books for which Lawless made original illustrations, if we except *Passages from Modern English Poets*, illustrated by the Junior Etching Club [1862]. *Lyra Germanica* contains three drawings by him: they are small, but they show him

M. J. LAWLESS: 'Rung into Heaven'

[*Good Words*, 1862]

M. J. LAWLESS: 'One Dead'
[*The Churchman's Family Magazine*, 1863]

at his best, and have a grace, and even a delicacy, which make us half inclined to blame cheap paper, hasty printing, and indifferent engraving, for most of the defects visible in his magazine work. On page 47 there is a lovely little study of a weeping girl; on page 90 a charming domestic idyll of an old lady and a child in church, reading from the same book; while, stretching down the margin of page 190, there is a long narrow design of a boy sitting under the wall of one of those Dürer towns the artist loved and drew in such bold decorative relief.

According to tradition the other book illustrated by Lawless is Formby's *Life of St. Patrick* (1862). Gleeson White refers to it, but adds, ' the labour in tracking it was lost; for, whoever made the designs, the wood engravings are of the lowest order, and the book no more interesting than an illustrated religious tract is usually.' It is rather strange he did not guess that he had somehow got hold of the wrong book, for as a matter of fact the names Maurand and Chazal actually appear, though very faintly, on several of the illustrations. Also, I should not be surprised if whoever gave him the hint actually knew of the real book, for though it is not the *Life of St. Patrick*, Formby is the author. I owe my own discovery of it to Mr. Harold Hartley, who showed me a portion of it, all he possessed, Part VII. The work is *Pictorial Bible and Church History Stories*, by H. Formby (Longman, Brown, Green and Longmans [1862]). It is undated, and this 1862 volume is the third. But the earlier volumes contain nothing by Lawless; all his drawings appear in Parts VI and VII of the third; and those that are dated are dated 1861, with a single exception, which belongs to 1862. Part VI contains two designs: ' St. Bernard with his Companions ' (p. 323), and ' Thomas à Beckett before Parliament at Northampton ' (p. 346). Part VII contains nine: ' St. Francis of Assisi ' (p. 364), ' Francis Distributes his Clothes to the Beggars ' (p. 377), ' St. Francis before the Sultan ' (p. 398), ' Meeting of St. Dominic and St. Francis ' (p. 413), ' St. Charles Borromeo ' (p. 458), ' St. Philip Neri ' (p. 461), ' Kill the Wretches ' (p. 479), ' The Carmelite Community ' (p. 501), and ' The Aged Mother ' (p. 502).

V.   FREDERICK SANDYS (1832-1904)

Though Sandys lived for more than seventy years his twenty-five drawings for the wood were all made well within our period, and they rank among the most important it produced. Rossetti considered him to be ' the greatest of living draughtsmen ': Millais's opinion of his work was equally high. He was born in Norwich on the 1st of May 1832, the only son of Antony Sandys, a portrait painter. The father was interested, scientifically as well as artistically, in the methods and technique of the old masters, and

[55]

the son inherited this taste, being particularly drawn to the early Flemish painters—Roger van der Weyden, Jan van Eyck, and others of their school —whom he preferred to the Florentines. Sandys's own earliest drawings were not imaginative designs but illustrations for a couple of local handbooks. The first of the great series of wood engravings was made in 1860, when he received a commission from Thackeray, then editor of the newly founded *Cornhill Magazine*, to supply an illustration for George Mac-Donald's *Legend of the Portent*. That his work was already held in high esteem, however, is proved by the fact that he received forty guineas for the block. Sandys himself described to Mr. Percy Bate the arrival of that first boxwood block, and of how puzzling he found it. 'He knew nothing of the correct way of preparing it; it was impossible to work on its smooth surface with either pencil or pen, and he finally drew "The Portent" line by line with a brush and Indian ink, and found the process so simple and the result so satisfactory that he always thereafter employed the same method.' The sable brush he employed was so fine, says Mr. Borough Johnson, 'that it became sometimes practically one hair; his other instrument was a quill pen cut by himself from the tip of the point upwards. He drew everything from life, seldom even making use of the lay figure for his draperies, and in fact did nothing without a model before him. It was his method to prepare most careful studies in pen and ink or pencil, before drawing direct on the wood block. He never used Chinese white to lighten or correct, but worked from a large slab of Indian ink.'

Sandys drew in pure black line, never forgetting that his drawing had to pass through the hands of the engraver, and that its ultimate appearance depended on the success with which the latter could reproduce it. He left as little to chance as possible; he did not experiment in tints; he knew the engraver's limitations and gave him no more than he could do—with the result that there are none of those repinings, varied by bitter jesting, which accompanied the production of each of the Rossetti blocks. He does indeed complain about the treatment of his 'Advent of Winter' ('It was my best drawing, entirely spoilt by the cutter '), but for the most part he is satisfied, and of the 'Danäe' he wrote, 'My drawing was most perfectly cut by Swain, from my point of view, the best piece of wood-cutting of our time.'

In the very first of these illustrations, 'The Legend of the Portent' (*Cornhill*, 1860), the style of Sandys is mature: there is no faltering of touch in the bold sweeping line; the thing is as perfectly achieved as the 'Helen' of 1866. In the next, 'Yet Once More on the Organ Play' (*Once a Week*, 1861), he openly proclaims his debt to the master who has most influenced and inspired him. The very signature is modelled upon Dürer's; but, for all that, the drawing remains his own—an amazing interpretation of the

[56]

F. SANDYS: ' Rosamond, Queen of the Lombards '
[*Once a Week*, 1861]

F. Sandys: 'The Little Mourner'

[Willmott's *Sacred Poetry*]

commonplace poem it accompanies. In the same volume (iv) of *Once a Week*, the illustration for *The Dying Heroes* is given in the index to Sandys, but it quite certainly is not his. 'The Sailor's Bride', however, on page 434, *is* his—a lovely thing, revealing more tenderness than he usually displays.

'From my Window', in vol. v, is conceived in an even more idyllic mood. It is the most graceful of all the Sandys designs, a drawing filled with atmosphere, and yet the woman's beauty has in it something of the austere severity and grandeur of a figure by Pier dei Franceschi. 'The Three Statues of Aegina' (vol. v) is a fine but less attractive drawing; while 'Rosamond Queen of the Lombards' (also vol. v) is among the supreme designs of the Pre-Raphaelite school, and indeed of the whole black and white art of England. There is more of Rossetti than of Dürer in the 'Rosamond'—in the tragic and voluptuous beauty of the Queen as she broods over the skull of her dead father, while in the background we see the limp supine form of the king, into whose drunken body she has plunged a knife. After Rossetti's manner, too, are the details—the lamp, the crucifix, the carved altar, the burning brazier. Its melody of line, its richness and imaginative power, place this drawing very high even among Sandys's best things.

Of the three designs in *Once a Week*, vol. vi, the Düreresque 'Old Chartist' is his most famous drawing. The subject here is taken neither from legend nor from the past, the old Chartist of George Meredith's poem is simply an English working man, leaning in meditation over a bridge, beneath which a brook flows through a woody landscape, and a water-rat 'washes his old poll with busy paws'. The second design, 'The King at the Gate', is not particularly interesting; but 'Jacques de Caumont' (p. 614) would be notable if only for the charming study of the child with the tray.

In the beautiful drawing of 'Harold Harfagr', vol. vii, p. 154, Sandys is once more at his best. Mr. E. J. Sullivan calls it 'one of the perfect and impressive compositions that this world has produced'. The other Sandys designs in the seventh volume of *Once a Week* are 'The Death of King Warwolf' and 'The Boy Martyr'. The latter seems to me, whether through faulty engraving or not, to be among the artist's very few failures. The lion is unsatisfactory, and to adorn the boy with a beard was surely not a happy thought.

Volumes vi and vii of *Once a Week* both belong to 1862, and in this same year, in *Good Words*, we find 'Until her Death', a drawing in which Sandys once more pays homage to Dürer, the Dürer of the 'Melancolia'. It is a glorious design, unsurpassable in its suggestiveness and in the grandeur of the attitude of the seated woman whose meditation has evoked the image of Death. Less tragic, because more melodramatic, is the 'Manoli'

(*Cornhill*, 1862), and though superb drawing does much to relieve the crude horror of the subject, one can scarcely place it in the first rank of Sandys's designs, but rather with ' The Portent ', which it more closely resembles, indeed, than any of the others.

To 1862 also belong the two lovely drawings for Willmott's *English Sacred Poetry*. ' Life's Journey ' shows a father finding his little boy who has been lost in the woods, and nothing more living and beautiful than the figure of the lost child can be imagined. ' The Little Mourner ' is again a drawing of a child. The poem is Dean Alford's, and describes how a girl kept watch, winter and summer, over the grave of her mother and sisters. The cemetery lies deep in snow, and beyond the walls we see the frozen hills and fields, the naked trees and houses. The drawing of the little girl is masterly, its exquisite purity of line—so sensitive and delicate in its strength —being hardly attained by any other draughtsman of our period. About this time, also, I should imagine, was made the powerful drawing of 'Jacob ', which appears in *Dalziel's Bible Gallery*.

The index to *Good Words* for 1863 gives two illustrations to Sandys— ' The Sheep and the Goat ' and ' Sleep '—but only the ' Sleep ' is his. Sandys in this drawing comes nearer to the naturalistic school, which sprang up in the immediate wake of the Pre-Raphaelites, than he does elsewhere, and if the attitude of the stooping figure is characteristic, the drawing as a whole is not beyond the scope of J. D. Watson. Nobody, however, could mistake ' The Waiting Time ' (*Churchman's Family Magazine*, 1863) for a Watson, dignified and impressive though that artist's work often is. But ' The Waiting Time ' is a great design, and such an epithet is hardly applicable even to the best of Watson's drawings.

Sandys's own favourite among his wood engravings was the ' Amor Mundi ', which appeared in *The Shilling Magazine* (1865) as an illustration for Christina Rossetti's poem. The ' Amor Mundi ' is a beautiful, slightly unpleasant, and extraordinarily suggestive drawing, depicting two lovers strolling down the easy path of sensuality to the hidden hollow where death lies waiting. Not Death as he is usually symbolized, but the dead and corrupted body of this very woman, now hanging in foolish soulless laughter on her lover's arm. A rat gnaws at the tattered wrist of the corpse, whose flesh Christina describes as ' pale ', but to which Sandys has given the terrible hues of putrefaction.

To 1866 belong ' The Advent of Winter ' (*Quiver*); ' Helen and Cassandra ' (*Once a Week*); ' Cleopatra ', for a poem by Swinburne (*Cornhill*); and ' If ' (*The Argosy*). Of these, the last, again for a poem by Christina Rossetti, is perhaps the most beautiful. The woman sitting by the shore, looking out across the sea, clutching the coarse sea grass in one hand,

F. Sandys: 'The Old Chartist'

[*Once a Week*, 1862]

F. SANDYS: 'The Waiting Time'

[*The Churchman's Family Magazine*, 1863]

F. SANDYS: 'Amor Mundi'

[*The Shilling Magazine*, 1865]

and biting her hair as she longs for her tardy lover, is a conception peculiarly characteristic. We find the biting of the hair repeated in the 'Proud Maisie' engraved many years later in *The English Illustrated Magazine* for 1891. Another engraving only published in later years, but which really belongs to our period, is 'Danäe in the Brazen Chamber'. This appeared in 1888 in the third volume of *The Century Guild Hobby Horse*, but was actually made in 1860 for *Once a Week*, to illustrate a poem of Swinburne's. One detail in the drawing, however, proved too realistic for the editor, and, since Sandys refused to emasculate Danäe's lover, the design was not published.

A similar timidity seems to have defeated a far more important undertaking, for in this case a whole series of drawings was involved. It was the Dalziels, as usual, with whom the idea originated. Their plan was to bring out a fully illustrated *Biblical Life of Joseph*, and with their customary acumen they chose Frederick Sandys as the man for their purpose. That he was willing to accept, and indeed had accepted the commission, we may gather from the following letter. 'I have not yet commenced the drawings of *Joseph*—it requires an immense amount of research, and it would be most unwise to spoil the series, and I promise you the drawings as soon as you reasonably can ask for them. When would you like to have the *Life* out—in twelve months? If so you shall have my drawings in time. I am coming to town in a week to make some drawings at the British Museum and to get some Jewish dresses. . . . I am doing all this that I may thoroughly, or, as far as it is my gift, make myself acquainted with Jews and Egyptians—to know all that is characteristic and beautiful. . . . Millais's " Moses " is not a bit what I want—it is not a Princess, a daughter of Pharaoh, he has drawn. . . . The more I look at the cutting of " Life's Journey " the more I am delighted and full of hope for " Joseph ".'

'Unfortunately', write the Dalziels, from whose *Record* I have just quoted a portion of Sandys's letter, ' he never sent in one drawing for the book.' That is the only comment they make, but Gleeson White assures us that several of the drawings were completed, and from his diplomatic reference to a ' too prudish publisher ' rejecting ' an artist's ideas ' we can only infer that the emotions of Potiphar's wife were not left unrecorded. The identity of the ' too prudish publisher ' remains hidden. Obviously, from their note quoted above, the Dalziels themselves had nothing to do with the rejection of the drawings, and Mr. Gilbert Dalziel tells me he cannot recollect ever having heard the matter discussed.

Two or three further designs by Sandys may be mentioned, though they do not belong to the series of wood engravings: ' The Nightmare ' (1857), a parody of Millais's ' Sir Isumbras at the Ford ', engraved on zinc and printed as a broadsheet; a frontispiece engraved on steel for Meredith's incomparable *Shaving of Shagpat*, and illustrating the tale of *Bhanavar the Beautiful* (1865); another steel frontispiece, for Miss Muloch's *Christian's Mistake* (1866); a very elaborate and Pre-Raphaelite drawing, ' Morgan le Fay ', reproduced as a supplement to *The British Architect* (October 1879); ' Miranda ' (*The Hobby Horse*, 1888); and an unfinished wood drawing, ' The Spirit of the Storm ', which appeared in the first number of *The Quarto* (1896). There are other drawings, of course—and among them several portraits—but I have given those which seemed to come most nearly within the purview of our present chronicle.

After her husband's death Mrs. Sandys issued a portfolio, *Reproductions of Woodcuts by F. Sandys*, 1860-1866, published by Carl Hentschel. This contains the twenty-five wood engravings neatly bound between folding wrappers. It is a convenient memorial of the artist's work, but the impressions leave a good deal to be desired. They have nothing like the brilliancy, sharpness, and depth of the original prints, and were probably reproduced from photographs of these, while the soft paper on which they are printed is itself unsuitable. Certainly the collector who takes the trouble to hunt up the actual engravings in the magazines where they appeared will not find his labour wasted.

VI. JOHN EVERETT MILLAIS (1829-1896)

Though we place Millais in the Pre-Raphaelite group, the majority of his illustrations belong really to the later school, and have far more in common with the drawings of Fred Walker than with those of Rossetti or Sandys. That he was a great draughtsman I suppose nobody will deny; that he occupies quite the position in relation to his fellow-illustrators allotted to him by Gleeson White, as a kind of demi-god among mortals, we may be more loath to admit. His finest imaginative designs do not surpass those of Sandys, and it is quite possible to prefer many of Charles Keene's drawings even to the drawings for *Framley Parsonage*. That is not, with the present writer at all events, to claim that the Keenes are better, it is merely to express a preference for a particular technique, for the broader, looser, impressionist method of Keene.

Millais never lacked appreciation, though when he was painting his best pictures he may have lacked popularity. His career was in truth as brilliant as that of the hero of a ' best-selling ' novel. Born in 1829, he had already been studying art for two years when, at the age of eleven, he became a student at the Royal Academy Schools. During the next six years he was the pet pupil, the infant prodigy, carrying off every prize for which he competed. At sixteen he painted his picture of ' Pizarro ',

J. E. MILLAIS: 'The Lost Piece of Silver'
[*The Parables of Our Lord*]

which was hung in the Academy's annual exhibition. The 'Lorenzo and Isabella' belongs to 1849, 'The Carpenter's Shop' to 1850. These dates seem incredible, but there they are. It is, however, with his work in black and white that we are concerned here. The wood engravings are so numerous that it is difficult to know in what order to take them. A chronological method presents no great advantage, because, in the style of the drawings, there is little if any development. The variations in manner are purely experimental and offer no clue to the exact date at which any particular drawing may have been made. The first wood engraving was made for *The Music Master* of 1855; the next designs appear in the *Tennyson* of 1857, and, since we have already considered these, it might be as well to reverse our usual order and take all the illustrations done for books before turning to the larger number scattered through the pages of *Once a Week*, the *Cornhill*, and other periodicals.

Millais's two designs for Willmott's *Poets of the Nineteenth Century* belong to the same year as the famous *Tennyson*; that is to say, to 1857; and one of them, the drawing for Coleridge's *Love*, is, I think, the most moving and impassioned he ever made. He made many drawings which in beauty of line and form equal it, but none, it seems to me, which shows the same quality of ecstasy. This picture of two figures clinging together in a darkened landscape, with the great white moon rising between the branches of the trees, strikes us indeed as being in no way inferior to the work of Coleridge himself. The drawing for Byron's *Dream*, though a lovely thing too, has not this intensely poetic quality. Rather strangely it brings together the two distinct groups of his illustrations—the boy belonging to the Pre-Raphaelite group, the lady being the lady we shall meet so often in *Mistress and Maid* and other tales of contemporary life. These two designs, with Madox Brown's *Prisoner of Chillon*, rise far above everything else in a book which nevertheless contains charming things of an older fashion.

Such is not the case with the single drawing Millais contributed to *Lays of the Holy Land* (Nisbet [1858]). 'The Finding of Moses' may be classed with his average work, and, though Gleeson White gives it first place among the illustrations in this not very interesting volume, I should be inclined myself to single out certain drawings by Thomas Dalziel, which in their own way achieve a small but genuine perfection. On the other hand, *The Home Affections* (1858), though also somewhat disappointing if we are looking for the newer school of design, contains two of Millais's masterpieces, 'There's Nae Luck About the House' and 'The Border Widow'; and the fact that the latter was by some oversight omitted from his *Collected Illustrations* makes the book particularly desirable. Two etchings contributed to *Passages from Thomas Hood*, illustrated by the Junior Etching Club, belong to 1858, and another appears in *Passages from Modern English Poets* —also illustrated by the Junior Etching Club—[1862].

In December 1861 Chapman & Hall brought out the first volume of *Orley Farm*, and in September 1862, the second; the title pages of both volumes being dated 1862. The novel had originally been issued in twenty monthly parts, the last of which is dated October 1862, and altogether it contains forty drawings by Millais, engraved by Dalziel. Of these drawings Trollope himself writes in his *Autobiography* that they are the best he has seen ' in any novel in any language '. Trollope was certainly most fortunate in obtaining Millais for his illustrator, a fact he himself fully realized. ' Mr. Millais ', he tells us in another passage, ' was engaged to illustrate Framley Parsonage [in *The Cornhill Magazine*]. The first drawing did not appear till after the dinner of which I have spoken, and I do not think that I knew at the time that he was engaged on my novel. When I did know it, it made me very proud. He afterwards illustrated *Orley Farm*, *The Small House at Allington*, *Rachel Ray*, and *Phineas Finn*. Altogether he drew from my tales eighty-seven drawings, and I do not think that more conscientious work was ever done by man. Writers of novels know well—and so ought readers of novels to have learned—that there are two modes of illustrating, either of which may be adopted equally by a bad and by a good artist. To which class Mr. Millais belongs I need not say; but, as a good artist, it was open to him simply to make a pretty picture, or to study the work of the author from whose writing he was bound to take his subject. I have too often found that the former alternative has been thought to be the better, as it certainly is the easier method. An artist will frequently dislike to subordinate his ideas to those of an author, and will sometimes be too idle to find out what those ideas are. But this artist was neither proud nor idle. In every figure that he drew it was his object to promote the views of the writer whose work he had undertaken to illustrate, and he never spared himself any pains in studying that work, so as to enable him to do so. I have carried on some of those characters from book to book, and have had my own early ideas impressed indelibly on my memory by the excellence of his delineations. Those illustrations were commenced fifteen years ago, and from that time up to this day my affection for the man of whom I am speaking has increased. To see him has always been a pleasure. His voice has been a sweet sound in my ears. Behind his back I have never heard him praised without joining the eulogist; I have never heard a word spoken against him without opposing the censurer. These words, should he ever see them, will come to him from the grave, and will tell him of my regard,—as one living man never tells another.' Well—that passage does as much honour to the writer of it as to its subject: it is the kind of thing (all too rare, alas!) that

J. E. MILLAIS: 'The Hidden Treasure'
[*The Parables of Our Lord*]

makes us think better of human nature and of this world which tries it so sorely.

The drawings for *Orley Farm* do not excel, in many cases do not equal, some of the earlier drawings made for *Framley Parsonage* and the tales of Miss Martineau, but they may be taken as representative. In vol. i the frontispiece and the drawing on page 227 of 'Felix Graham in Trouble' are particularly attractive: in vol. ii the best things are on pages 40, 149, and 206: while the rest maintain an excellent average. In none, I think, will you find the beauty of spacing, the lovely rhythmic line, the coolness and the breadth of the finest illustrations of Charles Keene. But one quality Millais could express which perpetually eluded Keene—if, indeed, he was ever conscious of it. It is the quality of breeding. Had I to illustrate my meaning by a solitary picture I should choose, I think, a drawing in *Once a Week* for Tennyson's *Grandmother's Apology*. Looking at Millais's drawing we know that it has taken many generations to produce this old lady and this little girl. Quite apart from accidents of beauty, they have a fineness, a distinction, an indescribable stamp of race, which none even of du Maurier's dukes and duchesses possesses. It is a kind of distinction that Charles Keene seems to have missed utterly, for if he had not missed it he could have reproduced it, since there was nothing that came within his vision which he could not express in drawing. Beauty, when he cared to record it, was always at his command; but his sense of class distinction, like Phil May's later, was curiously weak. His 'swells' are infinitely the least successful portraits in his gallery; Evan Harrington, the tailor's son, is perhaps as near an approach to an aristocrat as he ever reached.

In Mr. J. G. Millais's *Life and Letters* of his father he mentions three drawings for books made in 1862—one for *Maggie Band* (Sampson Low), and two for *Robinson Crusoe* (Macmillan). *Maggie Band* I have been unable to trace, but the *Robinson Crusoe* (though I have not seen it either) appears to be an edition edited by Clark for the 'Golden Treasury Series'. Earlier than these, however, are a couple of frontispieces engraved on steel for *Nothing New* and *The Valley of a Hundred Fires*, both issued in 1861, and a frontispiece for *John Halifax, Gentleman*—all belonging to Hurst and Blackett's 'Standard Library', for which, in 1864, he made a further drawing, this time a frontispiece to Victor Hugo's *Les Misérables*.

In 1862 Millais made four drawings for Sarah Tytler's *Papers for Thoughtful Girls*, one of which, 'Our Sister Grizel', is in his most charming vein. In 1863 he made a drawing for Wilkie Collins's *No Name*, and to the same year belongs a delightful vignette for the title page of that dainty little volume, *Wordsworth's Poems for the Young*. 1863, however, is chiefly memorable for the publication of his masterpiece, the famous *Parables of Our Lord*,

[71]

really issued then, though it is dated 1864. Of this superb work much has been written, but it is worthy of all the praise ever bestowed upon it. Here we have the artist determined to do his best, sparing himself no pains, making as elaborate studies for his designs as Rossetti or Sandys did for theirs. It is not surprising to find that we must go back several years in tracing the origin and history of the book. Another Dalziel project, the first positive allusion to it seems to be in a letter from Millais himself, dated August 1857, in which he accepts the commission, but at the same time makes it a condition that he must be given his own time in which to prepare the drawings. 'I should make it', he says, 'a labour of love like yourselves.' Originally the agreement was that he should do thirty drawings, but in the end this number had to be reduced to twenty, and even then the twenty were spread over some six years. In a letter quoted by the Dalziels Millais explains the delay. 'They are separate pictures, and so I exert myself to the utmost to make them as complete as possible. I can do ordinary illustrations as quickly as most men, but these designs can scarcely be regarded in the same light—each Parable I illustrate perhaps a dozen times before I fix, and the " Hidden Treasure " I have altered on the wood at least six times. The manipulation of the drawings takes much less time than the arrangement, although you cannot but see how carefully they are executed.'

The cutting, by Dalziel, was equally careful: again and again Millais praises it as perfect: nothing could be more exquisite, he says, than the rendering of ' The Unjust Judge '; and when the book at last appeared he expressed himself as delighted with it. Yet, commercially, it proved a disappointment. The issue during the previous year of twelve of the drawings in *Good Words* should, one would have imagined, have given it a useful advertisement; but neither critics nor public responded with the enthusiasm the publishers had expected. The twelve subjects that appeared in *Good Words* are ' The Leaven ', ' The Ten Virgins ', ' The Prodigal Son ', ' The Good Samaritan ', ' The Unjust Judge ', ' The Pharisee and the Publican ', ' The Hidden Treasure ', ' The Pearl of Great Price ', ' The Lost Piece of Silver ', ' The Sower ', ' The Unmerciful Servant ', and ' The Labourers of the Vineyard ': the remaining eight are ' The Tares ', ' The Wicked Husbandman ', ' The Foolish Virgins ', ' The Importunate Friend ', ' The Marriage Feast ', ' The Lost Sheep ', ' The Rich Man and Lazarus ', and ' The Good Shepherd '.[1]

[1] I learn from Mr. Gilbert Dalziel that his brother, Mr. Harvey Dalziel, on a recent visit to South Africa discovered in the Johannesburg Art Gallery two of Millais's original designs for *The Parables*. They are drawn on the wood-blocks in pencil and Chinese white, the subjects being 'The Good Shepherd' and 'The Importunate Friend'. This means that these two drawings, at any rate, must have been photographed on to two new blocks of exactly the same size as the ' originals ', and then engraved.

J. E. MILLAIS: 'The Wicked Husbandman'

[*The Parables of Our Lord*]

Familiarity with them cannot diminish our pleasure in these drawings. Given over to mice and damp, while Cruikshanks and Rowlandsons are treasured under lock and key, I have seen copies of this book stacked away in the lumber-room of more than one shop. It can be bought for two or three shillings, instead of the guinea at which it was published, nevertheless it remains among the treasures of English black and white art; and since so many copies have been allowed to perish, it may one day quite conceivably be among the rarest.

Of the twenty drawings, each is in its fashion admirable. We may have our favourites, but no two lists are likely to be identical. Millais has placed the design of ' The Sower ' first—a bare steep landscape of broken rocks and boulders, leading up to a small clump of those flat-boughed trees he loved, with a figure striding across the sky line, scattering the seed. ' The Leaven ' has the beauty of a charming pattern, and the beauty of the little girl in the background. In ' The Tares ' we see a wicked old man sowing the tares at night, while the creatures who symbolize evil, the sluggish snakes and glaring jackals, gather round him. In the ' Hidden Treasure ' the fine drawing of the oxen is even more striking than the drawing of the kneeling man, and a floating memory of this design seems to have influenced Houghton when he came to illustrate the ' Parable of the Sower ' in *The Sunday Magazine* five years later. ' The Wicked Husbandman ' is not at first sight very like a Millais—the technique, the treatment of the foliage, the brilliantly contrasted blacks and whites even suggest an early and particularly successful du Maurier; but it is a lovely drawing, and the variation from his customary manner is highly effective. ' The Foolish Virgins ' is a night piece; with light and shadow from a lamp playing over the beautiful faces of the girls kneeling in the rain as they beat against the closed door. ' The Good Samaritan ', besides its dramatic power and beauty of composition, has, in the donkey, another fine animal study. ' The Importunate Friend ' is subtle in its suggestion of character, the drawing of the cloaked figure superb. And again we have a composition as satisfying as it is unobtrusive. ' The Lost Sheep ' is a delicate landscape, extraordinarily beautiful in tone, with the figure of the shepherd and the sheep in the foreground. ' The Lost Piece of Silver ' is in pattern the most simple of all the drawings. The line has the flowing elastic quality of a water weed streaming in a current; the background is bare of detail; there is nothing but the stooping figure of the woman who holds the broom, with the square window behind, through which the stars and the moon are visible. A much larger engraving of this design appeared ten years later in *The Day of Rest*. ' The Prodigal Son ' is among the finest drawings of all. The pattern of the pagoda-like hut at the top of the picture is repeated in the exquisitely drawn cedar-trees: the contrasting tones are rich and full of colour: and how beautiful the sleeping sheep, the little pond, the dark and the fair heads of father and son clasped in each other's arms. Less appealing as a picture, ' The Unjust Judge ' as a character study is masterly. ' The Good Shepherd ', which seems less highly finished than its fellow designs, makes freer use of the white ground, the colour tending throughout to silvery greys.

The Dalziels printed fifty special copies of the *Parables* on India paper in 1864, but these were never issued to the public. Eventually the subscribers received them in an exceedingly sumptuous but somewhat unsightly form—a kind of album, with reproductions in facsimile of all Millais's letters on the subject. The album was dedicated to Poynter, and produced by Charles Dalziel at the Camden Press.

In 1864 Millais made a drawing for Trollope's *Rachel Ray*, and to the same year belongs *Lilliput Levée*, which ought not, however, to be mentioned here, as the Millais in it are reprints from magazines. To 1865 belongs *Little Songs for me to Sing*, a book of rhymes, with music by Henry Leslie, and illustrated with seven charming drawings of children and a vignette, all by Millais. A later, cheaper, and much enlarged edition of this book, Leslie's *Songs for Little Folks* (Cramer & Co.) has a frontispiece, ' St. Agnes' Eve ', which is not in the *Little Songs*. It is a beautiful drawing of a nun gazing out at a snowy winter landscape, and though I cannot place it elsewhere, I think it almost certainly must have been made originally for some earlier book than this—possibly, indeed, at the time he designed the ' St. Agnes' Eve ' for the Moxon *Tennyson*. *Dalziel's Arabian Nights*, in which he has a couple of rather indifferent drawings on pages 97 and 105, is also dated 1865.

Studies for Stories (1866), besides one drawing each by Houghton, Small, and Barnes, contains two designs by Millais: Mackay's *1001 Gems of Poetry* (1867), according to Gleeson White, contains one, but on looking it up I found it to be merely the ' Edward Gray ' reprinted from the Moxon *Tennyson*. The exact date of *Wace, ses œuvres, sa patrie*, par John Sullivan of Jersey, I do not know. The second edition, in which Millais's illustration appears, is, however, later than 1865. I have not seen this book— probably a pamphlet—but I found a proof of the drawing, a portrait of Wace, engraved by Swain, in the Print Room of the British Museum, and the actual print, used as an advertisement, in an album of broadsheets and leaflets in the Library.

Another wood engraving not particularly interesting except that it is little known, is the frontispiece to Goethe's *Egmont*, translated by A. D. Coleridge (Chapman & Hall, 1868). It too is engraved by Swain, and shows Egmont asleep, while Freedom, like an angel, hovers above him. Mr. J. N.

J. E. Millais: ' The Grandmother's Apology '
[*Once a Week*, 1859]

Hart put me on the track of this drawing. Finally, we have the four admirable illustrations made for Thackeray's *Barry Lyndon* (1879), one of which at least, ' The Last Days ', is a masterpiece. The drawing of that drunken figure seated at the table is the most realistic and the most terrible design Millais ever made.

Millais's first illustration for *Once a Week* appeared in the first number of that paper on the 2nd of July 1859, the remaining illustrations being by Leech, Tenniel, and Charles Keene—not a bad start. This little drawing of ' Magenta ', engraved by Dalziel, which shows a girl in a twilit room, still holding in her hand the newspaper in which she has just read the fatal news of the battle, is extremely characteristic, and despite a somewhat blurred printing is a most graceful and expressive design. Among the sixty-nine drawings contributed by Millais to *Once a Week* it holds a high place, having none of that scratchiness of pen work which detracts from the beauty of certain of the later illustrations. The second drawing, on page 41, for *The Grandmother's Apology*, I have already referred to. It seems to me an exquisite and flawless piece of work, the cat being just as successful as the little girl and her grandmother, while the engraving is perfect. Passing over the next drawing we come on page 306 to ' La Fille Bien Gardée ', a very simply expressed but very lively portrait of a girl reading, with a dog lying at her feet—the artist's own dog, one imagines, since he figures so often in the drawings. On page 316 we have another fine thing, this time tragic in theme, ' The Plague of Elliant ', in which a mother is seen dragging her dead children in a cart to their burying place. On page 482 ' A Lost Love ' is chiefly interesting because, without the signature, one would give it unhesitatingly to Matthew Lawless. On page 514 the ' St. Bartholomew ' is a very tender treatment of a mother and children, somewhat spoiled in the engraving.

In vol. ii we have six illustrations, none pre-eminent, although one of them, ' The Crown of Love ', the artist afterwards painted as a picture. Vol. iii contains seven drawings, among them two dainty little sketches, ' Violet ' and ' The Meeting ', and a third still more charming, ' The Iceberg ', of a mother sewing by her baby's cradle. There is a lightness and deftness about these drawings which make them particularly pleasing.

Of the two drawings in vol. iv both are below the artist's average, and of the two in vol. v, if one mentions the ' Swing Song ' it is because ' little Johnny, with the feathers in his hat ' foreshadows a host of the ' Bubbles ' and ' Cherry Ripe ' pictures in which the artist exploits the age of innocence.

Several of the twelve pictures in vol. vi are more interesting—especially that for the seventh chapter of Harriet Martineau's *Sister Anna's Probation*. Here the intricate, broken lines achieve something of the effect of a tapestry.

It is a beautiful drawing, and in this particular manner Millais never did anything better. Vol. vii has eleven designs, of which the first two, for another tale of Miss Martineau's, *The Anglers of the Dove*, are the most attractive; and to these might be added ' Margaret Wilson ', ' The Mite of Dorcas ', and ' Limerick Bells ', as maintaining his very high average.

From the eleven drawings in vol. viii one again selects three illustrating a tale by Miss Martineau. The story this time is *The Hampdens*, and the drawings are on pages 239, 267, and 365. In vol. ix there are nine drawings, all, with one exception, illustrations for Miss Martineau's *Son Christopher*, that on page 519 being a beautiful thing: and how infinitely more charming is the boy in it, as he sits buried in his book, for the reason that he is not prettified and idealized.

After 1863 Millais only made two more drawings for *Once a Week*— ' Death Dealing Arrows ', a symbolic design, which appeared in 1868; and ' Taking His Ease ', a drawing of a boy, which appeared in the Christmas Number of the same year—both rather commonplace.

To *The Cornhill Magazine* Millais contributed thirty full-page drawings and some initial letters, the first, ' Unspoken Dialogue ', being on page 197 of vol. i. The large drawings have this advantage over those he made for *Once a Week*, that they are printed separately from the text and on a specially prepared paper. They are also more careful than most of the later *Once a Week* designs. ' Last Words ', in the second volume, comes very near to his finest work. It is an interior, and it is strange how the tiny glimpse of land-scape through the window gives it an atmosphere of romantic poetry. Such an atmosphere one can hardly expect to find in the Trollope illustrations, however, and all the other drawings, with the exceptions of ' Horace Saltoun ' (vol. iii), ' Irene ' (vol. v), ' The Bishop and the Knight ' (vol. vi), and ' Madame de Monferrato ' (vol. x), are for Trollope's *Framley Parsonage* and *The Small House at Allington*—admirable things—in their own way unsur-passable.

In *London Society* there are only three drawings by Millais, but all are good. ' The Border Witch ', and the very charming ' Christmas Wreaths at Roxton ' belong to vol. ii; ' Knightly Worth ' appears in vol. vi (1864).

The first volume of *The Churchman's Family Magazine* (1863) contains only a couple of Millais, and they are not particularly interesting; but in *Good Words* there are thirty-two. He has nothing in the first two volumes, but for the serial, *Mistress and Maid*, in vol. iii (1862), he supplies twelve full-page illustrations which equal the best of the Trollope designs, and, taken together, form perhaps the finest series of drawings he made for any single novel. In the same volume he has two other contributions, ' Olaf ' and ' Highland Flora '. 1863 is the year of the *Parables*. In 1864 he has

J. E. MILLAIS: 'Son Christopher'

[*Once a Week*, 1863]

J. E. Millais: 'Irene'

[*The Cornhill Magazine*, 1862]

five drawings, three of which, ' The Bridal of Dandelot ', ' The Lark is Sing-ing ', and ' Scene for a Study ', are among his good things. Of the remain-ing two, ' Prince Philibert ' is a not very happy study of childhood, while ' Polly ', though it is a better drawing, is spoiled by its quite shameless appeal to the sentimentalists. Both these were reprinted in *Lilliput Levée*. After 1864 Millais appears only twice in *Good Words*. In the volume for 1878, fourteen years later, he contributes one of the illustrations to William Black's *Macleod of Dare*; and in 1882 he has an illustration for Trollope's *Kept in the Dark*.

Punch is not a journal in which we should look for the work of this artist, nevertheless it contains two drawings by him, one of which, a design for Burnand's *Mokeanna!* is well worth looking up, both because it is an excellent drawing in itself and because it is Millais's only experiment in grotesque. Burnand was always fortunate in his illustrators: for his later burlesques he had the incomparable Linley Sambourne, and for this, his first contribution, Gilbert, Charles Keene, du Maurier and Millais, all made wonderful designs. Millais's drawing for *Mokeanna!* appeared in 1863 in vol. xliv, page 115; his other *Punch* picture, ' Mr. Vandyke Brown's Sons Thrashing the Lay Figure '—showing two children attacking a lay figure in a studio—will be found in the *Almanac* for 1865.

In the *Illustrated London News* (December 1862) Millais has a large full-page drawing, ' Christmas Story Telling ', which is particularly inter-esting because it is, I think, the only drawing of this kind he made. It was engraved by Dalziel, and the proof will be found in the Dalziel collection in the British Museum.

In 1867 *St. Paul's Magazine* was started. It is not a very happy hunt-ing ground for our purpose, but as well as some illustrations by F. A. Fraser it contains the drawings made by Millais for Trollope's *Phineas Finn*. These appear in the first four volumes, and though Gleeson White says there are twenty-two there are really only twenty—two of the designs in the third volume being reprinted in the fourth. The *Phineas Finn* illustrations seem to me to be on a perceptibly lower level than those for the earlier Trollope novels.

Lastly, *The Sunday Magazine* (1883), on page 756, contains ' These Twin Girls ', by Millais. Curiously enough, the familiar signature is absent from the print though it appears in the proof.

VII. ARTHUR HUGHES (1832-1915)

Arthur Hughes was born in London in 1832 and received his art education at the Royal Academy Schools, exhibiting his first picture in

1854, the year before the *Music Master* drawings. He was also one of that enthusiastic little band of workers who, under Rossetti, produced the vanishing frescos of the Oxford Union. The story of that impulsive and light-hearted experiment is too well known to need repetition—how, in a state of happy and complete ignorance concerning the science of fresco painting, the task was begun, on brick walls covered with whitewash. The frescos, or rather the dissolving views, are said to have been very lovely during their few months of visibility; Rossetti's (unfinished, of course) the loveliest of all.

Though Arthur Hughes was eventually to make a great many black and white designs, his beginnings in this medium were desultory and tentative enough. He never, indeed, became a first-rate draughtsman, still less such a master as Sandys, Millais, Houghton, or Keene. But he had what is rarer than clever draughtsmanship, a spark of genius, and a personal charm so persuasive that it goes far to make up for a somewhat wobbly technique. In the *Music Master* drawings of 1855 he was not really expressing himself, nor has he made any advance in his next drawing, the solitary design he contributed two years later to Willmott's *Poets of the Nineteenth Century*. This is merely a pretty, Doyle-like arrangement of bluebells and fairies, such as any " gifted amateur " might produce; and for three years there are no more drawings. Then, in the Christmas Number of *The Queen* (1861), come a couple of designs, 'Hark the Herald Angels Sing' and 'Born on Christmas Eve', the latter a delightful thing, a genuine Hughes, showing an old man in spectacles playing on the violoncello, and a little boy, his head on one side, playing the triangle. Another two years' interval is followed by an illustration for *Margaret Denzil's History (Cornhill*, 1863), while with 'At the Sepulchre' (*Good Words*, 1864) the artist reaches a point beyond which— along this line at least—he never passed. The content of this drawing is entirely spiritual, and it possesses perhaps as much beauty of line and form as Hughes was destined to achieve.

'The Farewell Valentine', contributed to *London Society* (vol. vii, 1865), shows that he is not in the front rank as an illustrator of modern fiction: 'A Will of Her Own' (*Good Cheer*, 1868) is another drawing of the same kind: but 'Carmina Nuptiala' (*Good Words*, 1869) marks a return to the world of imagination, and 'Blessings in Disguise' (*Sunday Magazine*, 1869) is among his most beautiful designs. There follows a brief relapse: the title 'Not Mine' is singularly appropriate to the very commonplace drawing of a fashionable lady and gentleman holding hands which he contributed to *London Society* (1870); but 'The Mariner's Cave' and 'Fancy', in *Good Words* for the same year, emphatically *are* his, and the succeeding volume (1871) has four drawings in his best manner. Three of these were

[84]

ARTHUR HUGHES:
'At the Back of the North Wind'
[*Good Words for the Young*, 1870]

made for an illustrated musical edition of Tennyson's *Loves of the Wrens* (Sullivan supplying the music), and it was only after the cantankerous poet had discovered that he did not really want illustrations that the pictures were cut down and issued in *Good Words*.

In *The Sunday Magazine* for 1870 there is a delightful drawing, 'My Heart'; and in 1871 two other good things, 'The First Sunrise' and 'The Tares and the Wheat'. To the volume for 1872 Hughes gives 'Sunday Musings', 'Daria' (one of his most striking drawings, remarkable for the lovely figure of the weeping boy-angel) and 'Night and Day', one of his few landscapes: and to *Good Words* (1872) he gives the exquisitely fantastic 'Will o' the Wisp', 'The Carpenter', 'The Man with Three Friends', and two richly imaginative compositions entitled 'Vanity Fair'. A few later designs—very much later—appeared in *The London Home Monthly* for 1895, where he illustrated Hall Caine's *Graih My Chree* with five drawings, and Frederick Greenwood's *Good Night* with two; and in *The Graphic* (Christmas Number, 1887).

I have left, however, to the last the periodical which for Arthur Hughes enthusiasts is by far the most important. To the first five volumes of *Good Words for the Young* he contributed no less than two hundred and thirty-one drawings—fifteen more than Gleeson White places to his credit—as well as a very beautiful cover design made in November 1870. Here, in these pictures for children, he at last enters his own world—a world very close to that of Blake's *Songs of Innocence*. It would be easy, I dare say, for a drawing master to pick holes in Arthur Hughes's technique. He might point to deficiencies in knowledge—knowledge of anatomy, of perspective—he might point to deficiencies in skill—the very uncertain fashion in which the clothes are realized: he might continue his criticism into matters of light and shade and form:—and, when all is said, the drawings remain beautiful—fulfilling perfectly their aim, strong with the strength that comes from complete conviction. They are in the highest degree subjective; their source of inspiration is an emotion which in most people does not survive the period of childhood, but which in Arthur Hughes did survive it. These drawings have been conceived in a mysterious world, out of space, out of time—a world to which the artist *goes back*, so that he is not in the ordinary sense drawing for other children at all, but drawing for himself. It is true that the past to which he returns is one in which everything is created anew after the dreamer's desire. This particular dreamer happens to love all that is sweet, gentle, innocent; hence it is with these qualities that the human beings he meets are endowed. For they somehow *are* human—his little boys and girls—in spite of their half angelic sexlessness and strange air of dreamy gravity. They may be, and indeed are, superficially less real than the very earthy little boys of Charles Keene and Linley Sambourne, or even than the sophisticated children of du Maurier; but they are as faithful to the imaginative side of childhood as these others are to its street play and drawing-room manners. In George MacDonald's *At the Back of the North Wind*, Arthur Hughes found a subject after his own heart. It was George MacDonald, says Mr. Laurence Housman, 'who invented as a new form of literature the adventures of a child in his nightgown', but it is in Arthur Hughes's illustrations that this new form of literature comes most vividly to life. The artist was unhampered by George MacDonald's strong moral purpose. *He* is moral, also, but it is because he is faithful to the lovable qualities in the mind of his young hero. And yet this mind is not quite normal: it hovers perpetually on the borderline between sleeping and waking, vision and reality; and when the dream world overlaps the real world then the adventure begins. Whether we explain these adventures by saying that Diamond walks in his sleep, or by saying that he is a prey to delusions, does not matter in the least; they are for him real. The marvel is that such a story escaped the charge of morbidity, and no doubt only its faults saved it. It is saved, I mean, from such an accusation, by the interventions of the author in the character of wise parent, by the moralist who keeps a vigilant eye on that other collaborator, the poet, lest he should be carried away by the merely beautiful and fantastic possibilities of his subject. But it is in such beautiful possibilities that Arthur Hughes revels. He sees all things just as Diamond saw them, and his wisdom is no wiser than the child's. Arthur Hughes made many charming illustrations for fairy tales, but it is because *The North Wind* is *not* a fairy tale that it gives him his great opportunity. He made, on its appearance in *Good Words for the Young*, seventy-six drawings for it, and from the first—in which we see little Diamond, the coachman's son, peeping down from his bed in the stable loft at old Diamond, the horse who sleeps in the stall beneath him— to the last—in which he is lying white and still in a proper bed in a proper house—they show the artist at his finest. What they convey above all is the atmosphere of the unearthly side of the story, so that one becomes at last tempted to suspect, and to suspect, I think, unjustly, that it is the drawings, primarily, which create that atmosphere. Their beauty is at once so strange and so homely, seeming to bring into one world the cat purring on the hearth, and the wildest gleams of fantasy. What could be more perfect than that little engraving which shows Diamond kneeling up in bed to listen through the stable wall to his dear North Wind?—yet it is only one of many. North Wind herself varies in a dream-like fashion; she is now hardly more than the wind, or a whirl of vapour; she is now a lady who leads the little boy by the hand; she is now a goddess in whose hair he flies over the earth; she is

ARTHUR HUGHES:
' The Princess and the Goblin '
[*Good Words for the Young*, 1871]

now a colossal figure whose foot, as he clasps it, is as large as Diamond's whole body. Turn to pages 541 and 542 of the first volume of *Good Words for the Young* and study the four admirable drawings there. In the two that represent the great empty stillness of the cathedral at night, with the tiny figure of the boy lost in its vast loneliness, we have, I think, the highest kind of poetry: and what an immensity of space is suggested in a drawing that actually measures three inches by two and a half. Look, again, at the drawing of Diamond and the old horse on page 301 of vol. ii, and see with what magic the sympathy that exists between them is expressed.

The drawings for Henry Kingsley's *Boy in Grey*, which also began as a serial in the first volume of *Good Words for the Young*, though attractive, and perhaps more decorative, are far less intimate in quality than the drawings for *The North Wind*. In the second volume of *Good Words for the Young*, for a very homely tale of George MacDonald's, *Ranald Bannerman's Boyhood*, Hughes supplies thirty-six illustrations, as well as a number of fanciful designs for *Lilliput Revels*. In vol. iii (1871) he has thirty drawings for *The Princess and the Goblin*, and sixteen others, among them the lovely designs for *Barbara's Pet Lamb, Mercy*, and *King Arthur's Boar Hunt*.

The drawings for *The Princess and the Goblin* are for the most part purely fantastic, but George MacDonald's next story, *Gutta-Percha Willie*, is on domestic lines. It runs through the 1872 volume, but the illustrations are only nine in number. *Innocent's Island*, on the other hand, has twenty-four illustrations, and *The Wind and the Moon* one.

1873 brings us not only to the beginning of the end, but to the end itself. The very title of the magazine is changed: it now becomes *Good Things*. Arthur Hughes supplies twenty-four drawings, but nearly half of them are in the special Christmas Number. There are no more stories by George MacDonald, and if we omit the Hughes drawings, a few of which are in his best manner, there is nothing to interest us. After 1873 the magazine ceases to count.

But these five volumes, although the fifth shows so marked a falling-off, are among those the collector must possess. As a monument to the genius of one man there is nothing like them in periodical literature, and besides Arthur Hughes's contributions the earlier volumes contain capital things by Pinwell, Houghton, Small, Herkomer, Mahoney, Basil Bradley, F. A. Fraser, and others.

This, so far as I am aware, covers all, or nearly all Arthur Hughes's contributions to magazines. Turning to the books illustrated by him, the first—after the *Music Master* volume, *Poets of the Nineteenth Century*, and Woolner's *My Beautiful Lady*, for which he made a vignette—is *Enoch Arden* (Moxon, 1866). It contains twenty-five drawings and a cover design, all by our artist, though, with a few exceptions, not in his best manner. To 1867 belongs George MacDonald's *Dealings with the Fairies* (Strahan), a charming, dumpy little book with a dozen drawings. Palgrave's *Five Days' Entertainment at Wentworth Grange* (Macmillan, 1868) is a larger volume, containing a vignette engraved on steel and seventeen admirable wood engravings.

At the back of *Wentworth Grange* you will find an announcement of a new edition of *Tom Brown's Schooldays*, with illustrations by Arthur Hughes. The book, a quarto, was in fact published in the December of that year, 1868, though it is dated 1869. Some of these *Tom Brown* illustrations are well known, for until comparatively recently they were still reprinted with each new edition of the story; but others were dropped out of the later editions, and among those sacrificed are many of the most charming. The quarto contained fifty-eight illustrations, whereas the octavo reprints have only twenty-six. From contemporary editions, alas, all are gone, the thankless task of providing substitutes having been placed in the capable hands of Mr. E. J. Sullivan, for whom, however, this particular work can hardly have been a labour of love.

England's Antiphon (Macmillan, n.d.), originally published in three parts in October, November, and December 1868, and afterwards in book form, has three full-page drawings by Arthur Hughes, two in Part I and one in Part II; Mrs. George MacDonald's *Chamber Dramas* (1870) has a vignette; *National Nursery Rhymes* (Novello, Ewer & Co. [1870]) has a couple of characteristic designs, and the same publishers' companion volume, *Christmas Carols* [1871] three, of which the first, the frontispiece, is a large and very beautiful drawing. In the latter two books Arthur Hughes collaborates with other artists, but in those remaining to be chronicled he is the sole illustrator. *Parables and Tales*, by T. Gordon Hake (1872), has seven drawings, the 'Mother and Child' on the first page being among the artist's loveliest creations. The cover design for this book, Mr. Hart tells me, is by Rossetti. *Sing-Song* (1872), a book of nursery rhymes by Christina Rossetti, is decorated with a hundred and twenty small drawings: *Speaking Likenesses*, also by Christina Rossetti (1874), has twelve. Hughes also made a series of delicate and delightful vignettes for the title pages of the Uniform Edition of Miss Thackeray's stories, commencing with *Old Kensington*, and published during 1875 and 1876.

Here, I suppose, my catalogue should end, the subsequent illustrations carrying us far beyond our period. But, though the collection be a collection of wood engravings of the sixties, the collector will probably desire to add to it examples of the later work of his favourite artists, even when that work is reproduced by other methods. To complete my list of Arthur Hughes's

E. J. POYNTER: 'Moses Slaying the Egyptian'

[*Dalziel's Bible Gallery*]

illustrations I therefore add the following. *Babies' Classics* (1904)—an anthology of poetry, and a book more elaborately decorated than any we have hitherto noticed, each capital letter having its tiny drawing, to say nothing of the illustrations scattered through the text, the headpieces and tailpieces. Dr. Greville MacDonald's posthumous edition of his father's fairy romance, *Phantastes* (1905), is now for the first time illustrated with thirty-three designs by Arthur Hughes. 'For offering this new edition of my father's *Phantastes*', says Dr. MacDonald, 'my reasons are three. The first is to rescue the work from an edition illustrated without the author's sanction, and so unsuitably that all lovers of the book must have experienced some real grief in turning its pages. With the copyright I secured also the whole of that edition and turned it into pulp. . . . My third reason is that wider knowledge and love of the book should be made possible. To this end I have been most happy in the help of my father's old friend, who has illustrated the book. I know of no other living artist who is capable of portraying the spirit of *Phantastes*; and every reader of this edition will, I believe, feel that the illustrations are a part of the romance, and will gain through them some perception of the brotherhood between George Mac-Donald and Arthur Hughes.'

Lastly, we have three books, fairy-tales, by Dr. Greville MacDonald himself, *The Magic Crook* (1911), *Jack and Jill* (1913), and *Trystie's Quest* [1913]. In some of the illustrations for these later books there is perhaps only an echo of the old charm, but it is still a very pleasant echo. For more than half a century, between 1855 and 1913, Arthur Hughes was haunted by a vision of spiritual beauty, and that vision floats through his work to the end.

There remain four drawings I have been unable to identify. They were engraved by Dalziel in 1875—apparently for Roberts of Boston—and I found the proofs in the Dalziel collection in the British Museum. In case any reader should be able, and good natured enough, to help me, here are the subjects. The first is a picture of a shepherdess carrying a lamb. The second is a picture of Christ guarding a flock of sheep. The third shows an angel pulling aside the curtain of a bed on which a figure is reclining: a dove hovers on the stairs. The fourth is a picture of a boy riding through the clouds on the back of a goose. All these drawings, I fancy, are connected, and were made for one particular book.

VIII.   E. J. POYNTER (1836-1919)

Poynter is not among our most interesting illustrators. Born in Paris, he received his first art training there, going afterwards to Antwerp, where he was a fellow-student of du Maurier's. His first drawing, 'The Castle by the Sea', appeared in *Once a Week* on the 11th of January 1862. It is a careful composition, carried out in elaborate detail, and perhaps had not Charles Keene drawn that wonderful little boy on the opposite page it would appear better still. The drawing for 'Wife and I', further on, is less striking—the lady faintly reminiscent of Lawless.

In the next volume (vii) there are five Poynters, and among them a powerful design for *The Broken Vow* which immediately recalls Sandys. It has an amplitude not at all characteristic of Poynter's usual work, and the woman's head, and her attitude with the arm raised, are pure Sandys. Following this come two drawings for *A Dream of Love*, modern subjects treated in the Pre-Raphaelite manner: much better are the drawings for *A Fellow-Traveller's Story*. Volume viii (1863) has four Poynters, but after this there are no more in *Once a Week* till we come to 'Feeding the Sacred Ibis', a drawing in his *Bible Gallery* manner, which appeared as an extra illustration in 1867.

To *London Society* (1862) he contributed the not very felicitous 'Lord Dundreary' sketches, and a more serious and more successful drawing, 'The Kissing Bush'. Three designs for *The Painter's Glory* (*Churchman's Family Magazine*, 1863); 'The Sprig of Holly' (*London Society*, 1864); and a large 'Vision of the Departed Year' (*Illustrated London News*, Christmas, 1870) exhaust, or very nearly exhaust, the list of Poynter's magazine illustrations.

In *Jean Ingelow's Poems* (1867) he has a 'Persephone', and he also contributed four designs—'Mercy', 'Obedience', etc.—to *The Nobility of Life* (1869). All the plates in this latter work are printed in colour.

But what are by far Poynter's most important drawings will be found in *Dalziel's Bible Gallery*. The subjects here gave him an opportunity to do the kind of thing he could do best, and these careful designs, which appear to have been made between 1863 and 1865, are distinctly worthy of their place in an admirable collection. The first four belong to the Joseph series, and of these the 'Joseph before Pharaoh' and 'Joseph Distributing the Corn' are beautiful drawings. They are followed by a powerful design of 'Moses Slaying the Egyptian', in which, as indeed in most of them, one seems to trace the influence of Madox Brown. 'Moses Keeping Jethro's Sheep' is chiefly remarkable for the drawing of the goat crouching under the rock, from which it looks out with that enigmatic expression so characteristic of the caprine race: 'Moses and Aaron before Pharaoh' is a frankly decorative pattern; and 'Daniel's Prayer' is suggestive of all the mystery and magic of the East, the kneeling figure being somehow much more like a magician than a prophet.

A large and bold drawing, 'Labour and Science', probably used as an

E. BURNE-JONES: 'The Parable of the Boiling Pot'

[*Dalziel's Bible Gallery*]

advertisement or a cover design, belongs to 1868, and another excellent, though very different drawing, of a man playing on a spinet to two listening ladies and a second man, was made for Bell and Daldy in 1871.

IX. EDWARD BURNE-JONES (1833-1898)

The Burne-Jones illustrations can almost be numbered on the fingers of one hand if we do not include those he made many years later for the Kelmscott *Cupid and Psyche, Golden Legend, Chaucer, Sigurd the Volsung, Well at the World's End*, etc., some of which were cut by William Morris himself, and all of which lie beyond our present survey. The Kelmscott designs are frankly derived from medieval book decoration, and have nothing in common with the movement we are considering.

Against his early drawings, however—the drawings which do belong to our movement—Burne-Jones had an exaggerated prejudice. ' Those to a quite forgotten book ', writes Gleeson White, ' must not be mentioned; but it is safe to say that no human being, who did not know by whom they were produced, would recognize them.'

The passage leaves one doubtful as to whether Gleeson White himself saw them, or whether he is merely quoting the opinion of the artist, who seems to have felt almost as strong a dislike for the two eminently recognizable drawings published in *Good Words*, and even for the 'Boiling Pot' of the *Bible Gallery*. And though the book ' must not be mentioned ', as a matter of fact it *is* mentioned, and by Gleeson White himself, in the special Winter Number of *The Studio* devoted to *Children's Books and Their Illustrators*. Two of the drawings really *are* unrecognizable: in the third, a tailpiece, we get just a hint of the later Burne-Jones. On the other hand, they are all rather charming—certainly nothing to be ashamed of—a steel frontispiece and title page, the tailpiece engraved on wood. They are stiff, archaic, immature, romantic, but, as I say, charming and amusing. The book is *The Fairy Family* (Longman, 1857).

In November 1861 we find Holman Hunt writing to the Dalziels concerning a friend ' who I feel very strongly might be of great value to you in the illustrating of *Good Words*. He is perhaps the most remarkable of all the younger men of the profession for talent, and will, undeniably, in a few years fill the high position in general public favour which at present he holds in the professional world. He has yet, I think, made but few if any drawings on wood, but he has had much practice in working with the point both with pencil and pen and ink on paper, and so would have no difficulty with the material. I have not seen him lately, but remember that he has sometimes said that he should like to try his hand at drawing on wood, so without further ceremony I will enclose a letter to him which you may use at your own discretion. His name, as you will see by the enclosed, is Edward Jones.'

This letter is explained by the fact that Strahan, who published *Good Words*, had asked the Dalziels to look after its illustration; to act, in short, as art editors. Nevertheless, Burne-Jones's contributions to *Good Words* amount only to a couple of drawings—the 'King Sigurd' of 1862, and the 'Summer Snow' (attributed in the index to Christopher Jones) of 1863. Looking at these designs, one fails to understand the artist's strong desire to suppress them. Probably they have suffered at the engraver's hands, but they are far from being the feeble experiments one would expect from his attitude. The 'King Sigurd' is quaint, and perhaps even a little awkward, but in those girls' heads depressed into the picture the artist has already realized the type of feminine beauty he repeated throughout his life, and 'The Summer Snow' is a lovely drawing, showing, one fancies, an increased mastery over his material, while there is really nothing to indicate that the cutting has not been successful.

Very likely at the time these cuts were made Burne-Jones was less dissatisfied with them than he became later, for we find him entering with considerable enthusiasm into the Dalziels' plan for an illustrated Bible. He suggests several subjects he would like to do for it, including an 'Adam and Eve' 'sufficiently concealed in the thicket so as not to offend the prurient'. It is staggering to find that he had already managed to do this. Yet such is the case: one of his pictures was withdrawn from an exhibition held by the Society of Painters in Water Colours at the request of a sensitive and influential lady. In the end Burne-Jones gave only a single design to the *Bible Gallery*, 'The Parable of the Boiling Pot', a masterpiece of its particular school.

A drawing quite out of his usual style, called 'The Deliverer', and made for Mrs. Gatty's *Parables from Nature*, almost closes our brief list. This is really a Nativity, with little angels beating bells above the Manger, and the Wise Men approaching in the distance. It is a charming thing, but so unlike a Burne-Jones that one is almost inclined to doubt the evidence of the index. It is his, however, and Mr. Pennell reproduces the original drawing in his *Modern Illustrations*.

The last illustration on my notes was never, I think, published, but it certainly belongs to the sixties, and a proof of the engraving is in the Victoria and Albert Museum. It is a picture of Christ in the Garden of Gethsemane, and the face of Christ is the face of King Sigurd. The landscape, rather oddly, reminds one of the work of Mr. Laurence Housman.

E. Burne-Jones: 'The Summer Snow'

[*Good Words*, 1863]

SIMEON SOLOMON: 'The Feast of Dedication'
[*The Leisure Hour*, 1866]

X. SIMEON SOLOMON (1840-1905)

The ill-fated Simeon Solomon was born in London, his father being a prominent member of the Jewish community there. Young Simeon had a brother, Abraham, and a sister, Rebecca, both considerably older than himself, and both professional artists. We find Rebecca Solomon occasionally contributing to the magazines of the period, but something went amiss with her too, and in the end she came to disaster. It was Rebecca who schooled her young brother in Hebraic history and ritual, a love of which, mingled with a natural vein of mysticism, never left him. While still a young boy Simeon Solomon entered his brother Abraham's studio in Gower Street as a pupil, and before he was fifteen began to attend the Academy Schools. His progress was rapid, and he made many influential friends, who were attracted by the pleasantness of his temper and the charm of his humour. Success seemed assured. His first Academy picture, 'Isaac Offered', was exhibited in 1858, when he was just eighteen; and it was probably about this time that he came to know Rossetti and that little group of artists and men of letters who surrounded him. Swinburne wrote *Erotion* and *The End of a Month* for drawings by Simeon Solomon; Pater praised his work in a famous essay. It was Sidney Colvin who, writing in one of the reviews, first hinted at a vein of sentiment in the young artist's work which he advised him to abandon. So rumours are started, but till 1872 all seemed well: and then, quite suddenly, Simeon Solomon's career collapsed. All attempts to assist him failed; he refused commissions; he had gone under and he preferred to remain under. For a time he worked as a pavement artist, but in the end drifted to St. Giles's Workhouse. On a night in May 1905 he was found lying insensible in Great Turnstile, and was conveyed from there to King's College Hospital, where he died.

The wood engravings of Simeon Solomon are not numerous, but some of them are extraordinary. To begin with, he employed two absolutely different techniques, for nothing could be less like the Pre-Raphaelite method of his Biblical and Eastern designs than the impressionism of his studies of contemporary Jewish life. And it is these latter drawings, so much less elaborate but so much more original, that chiefly interest us. If in their individuality one sees the trace of an influence it is that of Rembrandt. The collector will find the ten 'Illustrations of Jewish Customs' in the *Leisure Hour* for 1866, and they are so completely unlike anything else that was being done at this time that he cannot afford to ignore them. They must have proved something of a puzzle to the orthodox engraver, though Butterworth and Heath have accomplished their task well. Nothing could be richer in its effect than 'The Fast of Jerusalem', while several of the drawings, such

[103]

as 'The Eve of the Jewish Sabbath', anticipate the melancholy poetry of Josef Israels. 'The Day of Atonement' is full of mystery, and in the lights and shadows of 'The Fast of Jerusalem' the mystery becomes weird, almost disquieting. Each one of these drawings is brimmed up with atmosphere— an atmosphere strange, sad, exotic, alien. It is an art different in conception and in execution from any we have encountered hitherto; it is a beauty created out of what is not beautiful, which may indeed account partly for its fascination. Its emotion is a kind of nostalgia, a homesickness, a sickness of the soul, but completely unlike the sensuous idealism of Rossetti, and still more unlike the weak, cloying idealism of Simeon Solomon's own later drawings.

What one might call two preliminary studies for these *Leisure Hour* drawings had been contributed by the artist as early as 1862 to *Once a Week* (vol. vii), in illustration of an article on *Jews in England*. He certainly made full use of these sketches for the *Leisure Hour* designs, the compositions being practically identical; and it is really through the technical handling of the later drawings that he gets so much more suggestion into them, though even the technical handling is foreshadowed in 'Lighting the Lamps', the second *Once a Week* picture.

Simeon Solomon's only other magazine designs are 'The End of a Month', a drawing of two heads, which appeared in *Dark Blue*; and 'The Veiled Bride', an example of his Pre-Raphaelite manner, which appeared in *Good Words* for 1862. All his remaining drawings on wood were made for *Dalziel's Bible Gallery*. For this work he made twenty designs, a greater number than anybody else, though only six of them appeared in the *Bible Gallery*, the others not being published till 1894, when they were printed in the new edition, called *Art Pictures from the Old Testament*. Some of these drawings are beautiful. The sturdy, intensely living little figure of Ishmael in the 'Hagar and Ishmael' is an exceptionally pleasing conception, full of pathos, and deeply human: the 'Abraham and Isaac' is less successful; but 'The Infant Moses' and 'Naomi and the Child Obed' are both de-lightful, while 'Melchizedek Blessing Abram', with its happily contrasted comeliness of age and youth, is at once a powerful and delicate design.

XI. H. H. ARMSTEAD (1828-1905)

H. H. Armstead is better known as a sculptor than a draughtsman but he made several particularly fine drawings on wood, drawings which belong to the Pre-Raphaelite school. The symbolic design of 'The Trysting Place', which he drew for the *Poems of Eliza Cook*, is highly characteristic. In it we see a pale lean cavalier, with a broad-brimmed plumed hat pushed

SIMEON SOLOMON: 'The Fast of Jerusalem'
[*The Leisure Hour*, 1866]

H. H. ARMSTEAD: 'The Fall of the Walls of Jericho'

[*Dalziel's Bible Gallery*]

back from his thin scattered locks, and a scythe in his hand, riding on a white horse towards a black open grave. He has ridden past the one tree standing isolated on a hill—past the church, past the crucifix by the wayside, past the belfry where an iron bell waves madly against the sky; and he is followed by a motley company, from the king in his richly brocaded gown, and the great lady with her tall head-dress, to the soldier and the youth and the young mother holding her child in her arms.

In Willmott's *English Sacred Poetry* Armstead has four drawings. The first, 'A Dream', pictures a black, winged fiend tearing the golden crown from a kneeling lady who is struggling to retain it. The demon is Sin, the lady Queen Virtue. The second design is the picture of a man reading his Bible in prison: the third, 'The Dead Man of Bethany', is a fine drawing of Mary and Lazarus: the fourth, 'Evening Hymn', shows a mother and her two daughters kneeling in prayer before a wide window filled with the evening light.

For *Good Words* Armstead made two designs. 'A Song which None but the Redeemed Can Sing' (1861) is an elaborate and beautiful composition of prancing horses and knightly figures, of young girls and women and children, moving in procession past a high-walled medieval town. Again the design is allegorical and Christian, but 'Sea-Weeds' of the following year is comparatively pagan, though the gentle mermaids who support the drowning man have little in common with the cruel sirens of legend.

In *The Churchman's Family Magazine* (1863) we find 'Fourth Sunday in Lent' and 'Angel Teachers'—the latter a very beautiful drawing of modern life, depicting one of those tall ladies Armstead admired, and two lovely children, by a field gate. In *The Sunday Magazine* for 1865 is a fine drawing (unindexed), austere to the point of bareness, of a man kneeling by a death-bed, 'Blessed are They that Mourn'; and lastly, in *Dalziel's Bible Gallery*, are 'The Fall of the Walls of Jericho' and 'Sun and Moon Stand Still', with two other designs not printed till 1894.

The great beauty of these drawings (for some reason very rarely mentioned) awakens regret that Armstead made so few. They are among the most distinguished our period can boast.

CHAPTER VI

WHISTLER AND CHARLES KEENE

1. JAMES MCNEILL WHISTLER (1834-1903)

HAD we nothing of Whistler's but his six wood engravings I think we might still claim that he was a great artist. They do not display all his qualities, of course, but they display his poetic imagination, his feeling for decoration, his beauty of line, his sense of composition, and that impeccable taste which in him, as Arthur Symons has said, was carried to the point of genius. All the wood engravings were made in 1862—two for *Good Words* and four for *Once a Week*. They are signed, not with initials or the famous butterfly, but in full. The *Good Words* designs illustrate a tale called *The Trial Sermon*. That on page 585, according to Gleeson White, 'shows a girl crouching by the fire, with a man, whose head is turned towards her, seated at a table with his hand on a lute'. The man—or boy—however, seated at the table, is not really looking at the girl. *Her* eyes are fixed upon him, with a wonderful expression of mingled sympathy, affection, and admiration, but *he* is looking into an imaginary world, and his hand is not resting on a lute but on the manuscript of the sermon which he has evidently been delivering to that most appreciative audience of one. The play of the firelight on the figure of the listening girl is marvellous, the whole picture has an indescribably sympathetic quality, a beauty more haunting than that of any of the famous Millais contributed to the same volume. And yet it was actually omitted, this and the other Whistler, from *Touches of Nature*, the collection of wood engravings selected from Strahan's magazines.

Of the *Once a Week* designs, the first illustrates *The Major's Daughter*. It will be found on page 712 of volume vi, and shows a girl on board ship, seated looking out over the sea. The second (vol. vii, p. 140), 'The Relief Fund in Lancashire', is a delicate, impressionist drawing with more perhaps of the quality of an etching than of a drawing on wood. The engraver's name is not attached to it, but whoever he was the task is well done. 'The Morning Before the Massacre of St. Bartholomew' is a more finished picture, a lovely thing, mysteriously conveying, like some of Charles Keene's work, an impression of cool clear water-colour. Here again the rapid touches of

Whistler: ' The Trial Sermon '
[*Good Words*, 1862]

WHISTLER:
' The Morning before the Massacre of St. Bartholomew '
[*Once a Week*, 1862]

the pen produce a line of marvellous elasticity, while the suggestion of texture in both dress and curtain could not be surpassed. Is it fanciful to see in the fine illustration for *Count Burkhardt* on page 378 a resemblance to Duse in *La Città Morta* ? The Italian actress fell into just the attitude of this woman in the drawing, though with her head slightly more raised: nor was her type wholly dissimilar from that of Whistler's nun, who, as she stands in profile by the open casement, might herself be gazing out over the dead city: even the gown drops in precisely the same unbroken line from throat to foot.

Of book illustrations by Whistler I have none to record except the two etchings contributed to *Passages from Modern English Poets*, illustrated by the Junior Etching Club [1862].

II. CHARLES SAMUEL KEENE (1823-1891)

Charles Keene was born on the 10th of August 1823. He was the son of a solicitor, and at the age of seventeen, two years after his father's death, himself entered a solicitor's office, that of his father's partner. He had already, however, shown a marked taste for drawing, and his mother, who believed in his talent, was determined to find more congenial employment for him. Very soon, therefore, we find Charles apprenticed to an architect, as a first step in the desired direction. Out of office hours he continued to practise drawing, always encouraged by his mother, who collected his sketches, showed them to dealers, and eventually discovered a purchaser for a few of them. It was indeed entirely due to Mrs. Keene's activity that Charles was at last introduced to one of the Whympers (of the well known firm of wood engravers), and became their apprentice:—a remarkable mother of a more remarkable son.

During the five years of his apprenticeship Charles Keene produced a few illustrations, surprisingly weak if we consider to what a pitch of virtuosity his technique was ultimately carried, but he developed slowly, and even ten years later many of his drawings are crude enough. He was a man of strong individuality, and from boyhood pursued his own way. His unconventionality, however, was not the self-conscious unconventionality of artistic cliques and coteries. It was unostentatious, entirely natural, like everything else about him. But he did not like putting on dress clothes, did not like shaking hands, did not like having his rooms tidied, did not like noises at night, and though all these antipathies are perfectly understandable they went far to make up a reputation for eccentricity. His sympathies were regarded as equally odd, because he was equally frank about them. He was fond of apple tart for breakfast; he was very fond of animals (the rats in the old house where he had his studio used to come every day to regular meals, making a crony of him much as they would of Doctor Dolittle); he was fond of playing chess, but because he often took a quarter of an hour over a move experienced some difficulty in finding opponents; he was intensely fond of making collections. In fact, he collected nearly everything, from flint implements to old cookery books, and his rooms became so crowded with curiosities and specimens that it was by no means easy to move about in them. He was fond of music, in a simple way, having a particular taste for part singing and playing on the bagpipes; he was interested in the volunteer movement, which he joined; and in spite of his Bohemianism he remained a staunch Tory to the end.

As for his work, it was carried on at all hours—persistently, tirelessly. When out for a walk in the London streets or in the country, he would stop when anything happened to interest him and make a drawing of it. For this purpose he had a special little ink bottle attached to his jacket, and carried steel pens and a sketch book in his pocket. His practice was constant, and his skill in time became phenomenal. I don't know whether he could draw Giotto's perfect circle, but it is said that he could draw parallel lines, straight or curved, of just the right thickness and distance from one another, practically with the same exactitude as if they had been drawn with a ruler or a compass. And he was constantly experimenting—experimenting in papers and in inks. He manufactured his own inks of varied shades and tints. The earlier drawings were usually made in pure black or brown, either with a pen or a brush used as a pen, but of the late drawings Mr. Pennell gives the following description.[1] 'They are drawn in black, blue, brown, and red lines, put down with pens, brushes, sticks, and his fingers; the various colours and methods are found combined in the same design, with very delightful results for everybody except the poor engraver. His paper alone was a serious drawback to excellence of reproduction. He liked to work on dirty brown scraps, upon the backs of old envelopes, or any odd pieces, in which the texture, the very imperfections, would add a quality that was amusing. And on these grey or brown bits, he drew with grey watery ink, with blue ink, with purple ink; he mixed up pencil and wash, pen and Chinese white, with which he gave modelling and relief to forms, afterwards to be photographed on to the wood, and engraved, as well as they could be engraved, by Swain, into pure black outline blocks, and printed upon pure white paper.'

That Keene did not take more into consideration what was possible and what was impossible to the engraver seems inconsistent with the fact

[1] *The Work of Charles Keene*, by Joseph Pennell. (Fisher Unwin, and Bradbury, Agnew & Co., 1897.)

CHARLES KEENE: ' Mokeanna!'

[*Punch*, 1863]

that on the drawing itself he spared no pains, and certainly, up till the eighties, we find many drawings reproduced with admirable fidelity. If a drawing did not come right he would begin it all over again, and Mr. Spielmann says he saw in Birket Foster's house the seventh version Keene had made of one of his *Punch* pictures. He left nothing to chance—except the engraving. If he wanted to draw a typewriter or an old boot he procured his original; if he wanted a turnip field for a background, out he tramped into the country till he found one. Frequently he made use of himself as a model, keeping a large mirror in his studio for the purpose—a habit that was not without its drawbacks, as the trousers worn by some of his 'swells' bear witness. To see how his work at times lost enormously in the engraving we have only to compare certain of the original drawings with the *Punch* pictures they subsequently became; that, on the other hand, Swain was often successful must too be granted. The drawings became bolder and bolder as the years went by, and with the drawings the signature. One could in fact date any example of his work fairly accurately from that famous C.K. alone—the particular stage it has reached in its development. Hence the charming study of a seated lady which Mr. Pennell reproduces on page 159 of his book, and thinks must be very early, I should have no hesitation in saying belongs not to the forties but to the eighties—unless the signature was added later, a most unlikely thing.

Keene's unsigned prentice work for *The Illustrated London News* would now be impossible to identify with any certainty. 'Bell Ringing' (20th December 1856), four illustrations for *A Wife at a Venture* (7th March 1857), and 'Snapdragon' (25th December 1858) are all his—the last drawing being much the best, though Jackson's engraving of it is poor enough. Fortunately he dropped the *London News* once he had established his connection with *Punch*. For the latter paper he made between two and three thousand drawings, but a complete iconography of his work has not yet been attempted. An appendix to Mr. Pennell's book gives valuable information, though in it we find the *London Society* drawings limited to four—a surprising under-estimation considering the importance of these designs. According to Layard, Keene's first *Punch* drawing was 'A Sketch of the New Paris Street-sweeping Machines', which appeared in December 1851; but Layard's catalogue of the *Punch* work, based on information supplied by Henry Silver, certainly requires revision. In the early years most of Keene's work was anonymous,[1] and he made far more drawings than his biographer attributes to him.

To praise these matchless *Punch* pictures is superfluous. Keene never

---

[1] He occasionally used a black mask as a signature—eight drawings, I think, are signed thus.

shared the popularity of Leech or du Maurier, or, later, of Phil May, though few will deny that he was the greatest of all Mr. Punch's artists. Yet it is strange how to this day some of his staunchest admirers cling to the idea that his humour was largely acquired. Even Layard, in his excellent *Life and Letters*,[1] accepts this view. At the same time he is transcribing passages like the following from a letter to Crawhall. ' He is married now and says his fishing is a good deal stopped! They were in great trouble about the first baby. It could not take milk and was a poor emaciated little bantling; but I consoled him when he told me, and congratulated him on the chance he had got—that there was no drawing at all in the ordinary fat maggot of a baby, but here was an artist blessed with a nice anatomical bony infant, such as Albert Dürer and the early German masters drew from, and gave such character to their Holy Families. I believe he took the hint, as I've heard he has made no end of nude studies from it; and only just in time, as they say it is fattening.'

Now what is significant here—seeing that Keene has been accused of having to rely on others for his jokes—is that this letter is funny in *exactly the same way* as the drawings are. It is the same *kind* of humour. Nobody denies, of course, that Keene was supplied with many subjects by his friends (Layard quotes pages of them, and one he has forgotten to quote, the famous ' bang went saxpence ', came to the artist through Birket Foster, who had it from John Gilbert), but the important thing is what he made of these subjects: Shakespeare, too, borrowed his plots. Keene's humour is essentially individual. He never, to my mind, drew anything funnier than the ' Rural Felicity ' picture (see *Punch*, 1865)—'Oh, Mum! 'adn't Master better go round with the lantern; there's a Moanin' Gipsy somewhere in the back garden! '—where the joke is so much his own that it is doubtful if the same subject presented by any other artist would be funny at all.[2] One regrets, of course, that he should have been more or less monopolized by *Punch*, since only one side of his genius found expression in comedy; but that he was naturally a great humorist not only his drawings prove, but also the scraps of letterpress printed below them, his ' legends ', as he called them. And he is immensely particular about these legends: they, too, in their own smaller way, are works of art. If a word is altered, if even a letter is altered in his dialect jokes, he is furious. He is so careful of them that, distrustful of his handwriting, he frequently prints the words, thus leaving no excuse for inaccuracy. Bitter is his anger when the ' sapient editor ' tampers

[1] *The Life and Letters of Charles Samuel Keene*, by George Somes Layard (Sampson Low, 1892).

[2] It is certainly not particularly funny as I give it here, but when drawing, title, and legend are all united it becomes a masterpiece.

CHARLES KEENE: 'Brother Jacob'

[*The Cornhill Magazine*, 1864]

with his text. 'I'll never forgive him,' he writes of poor Tom Taylor, who had changed 'faur sairer' into 'gey an' sairer': but his fiercest denunciations are reserved for F. C. Burnand.

'*American Angler:* "Guess, sir, I've been bumming around all day with a twenty-five dollar pole, slinging fourteen-cent bugs at the end of it, and haven't caught a darned fish."'

For this the 'exquisite delicacy' of Burnand led him to substitute:— 'What sport? Guess I've been foolin' around all day with a twenty-five dollar pole, slinging fourteen-cent baits at the end of it, and haven't caught a darned fish.' The alterations *are* stupid; but Keene is ready to take his editor's life.

One of his drawings was refused altogether (and it is an admirable drawing) on account of the words accompanying it. It represents a widow —an irresistible lady in Keene's best manner—who has been discussing her late husband with a sympathetic friend: 'But why should I grieve, dear? I know where he passes his evenings now.' The jest seems harmless enough, and the expression on the widow's face is as delightful as only Keene could make it: nevertheless, 'our Philistine editor said "it would jar upon feelings"'. Burnand probably knew his public better than Keene did, or it may be that something in this particular joke jarred upon his own feelings, for there is a side to that genial punster's nature which comes as a surprise to us when we read his autobiography. If the joke offended him it was far more likely to have been on the grounds of a fancied irreverence towards religion than for any moral reasons: indeed, the artist more or less forestalls moral objections by substituting 'evenings' for 'nights'.

Charles Keene died on the 4th of January 1891. His last *Punch* drawing, ''Arry on the Boulevards', an impressionistic sketch of a man reading a newspaper under the glaring lights of a café, and without any 'legend' attached to it, appeared on the 16th of August 1890. The beautiful softness of the original study has disappeared in the engraving, yet there are certain improvements—in the face of the waiter, for instance. The last drawing of all appeared in *Black and White*, 1891 (vol. i, p. 206), a sketch of his dog Frau asleep in a chair.

In the discussion of art Keene was unusually reticent. He would not discuss his own work at all, and in his letters there is infinitely more about his collections, his music, and the other interests of his life, than about art or artists. He appears to have admired Hogarth and Holbein, and among his contemporaries principally Whistler. Of black and white men his two favourites are Chodowiecki, a Russian painter and engraver who died in 1801, and of whose book illustrations he made a collection; and Menzel, whom he declares to be a follower in Chodowiecki's track. To Menzel he sent a selection of his own drawings, receiving in return a parcel of proofs and impressions of the German artist's designs on wood, together with photographs of his drawings and pictures, and half a dozen original sketches, a gift of which he was very proud.

Apart from *Punch*, the bulk of Keene's work was done for *Once a Week*. In *Good Words* he has only a single drawing, ' Nannerl the Washerwoman ', a masterly design, strong and beautiful, which appeared in 1862. To *The Cornhill* (1864) he supplied two illustrations for an anonymous tale of George Eliot's entitled *Brother Jacob*; the first an initial letter, the second a superb drawing, admirably engraved by Swain. In *London Society* all his work is first rate, and appears mostly in the Christmas Numbers. In 1865 he has two illustrations for *What Came of Killing a Rich Uncle*; in 1866 two for *How I Lost My Whiskers*; in 1867 two for *An Actor's Holiday*; in 1868 two for *Tomkins' Degree Supper*, two for *Smoking Strictly Prohibited*, and two for *Our Christmas Turkey*; in 1869 two for *Three Names*, one for *Lady Nelly the Flirt*, and two for *The Coat with a Fur Lining*; in 1870 one for *In the Solent* and two for *The Gipsy Model*; and in 1871, for *Full Fathom Five* either one or two, I cannot be sure, for though the index was there the Christmas Number itself was missing from the only copy of vol. xx I have seen. At any rate, instead of four designs, we find him contributing either twenty-one or twenty-two to *London Society*.

In *Once a Week* the humorous illustrations were left to Leech and Phiz. The former has some charming drawings, the contributions of the latter are poor even for Phiz. Keene, who from the first was a regular contributor, is here found as an illustrator of serious poetry and fiction. He supplies the illustrations for the first serial, Charles Reade's *A Good Fight*—later immensely elaborated and expanded into *The Cloister and the Hearth*. In these particular illustrations he adopts a medieval style to suit the period and the setting of the story, but in spite of this disguise we have no need to turn to the index to discover their authorship. In all, he is responsible for twenty-six drawings in the first volume (1859).

In vol. ii he again illustrates the serial, this time George Meredith's *Evan Harrington*. The medieval convention is of course abandoned, the drawings for *Evan Harrington* are as modern as the tale itself. And among them are some of the most beautiful examples of Charles Keene's early work. Gleeson White, apropos of the illustrations of the sixties, again and again expresses a regret I have never been able to understand. But the fashions then in vogue—the crinoline, the peg-top trousers—seemed to him so grotesque, so disfiguring, that in his choice of the engravings to be reproduced in his book he even made the avoidance of drawings in which these

CHARLES KEENE: 'Proof Positive'

[*Punch*, 1868]

'monstrosities' appear one of his principles of selection. It requires a Millais, he thinks, to introduce the crinoline 'so that its ugliness does not repel you'. This opinion seems to me astonishing. So far from sharing it, I should say that the crinoline is the most decorative adornment the feminine mind ever invented—incomparably, from the artist's point of view, superior to the formless wisps of clothing in fashion to-day. Nor is it so much to the drawings of Millais as to those of Charles Keene that I should turn in support of this view. Take the lovely drawing for chapter xvi of *Evan Harrington*;—is there anything repellent in the costumes of Rose and Evan? Again and again in Keene's drawings the crinoline is treated so that it has a positive aesthetic value, just as the chimney-pot hat has in several of Degas's and Manet's pictures. The drawings for *Evan Harrington* are, to my mind, equal to any that were ever made for a novel. Nor, when I say this, do I forget Millais's illustrations for Trollope, or Walker's for the Thackerays, father and daughter; but somehow Keene's *kind* of beauty appeals to me more than theirs.

In this second volume of *Once a Week* he has twenty-eight drawings: in vol. iii, including the further illustrations for Meredith's novel, he has twenty-one. Among the miscellaneous drawings 'The Emigrant Artist' shows a temporary and delightful return to his medievalism, with the very happiest results so far as the small boy and his granny are concerned. This particular design affords an excellent example of the way in which Keene could establish a relation between his figures, whether that relation be one of affection or the reverse. Note, too, what a world of expression he has put into the feet of the little boy.

In vol. iv the Keenes only number eleven, including the admirable and characteristic 'Beggar's Soliloquy', which in the index is wrongly attributed to du Maurier (the du Maurier is really on page 387, but both drawings are unsigned); and those who think he could not draw a beautiful woman might well turn to the lady on page 713 (*The Revenue Officer's Story*).

The number of Keene's designs sinks to eight in volume v, for the drawing on page 251, 'Business with Bokes', given to him in the index, is almost certainly a du Maurier, though not in that artist's more characteristic manner. Keene, however, supplies some fine illustrations for the short serial, *Lilian's Perplexities*, as well as one or two other designs.

In vol. vi he illustrates, as only he could, another short serial, *The Woman I loved and the Woman Who Loved Me*. This volume contains thirteen drawings.

The splendid illustrations for Mrs. Henry Wood's *Verner's Pride* (the fiction in *Once a Week* has sadly deteriorated) run through the next two volumes, with other occasional pieces, among which one notes in vol. vii the lovely drawing of a girl playing the piano (p. 295), as graceful and idyllic as anything of Walker's, and the humorous character drawing on page 463, so much in Keene's *Punch* manner, and so utterly beyond Walker. Vol. vii has thirteen drawings; vol. viii seven, among them the magnificent 'March of the Men of Arthur', one of his few romantic compositions.

In vol. ix 'The Viking's Serf' is another drawing of this kind. It, and the two illustrations for *The Heirloom*, are the only designs by Keene in this volume, for 'The Station-Master at Longley' (p. 169), attributed to him in the index, is obviously by Charles Green. His last drawing in *Once a Week*, 'The Old Shepherd on his Pipe', appeared as an extra illustration in vol. iv of the New Series (1867).

For Keene's first book illustrations we must go back to the days of his apprenticeship. According to Mr. W. H. Chesson, 'the number of books associated with the name of Charles Keene in the general catalogue of the British Museum is ten'. Mr. Chesson's own bibliography—given at the end of the Pennell monograph—contains sixty-three items, and to these I can add two books that have escaped him—one, I think, quite unknown. Not all the items on Mr. Chesson's list, however, need be mentioned here. It includes volumes which contain merely reprints of designs from periodicals, and others possessing little more than an 'association' interest:—*The Nature and Treatment of Gout*, which, on the authority of Mr. Henry Keene, contains some wood engravings of a technical nature (drawings of gouty deformities) made by his brother; and *Round the Table: Notes on Cookery*, which contains figures of 'How to Truss Fowls', 'How to Bone Fowls', etc., that Layard declares to be Keene's handiwork.

The earliest work recorded for which Keene made an illustration is *Dick Boldhero* (Darton, 1842),[1] which Mr. Chesson says has a frontispiece signed by our artist. I have never seen this book, nor does the British Museum, so far as I could discover, possess a copy; but, if the date is correct, the drawing must have been made soon after Keene went to Whymper's.

We have nothing between 1842 and 1847, the date of *Robinson Crusoe* (Burns), which contains half a dozen full-page illustrations of slight interest except to the enthusiastic collector. In the same year he contributed one small drawing to *Green's Nursery Annual*, a frontispiece to *The Wooden Walls of Old England*, and several illustrations to Mrs. Sherwood's *The De Cliffords* —all prentice work and all uncharacteristic. *The White Slave* (1852) contains eight illustrations equally unrecognizable, some of which are signed and some not. *A Story with a Vengeance* (1852) is better. The vignette in

[1] I take this date from Mr. Chesson's Bibliography, but the earliest edition of *The Adventures of Dick Boldhero* I have myself found recorded is dated 1846.

CHARLES KEENE: 'Hard Lines'
[*Punch's Almanack*, 1869]

this book is C.K.'s, and the initial letters on pages 1, 33, and 82. Probably, indeed, all the initials are his, though only those I have mentioned are signed. The same applies to the illustrations for *Marie Louise* (1853), three of which are signed and the rest anonymous. In *The Giants of Patagonia* (1853) the frontispiece only is signed. Here again Keene may be responsible for the remaining pictures; we have nothing to go on; since the signed frontispiece, wretchedly printed and engraved, is just as unlike him as anything else in the volume.

We now, however, come to a book containing several unmistakable Keenes—*The Book of German Songs*, by W. H. Dulcken (Ward, Lock, 1856). Not all the illustrations are his, though a fair proportion are, some initialed and some not—that on page 296, not initialed, being about the best of the group. The Keenes are engraved by Dalziel—in whose collection I found the proofs of a number of them—but the names of neither artist nor engraver appear in the book itself. To C.K. I should give the frontispiece, and the drawings on pages 35, 43, 58, 68, facing 92, 100 (very unlike him, but among the other Dalziel proofs), 115, 118, facing 126, 149, 167, facing 178, 191, 199 (?), facing 228, 242, 247 (another Dalziel proof of a drawing showing no characteristic touch whatever), facing 288, and 296.

A Narrative of the Indian Revolt, by Sir Colin Campbell (Vickers, 1858) appeared originally in thirty-seven parts. Among its ' nearly two hundred engravings ' are a couple by C.K.—large double-page drawings, roughly printed but effective. The ' Ride for Life', on pages 54 and 55, is a really powerful design of galloping horses: the other drawing is on pages 138 and 139.

Our two books of 1860 are more important still. *The Boy Tar*, by Mayne Reid, has twelve capital drawings, some of them—' Rowing to the Reef ', ' Tapping the Water-Butt ', 'An Ugly Intruder '—being of remarkable beauty. A few of these *Boy Tar* drawings appear later, anonymously, in children's picture books. Of the second book, *The Voyage of the Constance*, it may be as well to warn the collector that Gleeson White's account is incorrect, some accident apparently having happened to his notes. ' The *Voyage of the Constance*,' he writes, ' *a tale of the Arctic Seas* (Edinburgh, Constable, 1859), with twenty-four drawings by Charles Keene, a singularly interesting and apparently scarce volume which reveals powers of imagining landscape which he had never seen in a very realistic manner.' Now the date of *The Voyage of the Constance* is 1860, not 1859; it is *a tale of the Polar Seas*, not the Arctic Seas; it is published by Sampson Low, not Constable; and it contains eight drawings by Keene, not twenty-four. Nor can I detect anything very remarkable in the landscapes. The frontispiece is a charming

[127]

little winter scene, but we are in England, not at the North Pole. The best design, in fact, shows a schoolboy holding a pigeon and standing with one foot on a ladder that leans against an old creepered wall—a delightful thing, quite in the manner of some of the *Evan Harrington* drawings, though less successfully engraved, by Harral, who is rarely first rate.

Another book of 1860, Mrs. Webb's *Helen Mordaunt*, appears among Routledge's announcements as illustrated by Keene, but on looking up what seemed like a 'find', I discovered the illustrations to be by John Gilbert. To the following year, however, belongs a book which Mr. Chesson has missed. *Jack Buntline*, by W. H. Kingston (Sampson Low, 1861), has an excellent frontispiece by Keene, showing 'Jack and Sambo on the Raft'.

Sea Kings and Naval Heroes (Bell and Daldy, 1861) is illustrated by Charles Keene and E. K. Johnson. The drawings are unsigned, but those on pages 81 and 327, and the frontispiece, are Keene's. A charming design on page 197 is more doubtful. *Lyra Germanica* (1861) contains a drawing in the medieval manner of the *Good Fight* illustrations: *English Sacred Poetry* (1862) has two drawings; the first not very characteristic, and much more highly finished than is usual with Keene; the second a charming piece of line work, notable for the beautiful treatment of the trees. The original of this drawing must have been very lovely; in the engraving it has acquired a certain hardness.

The Cambridge Grisette, by Herbert Vaughan (Tinsley, 1862) is illustrated entirely by Keene. I have not read the tale, but the full-page drawings and initial letters are first rate, and Keene has made the heroine pretty enough to be a second Zuleika Dobson.

It was about this time, probably, that the Dalziels tried to engage his services for their proposed edition of *Don Quixote*. This was to be a big book, and the artist was to go to Spain to collect fresh material for his drawings. But though the idea pleased him at first, in the end his strange reluctance to bind himself by signing a definite agreement proved an insurmountable difficulty, and the project fell through.

Eyebright (a little book bound in green paper wrappers), and *Paul Duncan's Little by Little*, both 1862, have each a frontispiece by Keene; and Mark Lemon's *Jest Book* (1864) has a vignette, engraved on steel by Jeens. Layard, in his biography of C.K., publishes the first design for this vignette, and we can see from it how completely the delightful expression of the boy, as his face breaks into irrepressible laughter, has been lost in the engraving. *Legends of Number Nip*, by Mark Lemon (Macmillan, 1864), contains six delicate drawings. Mr. Chesson says, 'The cloth cover contains the words "Popular Edition" and the image of a winged imp in gold'; but the

CHARLES KEENE: 'Smoking Strictly Prohibited'
[*London Society*, 1868]

original issue has a brown cloth binding with an embossed scroll-work ornamentation in gold, no 'imp', and no 'popular edition'.

Tracks for Tourists, by F. C. Burnand (1864), contains sixty-eight sketches by Keene. This is an issue in book form of a series of Burnand's *Punch* articles, which in that journal appeared under the title of *How, When, and Where*. A particularly fine reproduction of 'The March of Arthur' will be found in Tom Taylor's *Ballads and Songs of Brittany* (1865).

Mrs. Caudle's Curtain Lectures (1866) is Keene's masterpiece in book illustration. Besides the sixty immortal designs in the text, there is, for frontispiece, a full-page picture of Caudle on his own doorstep, an excellent piece of colour printing, the original study for which will be found in Layard's biography. *Mrs. Caudle* has been re-issued more than once and in more than one form. The original issue with Keene's drawings is a small quarto bound in cloth, with a stamped design in gold. It is printed on a stout and very unusual paper, the colour being pale green. The illustrations show Keene at his best. Note the wonderful beauty of line in the picture of Caudle at the window on page 18, the splendid character drawing in the initial letter on page 54, and the delicate beauty of the boy on page 165. Yet Ruskin found this artist 'coarse', and Mrs. Meynell, even more sensitive, found him 'obscene'.

Legends and Lyrics, by Adelaide Anne Proctor (1866), has two fine designs by C.K. Both are large and elaborate drawings—the former, 'Settlers', is a picture of two men reclining in a sylvan evening landscape more suggestive of England than the far West; the latter, 'Rest', is an impressive battle piece, with the dead and wounded stretched under the light of the moon. Mrs. Gatty's *Parables from Nature* (1867) has also a highly finished design, 'Imperfect Instruments', which Mr. Chesson does not record.

Double Marriage, by Charles Reade (1868), has a frontispiece and vignette by Keene; and Thackeray's *Roundabout Papers*, republished in vol. xxii of an Edition de Luxe of his Works (1879), contains eight full-page drawings and ten initial letters. These *Roundabout* drawings are in C.K.'s later manner: that of 'The Evening Post' is a portrait of Thackeray himself elaborated, but hardly improved, from the first sketch made about 1860. *Our People* (1881) has already been described.

Robert [1885] is another reprint from *Punch*. All the pictures are by Keene, except two—that on page 75 being by Harry Furniss, and that on page 110 by E. J. Wheeler.

Songs of the North [1885] contains a design by Keene. *Imprisoned in a Spanish Convent*, by E. C. Grenville-Murray (1886), Mr. Chesson includes in his bibliography, and in his note to the book adds, 'It is difficult to say what was Keene's exact share in the volume.' As a matter of fact he has no share in it at all, since the only drawing by him—a picture for *M.P. in Spite of Himself*—is really an ancient design dished up again. It appeared in *London Society*, where it illustrated *Our Christmas Turkey*.

To a charity book, *Grass of Parnassus from the Bents o' Buchan* (Scott, 1887), Keene gave a few small sketches which were all lithographed on to a single page. In 1888 appeared a second series of the *Robert* papers (in which eighteen out of the twenty-one drawings are Keene's) and *King James' Wedding*, by J. Sands (Arbroath: T. Buncle). The *King James* is a most interesting volume. The illustrations, reproduced by photo-engraving, are not reprints but original drawings made for C.K.'s old friend, the author of the poems, and the whole book has the appearance of a private enterprise undertaken for the amusement of artist and writer. Two or three of the drawings follow the manner of Keene's ordinary illustrations, but the rest are in the nature of delightful experiments.

Eight of the *Once a Week* designs for *A Good Fight* were reprinted in a popular edition of *The Cloister and the Hearth*, while the whole fourteen appear in Andrew Lang's reprint of the *Good Fight* itself, published by Frowde in 1910. It would be quite unfair, however, to judge of the original engravings from this late reprinting of them. The larger drawings have suffered much by reduction in size, and, whether the roughish paper was unsuitable or not, all the impressions leave a good deal to be desired. This indeed is my chief reason for mentioning them here, since in most cases where I have referred to the magazine publication of a novel I have not thought it necessary to note its subsequent issue in book form.

The Fine Arts Society's *Catalogue of a Collection of Drawings by the late Charles Keene* (1891) contains two or three studies for *Punch* pictures, and both Layard's *Life* and Mr. Pennell's *Work of Charles Keene* contain an immense number of unpublished studies, etchings, and designs, all admirably reproduced on the finest paper. These two splendid volumes are worthy of the artist they commemorate, and indispensable to the student of his work.

The series of *Punch's Pocket Books*, from 1865 to 1881, should be added to the foregoing list. The *Pocket Books* are of interest, not only for the sake of C.K. but also for their illustrations by Tenniel, Linley Sambourne, and—more rarely—du Maurier. The seventeen volumes from 1865 to 1881 are those to which Keene contributed. In each he has a long, folding, etched frontispiece and title page coloured by hand. Lastly, there are the two etchings contributed by him to a couple of volumes illustrated by the Junior Etching Club—*Passages from Thomas Hood* (1858), and *Passages from Modern English Poets* [1862].

I have no note of drawings by Keene which must have appeared in *The Studio* and other art magazines since his death.

While working on these proofs I came upon another unchronicled drawing by Keene. It was made for Moore's *Canadian Boat Song* and appears in *Favourite English Poems* (Sampson Low, 1870). It may possibly have made an earlier appearance elsewhere, but it is in neither the 1862 nor the 1863 edition of *Favourite Poems*.

CHAPTER VII

THE IDYLLIC SCHOOL

FRED WALKER; PINWELL; J. W. NORTH

I. FRED WALKER (1840-1875)

I THINK Millais—the Millais of *Framley Parsonage* and *The Small House at Allington*—ought to head this group, but he was a member of the Pre-Raphaelite Brotherhood, and it was more convenient to consider all his work together. At any rate, such classifications need not be regarded too seriously: Pinwell, for instance, made a number of romantic drawings; Houghton and J. D. Watson made a large number of domestic ones; while the last artist even occasionally experimented in Pre-Raphaelitism. Fred Walker's work, on the other hand, is singularly uniform in manner and conception. In the drawings for *Denis Duval* he may clothe his figures in the costume of a bygone age, but the drawings themselves breathe precisely the same idyllic Victorian spirit as his modern illustrations. These have more in common with Millais's and du Maurier's—the du Maurier who illustrated *Wives and Daughters*—than with those of either of the other artists whose names head this chapter. Yet Walker developed independently. He began by copying the work of Gilbert, but by the time he had acquired any technique to speak of he had also acquired his own particular style, from which he never deviated, even to make an experiment. It was in one sense a naturalistic style—indeed the backgrounds of most of his designs were drawn directly on to the blocks from nature—but it was a naturalism that ruled out everything except the pleasing. There is little imagination in Walker's work; he possessed the type of mind for which the poetic is indistinguishable from the sentimental; therefore we like him best when he contents himself with reproducing charming aspects of ordinary domestic life—a pretty girl shelling peas, or an old woman lifting the kettle from the hob.

Fred Walker was born in Marylebone. When he was seven his father, a designer of jewellery, died, leaving the family in very poor circumstances. There were the usual difficulties about choosing a career for the boy, but at the age of fifteen a situation was found for him in the customary

FRED WALKER: 'Out of the World'

[*The Cornhill Magazine*, 1863]

architect's office.   In later life he always maintained that the Dalziels refused to take him as an apprentice; but the Dalziels are equally sure that he never asked to be taken, that he merely called on them to get an opinion on his drawings, and to ask about the prospects of an illustrator.   He also, twice, we know, took or sent specimen drawings to Maclise, and in 1858 we find him apprenticed to the Whympers (along with J. W. North and Charles Green), in which firm he worked three days a week for two years.   It was, the Dalziels say, during this period that they gave him some illustrating to do for various boys' books published by Routledge (books not recorded either in Mr. Marks's *Life of Walker* or elsewhere, and none of which I have been able to discover), and also for Dickens's *Hard Times* and *Reprinted Pieces*, though the Dickens drawings were not made till 1861.

Before this he had called on the editor of *Once a Week*, asking for employment, and bringing with him specimens of his work.   It was a step that must have cost Walker a good deal, for he was painfully, morbidly shy. Tom Taylor describes him as 'a nervous, timid, sensitive young fellow, frail and small of body and feverish of temperament', and Holman Hunt in his own conscientious fashion confirms this description.   'He was small and fragile, not more than five feet four, and truly delicate in the double sense of the word. . . .   Observing the feebleness of his frame, one naturally desired to remonstrate with him about the overtaxing of his fretful constitution by feverish habits.   Once or twice when I met him in the street in the small hours of darkness, he seemed to suspect possible admonitions, and hurried by as though to evade them.'

A legend has grown up connecting Walker with Pinwell, but in reality no friendship existed between them.   Walker was only once in Pinwell's house, and that was not till 1873.   On the other hand, an intimate friendship with J. W. North dates back to the days of their apprenticeship at Whymper's. His association with North and their sketching expeditions together, according to the Dalziels, were of the greatest value to him, North being a fine colourist, and Fred Walker's sense of colour being at first particularly weak.   Turning over the early illustrations, we cannot help feeling that his draughtsmanship too was weak:—most of these illustrations are commonplace, while some are positively bad.

What is supposed to be Walker's first illustration—for a story by Edmond About—appeared on the 14th of January 1860, in *Everybody's Journal*; his second appeared in *Once a Week* on the 18th of February of the same year.   They are feeble things, though it may be possible, with after-event knowledge, to read into the *Everybody's Journal* design just a hint of the later Walker: to the other, were it unsigned, we should never give a second glance.   He contributed, in all, eight illustrations to this, the second volume of *Once a Week*. In the third *Once a Week* illustration, 'An Honest Arab', we recognize the man with the pipe as a type he used later, but the picture is as uninteresting as those that preceded it. 'Après', on page 330, is better: nevertheless, on the whole, we may say that his contributions to *Once a Week* for the first half of 1860 are negligible. In vol. iii, for the latter half of the year, he has seventeen drawings, that on page 295 not being indexed. He is now beginning to find himself—particularly in the illustration for *Wanted a Diamond Ring*, while in another, on page 454, for *The Herberts of Elfdale*, we get the first of those delightful little boys that became a feature of his later work, Walker, in spite of the fame of his Philip, being much more successful with his boys and girls and women than with his men, who as a rule lack virility.

Vol. iv (1861) contains eleven designs. The index gives twelve, but I can hardly believe the 'Voltaire at Ferney' to be his. At all events it is not signed, so we may give him the benefit of the doubt—though it might be argued that 'The Fan', which *is* signed, is very little better. 'The Fan' certainly shows a marked falling-off from the last drawing of the previous volume, but with 'Bring Me a Light' he completely recovers his ground. In 'Dangerous' we have another and better drawing of the man who had appeared in the 'Honest Arab', and in 'The Jewel-Case' the man in a kilt will later on be redrawn with much more skill as Philip. The earlier of the seventeen drawings in vol. v need not detain us, but with the first illustration for *The Settlers of Long Arrow* we come at last to the real Walker. This charming design of a boy wading ashore from a boat has all the grace and felicity that a little later were to make the artist so popular. It was a favourite subject, and he returned to it more than once in studies for a large oil painting: he was in fact working at this very picture at the end of his tragically brief life, leaving it unfinished.

Volume vi (1862) contains thirteen drawings, in one or two of which (those on pp. 449 and 505) Walker is at, or very near his best. But he is also approaching the end of his connection with *Once a Week*: vol. vii contains only seven designs; vol. viii only one, 'After Ten Years', a delightful group of children; and vol. ix only one. Walker's sole remaining drawing for *Once a Week*, the famous 'Vagrants', appeared as an extra illustration in the first volume of the New Series, January, 1866.

It will hardly be claimed for more than a few of the *Once a Week* drawings that they equal the work he did for the *Cornhill* and *Good Words*. In Mr. J. G. Marks's *Life and Letters*[1] he quotes George Smith's account of the artist's first attempt to open a connection with the *Cornhill*. His very first visit produced nothing, because the clerk, misled by his extremely

[1] *The Life and Letters of Frederick Walker*. By J. G. Marks. (Macmillan, 1896.)

FRED WALKER: 'The Village on the Cliff'
[*The Cornhill Magazine*, 1866]

youthful appearance, merely told him that Mr. Smith was engaged. Walker, however, called again, and this time both he and his drawings got as far as the private office. The drawings were inspected, and Mr. Smith, after looking them over, asked him if he would be willing to re-draw Thackeray's designs for *Philip*, then beginning as a serial in *The Cornhill.* ' I understood him to accept the idea,' the publisher adds, ' but his nervous agitation was almost painful, and although I did my best to set him at his ease, he left without my being sure whether my suggestion was acceptable to him or not. I mentioned the subject to Mr. Thackeray, who said, " Bring him here, and we shall soon see whether he can draw." '

Thus the meeting was arranged, but during the drive to Thackeray's house in Onslow Square poor Walker became more agitated than ever. ' Mr. Thackeray saw at once how nervous and distressed the young artist was, and addressed himself in the kindest manner to remove his shyness. " I'm going to shave," said Mr. Thackeray ' (an announcement which makes us wonder if, like Mr. Moreen, he shaved in the drawing-room): ' " Would you mind drawing my back? " '

It is clear that Thackeray's treatment of Fred Walker was from the beginning charming: on the other hand the business arrangement they came to did not at all appeal to the younger artist, though he was too shy to say so. He wanted to invent his own designs, and after making a block or two from Thackeray's sketches expressed his dissatisfaction by the simple if not very happy method of returning the work sent to him. Now the shyest person in the world can at least write a note explaining his position, but this does not seem to have occurred to Walker. Accordingly, on the 11th of February 1861, we find Thackeray himself writing the note.

' Dear Sir—The Blocks you have executed for *The Cornhill Magazine* have given so much satisfaction that I hope we may look for more from the same hand. You told me that the early days of the week were most convenient for you, and accordingly I sent last Monday, or Tuesday, a couple of designs which, as you would not do them, I was obliged to confide to an older, and I grieve to own, much inferior artist. Pray let me know if I may count on you for my large cut for March.
' Believe me, very faithfully yours,
' W. M. THACKERAY.'

This letter did at last, as it was intended to do, elicit a definite expression of Walker's desires, and the ' older and much inferior artist '—who was of course Thackeray himself—immediately accepted the new arrangement. He did more. *The Cornhill*, from the beginning, had made it a rule not to

[141]

mention its artists' names, so Thackeray concluded the thirty-first chapter of *Philip* with these words: ' There was a pretty group for the children to see, and for Mr. Walker to draw '.

No happier way of introducing an unknown artist to the public could be imagined. One would have thought that the sentence might have been left as a permanent record of an extremely graceful act; but what are graceful acts compared with the joy of tampering with texts? So, after Thackeray's death we find the words altered, and in all later editions of *Philip* down to the present day the passage reads, ' There was a pretty group for the children to see and for an artist to draw '.

Thackeray still took the liveliest interest in the illustrations, but thenceforth he limited his collaboration to an occasional hint:

' Dear Mr. Walker,
    ' *Philip*. For August. The little sister, and the two little children saying their prayer in an old-fashioned church pew, not Gothic.
   ' The church is the one in Queen Square, Bloomsbury, if you are curious to be exact.
   ' The motto Pro Concessis Beneficiis.'

The design to which this refers is the beautiful and justly celebrated ' Philip in Church ', for which Mr. Gilbert Dalziel sat for the little boy.

As well as the *Philip* drawings, Walker has three others in *The Cornhill* for 1862: ' Maladetta ', and a couple of illustrations for Miss Thackeray's *Story of Elizabeth*. In the following year he has a third illustration for *The Story of Elizabeth*, two for *Out of the World*, and one for *Mrs. Archie*, all notable designs.

The drawings for *Denis Duval*, that unfinished romance in Thackeray's most delightful manner, appear in 1864. The first design, in which we see little Denis dancing for the Navy gentlemen, was made from a water-colour of Thackeray's. Neither it, perhaps, nor the duel scene that follows, is particularly characteristic of Walker, but the drawing of the two boys examining the pistol, and that of Denis's mother dressing his hair, are among his most charming things. It is strange to find that when *Denis Duval* came to be published in book form the illustrations were omitted.

In 1866 and 1867 Walker supplies six full-page drawings and some initial letters for Miss Thackeray's *Village on the Cliff*. In the latter year he illustrates the same author's *Red Riding Hood* and *Beauty and the Beast*, but the drawings for *A Week in a French Country-House*, which Gleeson White gives to him, are by Frederick Leighton. Of Walker's four remaining full-page drawings for *The Cornhill*—three in 1868 and one in 1869—I cannot

FRED WALKER: 'Philip in Church'
[*The Cornhill Magazine*, 1862]

pass in silence ' Waiting for Papa ', a masterpiece of pure and delicate line work.

Coming to *Good Words*, the first Walker we find is ' The Blind School ' on page 505 of the volume for 1861. Gleeson White refuses to give this drawing to Walker, suspecting a clerical error in the index, but our artist's hand, I think, is obvious in the figure of the middle girl of the three, and in the general pattern. It is a poor drawing, but it is certainly a Walker, and even foreshadows his later manner in a way that at least half a dozen of the early signed illustrations in *Once a Week* fail to do. On page 609, with ' Only a Sweep ', we come to a more characteristic if still somewhat immature design: and then suddenly, in the next volume (1862), we get three absolutely typical Walkers—two, ' The Summer Woods ' and ' Out Among the Wild Flowers ', being pastoral scenes, pictures of rustic boyhood and girlhood, realistic, yet chosen for their beauty—drawings characteristic not only of Walker but of this entire school, which found its poetry, as Wordsworth found his, in everyday life. The third drawing, ' Love in Death ', is tragic, showing a woman with a child in her arms fighting her way through the snow—a design of great beauty, worthy to illustrate a scene in one of Thomas Hardy's novels.

There is nothing in 1863, but 1864 has the eight illustrations for Mrs. Henry Wood's *Oswald Cray*. Looking at them, one could never guess how essentially common is the novel they illustrate, and a question immediately suggests itself as to the editorial inconsistency which could commission *both* the pictures and the text. Of course, in this particular magazine the Dalziels took charge of the illustrations, but the same thing occurs with other journals. Why was the taste in literature so very much lower than the taste in design? Why, having secured the concoctions of Mrs. Henry Wood, should one look about, and decide that *Verner's Pride* must be given to Charles Keene and *Oswald Cray* to Fred Walker? Why should a public that wanted good drawings be supposed to want bad writing? Why should one seek beauty here and be indifferent to its absence there? The drawings for *Oswald Cray* rank among the artist's best, and again, I think, the presentation of youth is their most beautiful and subtle feature. Take the picture on page 532 of the schoolboy standing at the table:—is he not really more successful than that seated lady he confronts, lovely as she undoubtedly is? and in ' The November Night ' drawing, does not its beauty depend largely on the boy following the man and woman through the foggy street, though here the stout servant maid standing on the doorstep with arms akimbo is equally masterly? Technically, in its light and shade, its spacing, its gradation between foreground and background, this latter drawing deserves the closest study.

[145]

Walker's only other contribution to *Good Words* is the 'Waiting in the Dusk' of 1867.

The remaining drawings for periodical literature are unimportant. For *Punch* he made two pictures. 'The New Bathing Company' appeared in the *Almanac* for 1865, and 'Captain Jinks' appeared in 1869. For *London Society* he made one design, an unsuccessful excursion into du Maurier's drawing-room territory, which appeared in the first volume. Mr. Marks, in his *Life of Walker*, also mentions a design in *The Leisure Hour* in the early months of 1860, but of this last I can find no trace. Possibly the drawing meant is the one already referred to, which appeared in *Everybody's Journal*. A few further designs were made more as advertisements than as illustrations. Such are the famous poster for *The Woman in White* and a couple of drawings for the programme of *Black Eyed Susan*.

A veil of obscurity hangs over Walker's earliest book illustrations—not only over those the Dalziels mention as having been done for Routledge, but also over a quantity of small drawings made for the S.P.C.K.—drawings which would appear to have vanished for ever. Gleeson White knew nothing of them, and I should have known nothing myself had not Mr. Harold Hartley actually seen them. Calling at the publisher's one day in the company of J. W. North, he looked over an album of proofs (since destroyed) —proofs of these very designs—about a hundred in all—many of them by Walker and some by North himself. What makes the tracking of them so difficult to-day is that they were not only unsigned but were also extremely immature. Nevertheless, I have turned up two S.P.C.K. books in which I believe Walker had a share. I put the more doubtful first: *Shipwrecks and Adventures at Sea* [1860]. The picture of 'The Loss of the Forfarshire' (p. 201) certainly suggests a very early Walker; and also that of 'The Loss of the Proserpine' (p. 5), though here I confess I am going only on the general grouping of the sailors—not a very secure foundation. And the remaining pictures are, frankly, anybody's. With *Scenes and Narratives from the early History of the United States of America* [1862] one feels oneself on slightly firmer ground. I think it highly probable that several of the illustrations here are by Walker, while that of 'John Marvel leaving Home' is remarkably like a North. *Reminiscences of the late Assheton Smith*, by Sir John Eardley Wilmot (1862), has a picture of a 'Hall Table at Tedworth House', which Edward Whymper told Mr. Hartley Walker drew when he was an apprentice. There is not much excuse, however, for mentioning 'hall tables' when I have omitted Charles Keene's 'trussing of fowls' and 'gouty deformities', and our next book luckily has a more genuine interest. *Tom Cringle's Log* (Blackwood, 1861), besides illustrations by Clarkson Stanfield and Harrison Weir, has two undeniable Walkers, engraved by

FRED WALKER: 'Oswald Cray'
[*Good Words*, 1864]

FRED WALKER: 'Esmond'
[Unpublished]

Whymper—'The Recapture of the West Indiaman' and 'Fishing in the Great Bahama Bank'—as well as one or two others that are possibly his.

But all are prentice work, and the volume we now reach, though equally unknown and actually of the same date so far as publication goes, marks a distinct advance. *The Twins and Their Stepmother* (Routledge, Warne and Routledge, 1861) contains four signed drawings by Walker, immature, but pleasing and sufficiently characteristic; indeed much more recognizably his than the early *Once a Week* pictures. A little later, I fancy, are the four illustrations for Dickens's *Reprinted Pieces* (published with *The Old Curiosity Shop* in 1861), and the four for *Hard Times* (published with *Barnaby Rudge* in 1862). Several of these Dickens designs are excellent, 'The Long Voyage' and 'The Schoolboy's Story' being particularly delicate and charming.

In 1862 Walker contributed three delightful examples of his earlier work to Willmott's *English Sacred Poetry*. Of these, 'A Child in Prayer' is one of his loveliest children, while 'The Nursery Friend' is among his most pleasing women. The illustration for 'The Portrait of a Minister', contributed to *English Sacred Poetry of the Olden Time* (Religious Tract Society), belongs to 1864. The boy and girl in it are said to be portraits of Walker's young brother and sister.

The next books on our list are among the most important of the period —*A Round of Days* (1866), and *Wayside Posies* (1867). Why the Dalziels should give the dates of these volumes as 1867 and 1869 I do not know, since it was they who planned them and printed them. They do not tell us when Walker made the drawings for *A Round of Days*. One gathers that it was two or three years before the book was published, the commission having originally been for a set of drawings on wood to form a companion volume to Birket Foster's *Pictures of English Landscape*. The rapidly increasing demand for Walker's paintings, however, proved fatal to this project. Half a dozen of the drawings were finished fairly promptly, but longer and longer intervals elapsed between the production of each, till finally the original scheme was abandoned. 'We published the engravings', the *Record* tells us, 'with those of other artists, mostly by G. J. Pinwell and J. W. North, first in *A Round of Days* and *Home Affections*, and afterwards in an India paper edition, as *Pictures of English Rustic Life*, by Frederick Walker and G. J. Pinwell.' For *Home Affections* read *Wayside Posies*; it is the work meant; *Home Affections* is a book of the fifties. But the first reprint is not *English Rustic Pictures* (which belongs to 1882), it is a book called *Picture Posies*, issued in 1874.

In *A Round of Days* there are six of Walker's drawings: in *Wayside Posies*, a finer book still (partly because of the closer bond uniting the artists, which gives it more unity of effect, and partly because of the abundant and splendid work of North and Pinwell), there are only five. Taking the two volumes together, the best of Walker's designs is the ' Broken Victuals ' on page 3 of *A Round of Days*. The simple beauty of the figures, the way they harmonize with the background—itself beautiful though it is but a kitchen wall—the complete satisfaction to the eye of the long parallel lines of fender and mantelpiece and picture-frame—all these things contribute to form a design that comes very near perfection. Walker, it is said, was perpetually dissatisfied with his work; and he was never, indeed, to become a supreme master such as Charles Keene, for whom, in the end, technical difficulties ceased to exist. Walker's drawings, on the contrary, were built up slowly and carefully, tentatively at first, and only through much patient labour did they attain their final effect of grace and beauty. But he had a profound sympathy with Greek art, and in his own smaller, different way attempted to carry on the Greek tradition. It is the tradition, one might add, of all the most typical work of the school that followed the Pre-Raphael-ites, and when I call it Greek I mean no more than that it is founded directly upon nature, that it accepts life as it is and turns it into beauty. But that is exactly what the art of the Greeks does, and what the pseudo-classical art of an Albert Moore, a Leighton, or a Poynter does not do.

Walker's remaining book illustrations are few. In an edition of *The Ingoldsby Legends* published by Bentley in two quarto volumes (1866), and containing as well as the illustrations by Tenniel and Cruikshank a few extra designs, he has a drawing on page 165 for ' The Lady Rohesia '. It is a poor drawing, obviously extremely early, though when it was actually made I do not know. As a matter of fact, in the index it is attributed to Tenniel, but in later reprints it figures as an anonymous design. *The Story of Elizabeth* (1867) contains, as well as the three drawings which appeared in *The Cornhill Magazine*, an elaborate title page that is really a full-page drawing. The very fine design, ' Hogarth's Model ', published in a post-humous edition of Thackeray's *English Humourists*, is, I should say, later than this, while a frontispiece to William Black's *Daughter of Heth* (1872) is probably the last illustration he made.

II. GEORGE JOHN PINWELL (1842-1875)

The work of an artist like Pinwell is always liable to be over- or under-estimated. It is an art extremely personal in its manner and therefore in its appeal; it is an art hampered constantly by an imperfect technique, and yet its very failures are frequently more interesting than the successes of cleverer draughtsmen, while its successes are lovely as April primroses.

FRED WALKER: 'Broken Victuals'

[*A Round of Days*]

Pinwell was conscious of his limitations, conscious of an insufficient training, conscious that he would never paint or draw the pictures of his dreams. Those imagined pictures, one fancies, would have been far more like Whistler's than like Walker's. To me, at any rate, the work he actually accomplished frequently suggests an affinity with Whistler, though it is with Walker that he is invariably coupled. But Pinwell's designs are never pretty, his type of feminine beauty is what the average man who rejoices in the sweetness of Walker's women would describe as plain, and he had a decorative sense far superior to Walker's. They both drew pictures of English rustic life, but Pinwell, again, has a wider range, is infinitely more imaginative, and his work, above all, has a subjective, a lyrical quality, so that everything comes to us reflected through his temperament, which was inclined to sadness.

George John Pinwell was born at Wycombe, in Buckinghamshire, in 1842. He received practically no education, his father having died when he was a child, his mother being a rough, illiterate woman, and he himself having been sent out to work when he should have been at school. Here comes in Harry Quilter's story of him as ' butterman's boy in the City Road, whose duty, among other things, was to stand outside the shop on Saturday nights shouting Buy! Buy! Buy!' The story may or may not be true, since of those early years we know absolutely nothing. We assume that he must have been a sensitive, rather dreamy boy, not very happy in his home, and with ambitions to become an artist; but even such fairly safe deductions are too bold for Dr. Williamson, his official biographer. It is an odd production, this, the sole existing monograph [1] on a neglected artist. As a source of information it is negligible, [2] as a criticism it merely echoes fragments of Gleeson White, as a character study it is infantile. ' Undertaken largely for the satisfaction of Mrs. Pinwell ', its main purpose seems to be to persuade us that ' Pinwell could hold his own in the most refined society ', and in this it fails. That such a point should have been raised at all is singular, for it is the last that would be likely to suggest itself to the reader. Dr. Williamson, however, is so bent on establishing ' the purity of Pinwell's domestic life ', on denying contemporary allegations concerning his sobriety and his grammar, that he would arouse suspicions in the least suspicious. Fortunately neither the grammar nor the purity is of much consequence

[1] *George J. Pinwell and His Works.* By George C. Williamson, Litt.D. (Bell & Sons, 1900.)

[2] Even the titles of the illustrations cannot always be relied on. What purports to be a ' Scene from the Illustrated Goldsmith ' (facing p. 11) is in reality a drawing called ' Vanity ', from *Golden Thoughts from Golden Fountains.* The bibliographical notes are copied from Gleeson White, the errors slavishly repeated.

to-day; all that really matters is that Pinwell survived the rough shaking of his boyhood, escaped from the butterman (even if he is only a symbol), and obtained employment with a firm of embroiderers for whom he made designs. At the same time he attended night classes at St. Martin's Lane School, and eventually, when his mother married again, found himself comparatively free to do as he pleased. The only art training he received was snatched in these off hours—at St. Martin's Lane School and later at Heatherley's Academy. The Dalziels mention that he called on them and that they commissioned him to make ' sets of illustrations for boys' books ', but, as in the case of Fred Walker, they tell us neither the date of the visit nor the titles of the books. The earliest books with illustrations by Pinwell of which I have a note are *The Happy Home, Hacco the Dwarf*, and *Lilliput Levée*. The drawings for *Hacco the Dwarf* Gleeson White believes to be Pinwell's ' earliest published work ', but with this I venture to disagree, nor do I see how any of these children's tales can be among the ' boys' books ' referred to by the Dalziels, unless that description is of the loosest kind.

We shall begin, at all events, according to our usual plan, with the drawings made for magazines. They are so numerous that a complete list of them would occupy several pages. Gleeson White says that between 1863 and 1869 Pinwell contributed occasionally to *Punch*, but the only *Punch* drawing I have succeeded in tracing appeared on the 6th of June 1863: on the other hand he did contribute two or three things to *Fun*—later—among them an excellent drawing for the Almanac of 1871—and possibly to *Judy*, the files of which I have not very carefully examined, though I came upon one Pinwell, in 1872, again for the Almanac. But both *Fun* and *Judy* are depressing in the extreme: with the exception of E. G. Dalziel everybody seems to have used them as dumping grounds for their very worst drawings.

With *Once a Week* Pinwell established a more or less regular connection, though the serial stories were never entrusted to him. His first illustration appears in vol. viii (January the 31st, 1863), and is for a poem of Walter Thornbury's called *The Saturnalia*. It is a powerful design, but we feel it should be signed T. Morten, not G. J. Pinwell. This drawing of apes and peacock feathers and dancing girls of Pompeii is, however, so utterly remote from the kind of subject Pinwell himself would have chosen that it would be surprising if we found much of his peculiar personal quality in it. In fact, of the seven designs contributed to vol. viii the only one in which we find the artist more or less himself is ' Seasonable Wooing '. Those on pages 392 and 477 are indeed obvious Pinwells, but they are Pinwells that have not come off. How far the failure of the child in the latter may be due to Swain's interpretation it is impossible to say, for even a casual inspection of Pinwell's original drawings is sufficient to show us

G. J. PINWELL: 'The Swallows'

[*Wayside Posies*]

that he suffered more than most artists when his work came to be cut. *Once a Week* for the latter half of 1863 also contained seven designs.

Volume x (1864) has fifteen, among them 'The Blacksmiths of Holsby', a fine example of his decorative treatment of figure and landscape. In vol. xi we have only four drawings; in vol. xii three ; and in vol. xiii one.

Pinwell has now become an infrequent contributor, though further designs will be found—one in vol. ii of the New Series (1866), three in vol. iii, including the extra plate, 'Come Buy my Pretty Windmills', and the drawing for *Joe Robertson's Folly* on page 225, which is already characteristic of his later manner—the manner that is to some so attractive, and to others just the reverse. Volume iv of the New Series contains the admirable 'Evening-Tide', which might be chosen as a test piece for the true Pinwellite ; and vol. iii of the Third Series (1869) 'A Seat in the Park', a fine subject picture from which he probably made a painting.

The Cornhill, I think, contains only five examples of Pinwell—three for *The Lovers of Ballyvookan* (1864), and two for *Out of the Forest* (1870).

In *Good Words* there are a great many designs. The first, 'Martin Ware's Temptation', appears in 1863. There are four in 1864; none in 1865 ; one in 1866 ; and then, in 1867, we come to the twelve strangely fascinating illustrations for George MacDonald's *Guild Court*, as well as a couple of other drawings. For the *Guild Court* designs the present writer will always feel a special affection: they formed the nucleus of a schoolboy's collection: in fact it would hardly be an exaggeration to say that it was through them he first discovered the existence of pictorial art.

All this cataloguing is no doubt tedious, but I would add that (apart from those which appeared in the extra Christmas Numbers, called *Good Cheer*) there are thirteen Pinwells in *Good Words* for 1868; none in 1869 ; three in 1870; four in 1871; and after that no more till we reach 1875, the year of his death, when for Jean Ingelow's *Fated to be Free* he supplies no less than thirty-four designs, some of which seem to show him breaking quite new ground. The illustrations on pages 43 and 108 are particularly fine studies of old age, not in the least like any types he had previously drawn. Of course, the former types are there too—even exaggerated in more than one instance—and the old plaintive, troubled, yet intensely quiet Pinwell atmosphere. It would be superfluous to describe these illustrations as mannered, because all Pinwell's later work is mannered.

From its foundation in 1865 Pinwell worked fairly regularly for *The Sunday Magazine*, his big year being 1869, when he made thirty-four drawings for *The Crust and the Cake*. In this journal he has many fascinating things—things varying from the simple beauty of 'For a Sick Boy' (1865) to the strangeness of 'The Gang Children' (1868) in which to some extent he anticipates the style of Hubert Herkomer. In 1868, too, we find a couple of drawings for *Madame de Krudener*, in the graceful eighteenth-century vein of his *Goldsmith*. The last *Sunday Magazine* drawing appeared, I believe, in the Christmas Number, *Paths of Peace*, in either 1872 or 1873.

A few lovely Pinwells appeared in *The Quiver* from 1866 to 1868, where, unfortunately, they had neither the advantage of good paper nor careful printing, so that the re-issue of several of them in *Idyllic Pictures* is particularly welcome. Gladly would we have had them all; especially since among those omitted are two of the most beautiful—' Home ' (1867), in which the woman might have been drawn by Whistler, and ' She is Gathering Pears in the Garden ' (also 1867). The treatment of the pear-tree against the wall in the latter picture is a beautiful piece of decoration, though the wall itself is ruined by the print on the reverse side of the too transparent page. The drawings actually selected for *Idyllic Pictures* are there, one supposes, because of some fancied wider ' human appeal ' in them. This human interest, this appeal if you like, is of course a feature of the work we are considering. Our artists themselves believed in it, and they were not afraid of the commonplace. They had no desire to ' bewilder the bourgeois ', they were interested in the whole of life. It is remarkable, for example, how seldom a merely erotic passage is chosen for illustration. No particular age is favoured, but the entire human comedy is there, from the cradle to the grave.

For *The Churchman's Family Magazine* and *London Society* Pinwell did little. In the former he has a couple of small drawings, ' By the Sea ' (1863) and ' March Winds ' (1864); in the latter he has half a dozen things per-haps, but they are not among his best. ' Black Rock ', however, his solitary contribution to *Good Words for the Young* (vol. i, p. 255), is an extremely good drawing, in which he attains more breadth and freedom than usual. He also contributed, though very infrequently, to *The Sunday at Home*. In its pages we find ' The German Band ' (1863), ' How to Use an Almanac ' (1864), and possibly others, for I confess I have not made an exhaustive examination of this very unattractive journal. In *The Leisure Hour* for 1865 he has an admirable drawing, ' Hop-Picking '—an impressionistic sketch full of colour and atmosphere, and well worth looking up, though as a rule *The Leisure Hour* proves nearly as barren a hunting-ground as *The Sunday at Home*. There is a drawing in *Cassell's Magazine* for May 1868; another in *The Argosy* for 1866; but much more interesting are those in the early volumes of *The Graphic*, chief among them being ' The Lost Child ' (1870), a subject he had already treated in *The Sunday Magazine* for 1865; a fine engraving by Dalziel of that lovely picture ' The Sisters ' (1871); and ' A Country Visitor ' (February 1873).

G. J. Pinwell: 'Home'
[*The Quiver*, 1867]

G. J. PINWELL: 'The Island Bee'

[From the original drawing in the possession of Mr. J. N. Hart]

G. J. Pinwell: 'The Island Bee'

[*Wayside Posies*]

Of the illustrated books *Hacco the Dwarf* is the accepted first—apparently because somebody once said it was. So far as I myself have been able to discover (taking *The Publishers' Circular* and *The English Catalogue of Books* as my guides) the early Pinwell volumes appeared in the following order: *The Happy Home* (November 1863), *Hacco the Dwarf* (November 1864), *Lilliput Levée* (December 1864), and the illustrations themselves support this dating. Both *The Happy Home* and *Hacco the Dwarf* were issued at two prices, the more expensive editions having the plates hand coloured. The illustrations in *The Happy Home* are quite uncharacteristic: those for *Hacco* (the book is post-dated 1865) are distinctly better; indeed, the drawing of 'Maud and Robert' on page 170 is a charming thing, and an unmistakable Pinwell. *Lilliput Levée* (1864) is a small slim quarto bound in maroon cloth (the square green edition uniform with *Dealings with the Fairies* is later), and most of the pictures are reproduced in a reddish-brown tint by some lithographic process similar to that employed in *The Postman's Bag*. The Pinwells are originals, the Millais reprints.

Our Life Illustrated by Pen and Pencil [1865] contains a couple of Pinwells. It is a mediocre volume, but is worth having for the sake of these two designs, and for one or two vignettes by Barnes and Watson, and a rather fine du Maurier, 'Paul in Prison'.

For *Dalziel's Arabian Nights* Pinwell made ten drawings, all belonging to the earlier numbers. The most notable is 'The Prince and the Ogress', a composition singularly rich in its contrast of black and white, the mysterious darkness of the forest being suggested with great imaginative power. It cannot, of course, be compared with the more amazing of the Houghton designs, but it rather more than holds its own with those of any of the other artists who collaborated to produce this great book.

For *Dalziel's Illustrated Goldsmith* (1865)—also brought out serially in parts—Pinwell made the whole of the drawings, one hundred in all, and the book is usually regarded as his masterpiece. In a sense, perhaps, it is—the sense that it is a more sustained flight than any he attempts elsewhere: but, taking the drawings separately, they are to my mind neither so beautiful nor so interesting as many of those he made later. They are costume pieces, and personally I prefer Pinwell when he is drawing from contemporary life: on the other hand they are entirely free from what Gleeson White describes as 'that curiously immobile manner of his later years'. The *Goldsmith* is one of the big books of the period, and establishes Pinwell's reputation as a first-rate illustrator. He found his richest material in *The Vicar of Wakefield*, but in the introduction there is a remarkably fine drawing of 'Goldsmith Wandering through the Streets', which shows a touch of Hogarth. The title page of *The Vicar* is a charming design, and wonderfully graceful is

[161]

the picture of Mr. Thornhill playing the guitar. The grouping in the larger designs is always admirable, and what could be more attractive than the drawing of Moses on page 49, or the figure of the woman posing as a model on page 64, or the little boy with his kneeling mother on page 121? —one picks them out very much at random from a score of others possessing an equal distinction.

We now reach a practically unknown volume, *The Adventures of Gil Blas* (Routledge, 1866), which has eight unsigned illustrations by Pinwell. I came upon the proofs of these drawings in the Dalziel collection, and, as so often happens, a few days later picked up a copy of the book itself in a shop in the Charing Cross Road. This copy, however, differs in two respects from the copy in the British Museum—it is undated, and has Pinwell's name on the title page. Probably, therefore, it is only a reprint, though the book seems rare enough in any form.

The Spirit of Praise [1866] has a couple of beautiful drawings, and Buchanan's *Ballad Stories of the Affections* [1866] four, including the delightful ' Maid Mettelil '.[1] There are six designs in *A Round of Days* (1866) and eighteen in *Wayside Posies* (1867). The drawings in *Wayside Posies* in particular show him at his best. Certain of them—the ' Shadow and Substance ', for instance—are of the highest decorative originality, and all are very lovely things: in the beautiful drawing of ' The Swallows ' we have a portrait of the artist's wife. They are more individual than the *Goldsmith* drawings. From now on he gives us something which, whether we like it or not, is altogether different from what anybody else gives us. It is quite possible, I know, that to many people the twenty blocks he made for *Jean Ingelow's Poems* (1867) will seem deliberately eccentric—particularly the superb series for *The High Tide*. Millais's, or Walker's, or du Maurier's drawings are everybody's drawings, but these are not everybody's drawings: —their beauty is hard, crabbed, recondite. But how well it lasts! For me these strange, rather stiff, and intensely mannered designs are among the most fascinating of the whole period. The first edition of the *Jean Ingelow* is now very scarce, but there were several reprints, and I have seen an American edition which must have been practically contemporaneous.

Golden Thoughts from Golden Fountains [1867] contains two drawings. The first edition of this book is easy to recognize in spite of its being undated. In the first edition the designs are all printed on a sepia background: in the reprints, with the exceptions of the full-page plates, they are in black and white. Buchanan's *North Coast* (1868) contains six Pinwells, all good,

---

[1] A large, unfinished, and very beautiful water-colour drawing of ' Maid Mettelil ' is now in the possession of Mr. J. N. Hart. It was one of the last works on which Pinwell was engaged.

G. J. PINWELL: ' The Goose '

[*Wayside Posies*]

G. J. PINWELL: 'The High Tide'

[*Jean Ingelow's Poems*]

and in the same year appeared his illustrations for a popular edition of Dickens's *Uncommercial Traveller*. Two of the four illustrations are actually dated 1868, but the proof of the frontispiece, ' This is a sweet spot ', was pulled as early as 1865, if one can trust the Dalziel album for that year. Charles Reade's *It is Never too Late to Mend* (1868) has a lovely frontispiece and vignette; *Leslie's Musical Annual* (1870) also has a fine drawing; and Novello's *National Nursery Rhymes* [1870] has one for ' Simple Simon ' in which we see the artist very pleasantly caricaturing his own manner. To *Sunlight of Song* (1875) Pinwell contributed an illustration, but the only drawing he made for *Dalziel's Bible Gallery*, the amazing ' Spies Bringing in the Grapes ', was not published till the reprint of 1894. This, I fancy, covers nearly all the black and white work of an artist to whom the world has not yet done justice, an artist who never ran after popularity, but who was endowed with one of the most delicate and poetic talents of his generation.

III. JOHN WILLIAM NORTH (1841-1924)

J. W. North, Fred Walker's intimate friend, was a landscape artist who introduced figures only by the way, and in his paintings some of these figures were put in by Walker. To modern taste North's broader, truer method is infinitely more satisfying than the painstaking minuteness of a Birket Foster, but in his own day his work never attained popularity, and was underrated even by his fellow-artists. In 1870 we find Walker writing to condole with him on the rejection of his pictures by the Royal Academy, and it was not till 1871 that he was elected a member of the Old Water-colour Society. The two artists worked side by side, and in a pettier mind than North's the early ' boom ' of Walker and the universal applause with which his pictures were greeted by both critics and public might have aroused a feeling of jealousy. But North was not jealous. It is quite plain that in their journeys and sketching tours all the troublesome details of manage-ment, of looking after accounts, of securing rooms, fell upon his shoulders. In Walker's letters to his ' dearest Mummy ', he makes no attempt to dis-guise the fact. ' Old North ' (who was really his junior by a year and a half) ' is very nice—quiet and considerate in small things; which is to me very refreshing.' ' I am taking great care of myself; especially changing my boots, etc. North would make me if I didn't of my own accord.' Probably even at this time North had a prevision of how short was to be the career that had opened so auspiciously.

His own conscientious, sincere, and quiet work was of a kind that makes its way slowly. His landscapes are the most beautiful, at once the broadest and most delicate, that the black and white art of the sixties can boast; but the demand for them was small, and editors were not eager to give him commissions. In all the volumes of *Once a Week* he figures only five times—in vols. ix, xii, and ii and iii of the New Series, though of these five drawings ' The River ' and ' Then and Now ' in vol. xii, and ' Luther's Gardener ' in vol. ii (New Series) should have been sufficient to establish his reputation. The last drawing is a particularly charming thing. It is quaint; but then it illustrates a poem by Walter Thornbury that is itself distinctly quaint—all about ants and beetles and spiders and woodlice and earwigs.

To *Good Words* in 1863 North contributed ' Autumn Thoughts ', and to the same magazine in 1866 ' The Island Church '. In the *Sunday Magazine* for 1865 he has ' Winter ', a lovely picture of a farm half buried in snow, with hedges and trees rising black and naked from the surrounding whiteness, and a boy and girl, muffled up against the cold, in the foreground. I should also, in the same volume, be inclined to give him the unindexed ' Church of Our Fathers ' on page 869, though if that is a signature in the left-hand corner it certainly is not his. In *The Sunday Magazine* for 1867 he has three excellent pictures, a landscape and two sea-pieces.

Our Life Illustrated by Pen and Pencil has an unimportant little vignette by North, and he is represented in *The Months*, an undated and uninteresting book published by the Religious Tract Society. *English Sacred Poetry of the Olden Time* contains ten of his drawings, all, however, belonging to a period when he was still imitating Birket Foster; nor is there anything outstanding in his contributions to *The Book of Sacred Poems* [1867], a large and dull anthology. In the latter book the names of the artists are grouped together on the title page; otherwise there is no clue to who made the drawings, many of which are unsigned, while the engraving is frequently poor. In spite of the well-known names the book is more or less negligible, such honours as there are going to M. E. Edwards, who comes nearer her true form than anybody else. The unsigned drawing, ' Side by Side ', on page 17, which puzzled Gleeson White, I think we may give to J. D. Watson.

But the five Norths in *A Round of Days*, and the nineteen in *Wayside Posies* are all gems. If one had to pick out a single design from them perhaps it would be the ' Reaping ' in *Wayside Posies*, which also, incidentally, is one of Dalziel's most perfect engravings. The dark figures against the sky, and the sky itself, with the light of sunset flushing it, are marvellously realized. Turn from this drawing to the sunlit elfin grace of ' The Nutting ' and you will see what variety of tone and colour and atmosphere North could get. ' The Nutting ' is as full of sunlight as a landscape by Monet.

And yet, fine though these engravings are, they cannot vie with the original drawings, all of which were drawn with a brush. Many of them are

J. W. NORTH: ' Reaping '
[*Wayside Posies*]

J. W. NORTH: 'The Home Pond'

[*A Round of Days*]

very slightly tinted, and all have an extreme delicacy that no engraver could hope to reproduce. Take, for instance, the engraving of 'The Old Shepherd', on page 69 of *A Round of Days*. It is beautiful there, but how much more beautiful as it came from the hand of North. Particularly the bush and the dog in the foreground have, in the engraving, lost their wonderful surface quality, which in the original is soft as the down on a butterfly's wings.

North's twenty-four drawings in *Jean Ingelow's Poems*, and the three in *The Spirit of Praise*, though not in every case quite maintaining this high level, include some exquisite examples of his work, while of the remainder not one is poor. For the *Poetical Works of Longfellow* (Warne's 'Chandos Poets') he made a single design. The date of the first edition of this book, which is undated, I have not traced, but the proofs of the illustrations were pulled in 1866. Lastly, a set of seven very fine proofs was sent by the Dalziels on the 11th of June 1864 to America. These must, I should think, all have been intended to illustrate the same work. The proofs are in the Dalziel collection, but the book itself I have not identified.

CHAPTER VIII

JOHN DAWSON WATSON (1832-1892)

TO attempt to draw a distinguishing line between talent and genius is neither very profitable nor very safe, yet who, in private, does not do so? In the graphic arts, we tell ourselves, one is a matter of hand and eye, and the other of emotion and imagination. So we give the talent to Walker and the genius to Pinwell, the talent to Leighton and the genius to Rossetti, the talent to du Maurier and the genius to Charles Keene. As a matter of fact, it cannot really be so easy as all that, and in the last pair chosen we already see our test beginning to fail, since the supremacy of Keene does primarily lie in the possession of a marvellous technique. It will be sufficient, therefore, to describe J. D. Watson as a sound draughts-man, whose work frequently surprises us by its power and beauty, though nowhere perhaps does it reveal a very striking individuality. Watson was, in the beginning at any rate, deeply imbued with the spirit of his period, and that spirit was a salutary one; but he was not an imaginative artist, and his legendary, allegorical, and religious illustrations seldom rise above mediocrity. Set him to illustrate some homely scene and he will treat it with dignity, simplicity, and a charm that often passes into poetry; but his Knights and Crusaders, his Spirits of Christianity and his Dreams of Sin, have all the triviality and dullness of pot-boilers. Why he should have been called upon for so many religious pictures is hard to see, for quite plainly they were not in his line. The lovely ' Sabbath Day ' in *Good Words* (1862) is not really a religious picture, the religious element consists solely in the fact that we are in a delightful old church. That the artist who made this particular drawing should also have made some of the others—the later designs in *The Quiver* for example—is strange and disappointing. Are we to explain it by the fact that Watson became a successful painter in water colours? His later black and white work, at all events, shows a marked falling off in quality; most of it seems mere hack work in which he has taken no interest, while even the few good things come nowhere near the standard of the early drawings.

Watson scarcely counts among the *Once a Week* artists. He made three drawings for that paper (one in vol. viii and two in vol. ix), but it was

J. D. Watson: 'The Aspen'

[*Good Words*, 1863]

to *Good Words* and *London Society* that he gave his best work. His first drawing in *Good Words* (1861) is for *The Toad*, a translation of Victor Hugo's poem. An excellent drawing it is, with a touch of Pre-Raphaelitism in it, as Pre-Raphaelitism was expressed by Holman Hunt; but the five remaining designs in the same volume show that he had already perfected the manner with which we are more familiar. The style of *The Toad* probably was adopted to harmonize with a certain naïveté in his subject, and we shall find him experimenting with it again in a few later though still very early drawings.

Good Words for 1862 contains eight Watsons, among them 'The Sabbath Day' I have referred to, a picture of a children's service, and as beautiful a drawing as he was ever to make. Or almost as beautiful, for 'The Aspen' of 1863 perhaps surpasses it. What is there in this naturalistic drawing that makes of it a thing positively steeped in poetry? Two figures, a young mother and a child, their backs turned to us, wandering at dusk through an old demesne. If we turn to the verses by Gerald Massey it is supposed to illustrate, the glamour instantly disappears. The picture most emphatically has nothing to do with those verses, which are trite in the extreme, while the drawing is charged with an emotion that has been a human inheritance from the beginning of time. Part of its rich dense atmosphere may be accidental; it has acquired, with the darkening paper of the old magazine, a mellowness, a depth, that add amazingly to its mysterious autumnal quality; for when we see it reprinted on the white paper of *Touches of Nature* it is less striking. The toned paper of *Good Words*, the soft tone of time this particular drawing has gradually absorbed, makes just the little difference that in its power of suggestiveness is so great. And when I spoke of Watson being imbued with the spirit of his age I might have added that that spirit is reflected in its essence in this drawing, as in Whistler's 'Trial Sermon', as in Houghton's 'Making Poetry', as in many things of Pinwell's. Watson has five other good designs in the volume for 1863, but I have singled out my favourite, and I shall leave it at that. Beauty —beauty of this kind at any rate—is essentially a work of collaboration, and unanalysable—depending on the creation by the artist in the spectator of a particular state of mind. Just *how* that state of mind is produced is, I think, impossible to know; nor do I suppose it can be produced *at all* except in a nature predisposed to it:—I mean, except where the germs at least of a similar understanding, experience, emotion, sympathy, already exist.

Some of Watson's finest drawings appeared in the early numbers of *London Society*. The boldest and best of these contain only one or two figures, drawn as large as the size of the picture will permit. Two out of the three in vol. i (1862), besides being among the artist's best designs, show

Dalziel's engraving also at its best, and are printed, it would seem, with a special care, so rich is their appearance. In 'Ash Wednesday' we see a man kneeling, with his face hidden in his arms, his whole attitude expressive of an overwhelming grief: 'Romance and a Curacy', though less tragic, is an equally impressive composition. Note the beauty of the background, the picture on the wall, and, in both designs, the drawing of the hands. The third drawing, 'Spring Days', though excellent, is not the equal of these; nor, with the exception of 'Married',[1] are any of the drawings in the second half of 1862.

Further Watsons will be found in *London Society* for 1863 and 1864, the latter year containing the exceptionally good 'Blankton Weir' and the beautiful 'Duet' of vol. v. In 1865 he contributes two delicate little drawings for *Green Mantle*, and a third, a full page, which is less satisfactory. In the Christmas Number for 1866 he has the admirable 'Given Back on Christmas Morn'; but after this, though he continues to work for *London Society*, his drawings decline in interest.

In the first volume of *The Churchman's Family Magazine* (1863) the 'Sunday Evening' is an excellent thing, while not far behind it come three or four others. Only one drawing by Watson I have noted in *The Sunday Magazine*—'The Cottar's Farewell', in March 1867. In the short-lived *Shilling Magazine*, however, he illustrated Mrs. Riddell's serial, *Phemie Keller* (1865) in his best manner, and other periodicals to which he contributed are *The Illustrated London News* (Christmas Number, 1861), *The Band of Hope Review*, *Cassell's Magazine*, *Tinsley's Magazine* (1868-69), *The British Workman* (1863 on), *The Quiver*, *The People's Magazine* (1873), and *The Graphic*, where in 1871 appeared his powerful 'Fugitives from Chicago'.

When George Routledge asked the Dalziels to find somebody to illustrate a proposed new edition of *The Pilgrim's Progress*, he made the stipulation that the artist must be 'a new man'. This desire for novelty may have been prompted by remembrance of the ubiquitous John Gilbert, always ready to illustrate anything and everything; and it speaks highly for the courage of the engravers that on the strength of a couple of drawings in *Good Words* they should have placed the commission (and it meant a hundred designs) in the hands of the then young and unknown Edinburgh artist, J. D. Watson. The Dalziels have told the story in their *Record*, and how this was the work that first brought Watson to London.

But as a matter of fact, even earlier than this they had engraved some

---

[1] When they came to be reprinted in *Pictures of Society* these drawings, as usual, received new titles. Thus, 'Romance and a Curacy' becomes 'Evenings Long Ago', 'Ash Wednesday' becomes 'Prayer', and 'Married' becomes 'Too Late!'

J. D. WATSON: 'Ash Wednesday'

[*London Society*, 1862]

designs made by Watson for now unprocurable nursery tales. In their album for 1859 there are the proofs of his drawings for *Cinderella*: several for *The Three Bears* also suggest his work, and a picture of a mother telling a story to a group of children (intended perhaps to advertise this whole series of toy books) is certainly his.

Watson's *Pilgrim's Progress* (Routledge, 1861), like his *Robinson Crusoe*, is now among the rarer books of the period. You must search long and patiently for a ' first '; longer and more patiently perhaps than the book itself deserves. For the illustrations, though beautifully engraved and printed, are disappointing. In spite of a few charming things, the general impression is monotonous and dull, while even the best designs fall far below the magazine drawings I have singled out. The text appears to have been a burden rather than a source of inspiration to the artist (Watson had little luck with his texts), and when he could get away from its influence, as in the picture of ' The Shepherd Boy ' on page 291, we feel much the same relief as he seems to have felt himself. This, and the drawing in the Memoir of ' Bunyan Parting with his Wife and Children ', and the drawing of ' Mercy Left Without the Gate ', show Watson's true quality; but for the remainder we can hardly say more than that they are good average work. It is easy to tell when a book has found its true illustrator, and there is nothing in this book to warn a later artist off the field.

To this same year belong the two or three pleasing illustrations made for Norman Macleod's allegory *The Gold Thread*, and the six illustrations for *Eliza Cook's Poems*. The most striking drawings in the latter book are ' The Farm Gate ', and a strange design called ' The Sexton ', in which Watson combines a sinister and Holman Huntish grave-digger with some round-faced innocents of his own devising, who view their companion not without alarm. 1861 was in fact a fertile year with Watson: *Eildon Manor* contains four beautiful drawings by him; *Accidents of Childhood* contains twenty (charming things, approximating to the naïve style of ' The Toad ' design in *Good Words*); and *The Maze of Life* four.

Willmott's *English Sacred Poetry* (1862) is another capital Watson volume, and one would not exchange the twenty-eight drawings he made for it for the hundred in *The Pilgrim's Progress*. Some of these illustrations, such as ' Sunday in the Fields ', show him in his most idyllic mood, and the delicate little landscapes for Gray's *Elegy* make one regret that he did not do more in that line. Perhaps the most successful drawing of all, however, is the ' Moonlight ' on page 257, a picture of a shepherd and his dog going out into the moonlit fields, with just a narrow strip of landscape visible through the open cottage door. It is a design that takes us straight back to the finer things of the Moxon *Tennyson* and *Poets of the Nineteenth Century*,

[169]

and one sighs to think of what Watson might have accomplished had he been gifted, or burdened, with a more exacting artistic conscience.

Like *The Maze of Life*, *Accidents of Childhood*, and *Eildon Manor*, *Bennett's Poems* (Routledge, 1862) is an unknown and unchronicled Watson volume, in which we find four excellent designs. J. H. Burrow's *Adventures of Alfan*, and Mrs. W. R. Lloyd's *Flower of Christian Chivalry* belong to 1863; *The Golden Harp* (Routledge, n.d.) to 1864. For some unstated reason Gleeson White takes the illustrations in this last book to be clichés, though a mere glance through the rhymes and poems is sufficient to show that the drawings were made for them. These drawings are certainly in Watson's earliest manner; nevertheless the proofs were pulled in 1863. *The Golden Harp* is a children's book; it contains a large number of designs, and is among the more successful examples of Watson's art as an illustrator.

This can hardly be said of the large and elaborate *Robinson Crusoe* (Routledge, 1864), for which, as for its companion volume, *The Pilgrim's Progress*, he made a hundred drawings. But again he has been saddled with a text that does not suit him. There are a few good things, undoubtedly, but on the whole the drawings, like the drawings for *The Pilgrim's Progress*, are dull and lacking in variety.

In 1864 Watson gave three perfunctory scribbles to *English Sacred Poetry of the Olden Time*, while the ' Casabianca ' in *Our Life* [1865] is equally mediocre. From now on, indeed, he becomes more and more content to rely on his facility, though the three drawings for *Dalziel's Arabian Nights* are better, and those for an anthology entitled *What Men Have Said about Women* (1865) better still. In this year he also contributed to *The Pleasures of Memory*, a volume interesting only from the fact that the larger drawings are produced by ' a new process ' explained in a note; and supplied a frontispiece engraved on steel for *Barbara's History*.

Ellen Montgomery's Bookshelf and *Melbourne House*, both illustrated in colour, I can only date approximately 1866, and to the same year belong two illustrations for *Ballad Stories of the Affections*, two for Foxe's *Book of Martyrs*, one for Adelaide Proctor's *Legends and Lyrics*, and five for *A Round of Days*. A question at the same time arises as to when some of these drawings actually were made. Watson's earliest work is always, or nearly always, signed with a monogram; later he signs with his initials. But in the *Golden Harp* drawings, with the single exception of the frontispiece, he uses the monogram, and uses it again to sign ' Amongst the Mowers ' on page 26 of *A Round of Days*.

Little Songs for Little Folk (1867), mentioned by Gleeson White as illustrated by Watson, I have failed to trace, unless it is *Little Lays for Little Folk* (1867), in which case, though it contains many admirable drawings,

J. D. Watson: 'Romance and a Curacy'
[*London Society*, 1862]

Watson is not among the artists who made them. In this year, however, he contributed a charming picture of a child kneeling, to illustrate *Advantages of Early Religion*, in the Nisbet edition of Watts's *Divine and Moral Songs*, and several designs to *The Illustrated Book of Sacred Poems*, among which, as I have said, I think we may place the anonymous ' Side by Side '. He also contributed to *The Savage Club Papers* (Tinsley, 1867), to *Cassell's Illustrated Readings* (1867), and to *Old Friends and New Friends*, by H. W. Dulcken [1867].

The *Word: the Star out of Jacob* (Nisbet, 1868), and *The Nobility of Life* (Warne, 1869) have the plates in colour. *Pictures from English Literature* [1870], *Wild-Cat Tower* (1877), a boys' book, and *Princess Althea* (1883) close my list.

But there was a suggestion, I thought, of Watson's hand in one or two designs for *Aunt Mavor's Alphabet* (Routledge, 1862?), only the proofs of which I have seen, and there are three other volumes published by Routledge of which I have no knowledge at all beyond that supplied in the publisher's advertisement. *The Boys' and Girls' Illustrated Gift-Book*, *The Child's Picture Story-Book*, and *Popular Nursery Tales and Rhymes* were all three sold, not at a penny plain and twopence coloured, but at five shillings plain and nine shillings with the plates in colour, and Watson is among their illustrators. That the drawings are clichés, however, I take to be nearly certain. I examined a host of similar picture books buried in the catacombs of the British Museum, including all that were associated with Watson's name, and not one contained a new drawing. The same designs—the impressions steadily decreasing in value—were repeated from book to book, though the scraps of prose and verse they were supposed to illustrate varied.

CHAPTER IX

GEORGE LOUIS PALMELLA BUSSON DU MAURIER (1834-1896)

DU MAURIER was born in England of a French father and an English mother, but he was educated in France. The father was devoted to science, and his ambition was to see his son achieve success as a scientist, so, at the age of eighteen, we find George du Maurier studying chemistry at the Birkbeck Laboratory of University College, where he remained for two years. His father then set him up as a chemist on his own account, and another two years went by, bringing us to 1856, the year of the father's death. In 1856 du Maurier went to Paris, and there he finally decided to devote himself to art. For a year he studied at Gleyre's studio, Whistler and Poynter being among his fellow-pupils: from Paris he went on to Antwerp; and it was while he was working at the Antwerp Academy that the sight of his left eye suddenly failed him. The eye grew worse, and the Dusseldorf specialist he had been recommended to consult told him there was no hope of saving it. It was a distressing time for the young artist, who was haunted by the fear that the right eye too might become affected. Fortunately this did not happen, and in 1860 he returned to London, where, for a while, he shared rooms with Whistler.

It has been said that du Maurier's first published drawing appeared in *Fun*, but the *Fun* picture, which I have not seen, cannot have been much earlier than the illustrations for *Faristan and Fatima*, a burlesque Eastern poem, which appeared in *Once a Week*, September 1860. They are signed M.B., and if not important are at all events easily recognizable as his work. The *Faristan and Fatima* drawings were followed by two others, the second of which is a very poor thing; and then, with ' Non Satis ', signed in full, the artist at last produced a thoroughly characteristic design. His remaining illustrations in *Once a Week* for 1860 are negligible.

In vol. iv (1861) the drawing on page 41, attributed to du Maurier both in the index and by Gleeson White, is by Charles Green. The same authorities give him ' The Beggar's Soliloquy ' on page 378, an obvious Charles Keene, but omit to give him the ' Night Ride to the Guillotine ' (p. 387), which is really his. Of the six designs in vol. iv, however, the only

G. Du Maurier: ' Hurlock Chase '
[*The Leisure Hour*, 1864]

G. Du Maurier: 'Wives and Daughters'
[*The Cornhill Magazine*, 1864]

one of importance is ' On Her Deathbed ', a drawing that shows him very nearly at his best. In vol. v there are also six, the more important of which illustrate his own *Recollections of an English Gold-Mine*, the initial letter being a particularly happy little sketch.

Volume vi (1862) contains ten designs, of which that on page 24 looks like a very good thing spoiled by the engraver. Volume vii contains twelve. Of these last, the figure in the foreground of ' Miss Simms ' (p. 166) is remarkably suggestive of Poynter, but the drawings for *Santa* are all du Maurier's own, and those for *The Notting Hill Mystery* are still finer examples of his dramatic power. The serial he is illustrating is a ' shocker ', but note the beauty he has got into the picture on page 617, with its Pre-Raphaelite colour and richness of detail. *The Notting Hill Mystery* was continued through the next volume, and never, I should think, has a story of this class found such illustrations—illustrations that cover its poor horrors with a veil of dark romance at once sinister and poetic, and that linger in the memory long after the tedious and involved plot is forgotten.

Twelve drawings belong to vol. viii (1863), in which *The Notting Hill Mystery* is concluded and Miss Braddon's *Eleanor's Victory* begun. Du Maurier is now at the height of his power and is getting the kind of work he can do best. Those who associate his name with the *Punch* drawings of the eighties and nineties, the smart studies of smart society, can form no conception of the combined delicacy and richness of many of his early designs. Volume ix has eight drawings, all for *Eleanor's Victory*; vol. x (1864) six, including the admirable ' Veiled Portrait '; vol. xi two—the second particularly good—for *Philip Fraser's Fate*.

' Little Bo-Peep ' in vol. i of the New Series (1866) shows him in his less interesting if more familiar rôle of charmer. It is a pretty picture, but du Maurier, like Millais, could never be trusted in the nursery. Both introduce a vein of sentiment that makes us vaguely uneasy, and, with du Maurier, our feeling of discomfort at times becomes acute. We are reminded of certain passages in the works of Sir James Barrie: the sentiment is no doubt irreproachable, but somehow it produces the effect of a fault in taste. Houghton or Pinwell or Charles Keene can draw a child as naturally as they draw a dog or any other animal; du Maurier cannot: Millais could, but in his later work would not.

The lovely drawing for *The Ace of Hearts* in the Christmas Number that preceded the New Series of *Once a Week* makes us regret that du Maurier was never called on to illustrate the masterpieces of the eighteenth century. The manners, fashions, and costumes of that sophisticated age— elaborate and slightly tinged with artificiality—would have suited him to perfection. In vol. ii of the New Series he has a couple of excellent designs;

[175]

and to vol. i of the Third Series (1868) he supplies nine large drawings for Charles Reade's *Foul Play*. These are boldly and frankly melodramatic, but they are perfectly in keeping with the work they illustrate. Beauty is there too, and the tropical landscapes are pictured with just the imaginative exuberance such full-blooded, almost boyish romance demands.

In 1883 Henry James committed himself to the remarkable statement that '*Punch*, for the last fifteen years, has been, artistically speaking, George du Maurier'. Linley Sambourne and Charles Keene are artists who express themselves in terms of ugliness; they see, he says, '*en laid*'. Of Charles Keene, indeed, we learn that 'his sense of the beautiful, of the delicate, is inferior even to Leech's'. One cannot help wondering what in this instance a sense of the beautiful precisely means? Not surely a belief that beauty is to be found only among the upper classes and in drawing-rooms! Yet, from the late seventies on, the work of du Maurier had become more and more a mere comment on fashionable society, and the artist in him had more and more given place to the journalist, or, to put it flatteringly, the novelist. This dual element is striking. It has been said, and said repeatedly, that *Punch* did not give du Maurier an opportunity to do himself justice; but he was by no means limited to *Punch*, the illustration of the *Cornhill Magazine* passed largely into his hands, and his later designs there show the same deterioration. He works hurriedly, scratchily, and according to a narrow formula; his figures lose their freshness and individuality; even his children tend to become unpleasantly adult in appearance, while he is content to draw the same face over and over again, so that we find the well-known lady of *Punch* figuring as the heroine of all the novels he illustrates, from *The Hand of Ethelberta* to *The Martian*. This second and more prolific half of du Maurier's career is, for his true admirers, depressing to contemplate. His natural mode of expression was akin to that of the Pre-Raphaelites he satirized so amusingly, and when he abandoned his first manner his work lost its beauty and gained nothing. We no longer get the decorative massing of black on white by which he achieved so rich an effect; detail is sacrificed and delicacy with it; the literary side of his art now comes to be everything, and to present some social triumph of Mrs. Ponsonby de Tomkyns gives him greater pleasure than to create a beautiful design. In his own selections from his drawings literature completely triumphs; those chosen are those that display his cleverness rather than his sense of beauty; nearly all the most beautiful drawings indeed are omitted, while none is included simply for its beauty. But du Maurier's cleverness is a poor substitute; his mind was superficial, his judgments, ideas, and conceptions were simply those of the average man of the world. It was the novelist in him, of course, that appealed to Henry James, but though du Maurier drew

G. Du Maurier: 'The Awdries'

[*The Leisure Hour*, 1865]

his material from the same world as James did, the result is vastly different. He has neither James's intellect, nor his imagination, nor his subtlety, nor anything approaching his genius. His observation never penetrates beneath the surface: in fact, if we are to judge of his work from those volumes of selected drawings which he himself published, we must pronounce it as of only second-rate interest.

'On the mantelpiece in my study at home,' he writes, 'there stands a certain lady. She is but lightly clad, and what simple garment she wears is not in the fashion of our day. How well I know her! Almost thoroughly by this time—for she has been the silent companion of my work for thirty years. She has lost both her arms and one of her feet.'

The playful confession is suggestive: we cannot help suspecting this 'companion of thirty years', this cast of the Venus of Melos, to be partly responsible for a peculiarity in the artist's work. He was very susceptible to the charms of women, but everybody looking over his drawings must have noticed how his ladies tend to become exaggerated in size, approaching the ample proportions of goddesses, of this particular goddess, and acquiring at the same time something of her marmoreal aloofness.

Du Maurier's first drawing for *Punch* appeared in 1860, and the later drawings run into thousands. The society pictures are the most widely known, and, since for our present purpose they are the least significant, I cannot do better than refer the reader to an admirable summary and analysis of this side of the artist's talent to be found in that essay in Henry James's *Partial Portraits* from which I have already quoted. The work in grotesque, however, must be mentioned here, because in it we find du Maurier accomplishing some first-rate things. The drawing for *Mokeanna!* (1863); the whole *Camelot* series (1866), Pre-Raphaelite parodies, with much of the charm of the originals; 'A Little Christmas Dream' (1868); and 'Old Nick-otin' (1869) are typical. From 1866 to 1876 is the decade of du Maurier's finest *Punch* drawings. During that decade he made designs of the most delicate beauty. Among them I would instance 'Caution', 'Uncle Tom the Bachelor' (a masterpiece of pen painting), and 'Berkeley Square'—all belonging to 1867. Note, too, the delightful treatment of an urban landscape in 'The Benefit of the Doubt' (1874), and the spacing and skilful disposing of the masses of white that give its exquisite summer freshness to 'Independence' (1875).

In *The Leisure Hour* for 1864 du Maurier illustrated *Hurlock Chase*. These twenty-seven large and comparatively unknown drawings are, in spite of Robinson's mediocre engraving and the poor quality of the paper on which they are printed, in their way almost as fine a series as he ever made for a novel. Their breadth is unexpected, their dramatic quality—for the

[179]

story is of the adventure type—convincing; and they are entirely free from the mannerisms, the short cuts and general carelessness he developed later. *Hurlock Chase* was issued in book form in 1876, but with only thirteen of the illustrations, and these reduced in size.

According to all accounts du Maurier's contributions to *The Leisure Hour* end here, but I think we may with safety extend the list. That magazine did not publish the names of its artists, and du Maurier, who usually signed his work, in its pages preserved the rule of anonymity. Nevertheless, the illustrations for *The Awdries* (1865) are almost certainly his, and, in the same year, I should give him those for *The Graemes of Glenmavis*, *A Week in the Austrian Tyrol*, and probably *A Rattlesnake at the Diggings*.

In *The Sunday at Home* for 1864 we find him illustrating *The Artist's Son* with designs that smack faintly of Fred Walker. He also supplies two excellent drawings for *John Henderson's Siller and Gowd* and a more characteristic and very beautiful one for *The Strange Hammer*.

That du Maurier should have contributed to such comparatively undistinguished magazines as *The Sunday at Home* and *The Leisure Hour*, while he has only two drawings of any importance in *Good Words* and none at all in *The Sunday Magazine*, is surprising. The *Good Words* designs are ' A Time to Dance ' (1861) and ' Under the Elms ' (1872). In both we have a woman seated (the attitude being almost identical), but the former has a massiveness, a simplicity, and a severity unusual in this artist's work, while the latter, though it shows a marked declension from this high ideal, is nevertheless a most accomplished and intricate drawing in which every blade of the flowered grass has been put in with a patient minuteness.

Du Maurier has a few illustrations in *Entertaining Things* (1861-1862). I have never come across a copy of this magazine outside the British Museum, and its rarity will probably lend it a mysterious virtue in the eyes of the collector. As a matter of fact it possesses no other, for though Morten, du Maurier, and Houghton are among its artists, their drawings are so wretchedly engraved as to be hardly recognizable.

From the second volume on, du Maurier contributed fairly frequently to *London Society*. Volumes ii, iii, iv, vi, vii, ix, and x all contain drawings by him. Those in vol. vii are particularly good, but the admirable ' Two to One on the Major ' in vol. ix (1866) is perhaps the finest of the *London Society* designs. In *Every Boy's Magazine* (October 1863) he has an illustration for *The Pacha's Pet Bear*; and there are a few full pages in *The Graphic*, commencing with the first volume.[1] The French journal, *L'Art*, also pub-

---

[1] Note, besides those I have mentioned in an earlier chapter, the ' Musical Rehearsal ' (September 1872), in which will be found one of the most beautiful women du Maurier ever drew.

G. Du Maurier: 'Harry Richmond'
[*The Cornhill Magazine*, 1870]

lished five of his designs, engraved by Swain. These are ' Portrait de Mistress Gilbert Scott', an excellent example of his more decorative manner; ' Le Leçon de Danse ', ' Souvenir de Dieppe ', ' Promenade d'Hiver ', and ' Madame est Servie '.

I have not counted them up, but du Maurier must have made more drawings for *The Cornhill* than any other artist. He appears as early as 1863, and in the last years he and William Small between them monopolize the illustration. His first design, ' The Cilician Pirates ', though a remarkably good one, is far more akin to the work of the *Bible Gallery* group than to that of the later du Maurier. It is an experiment—Poynter plus du Maurier —the latter supplying little more than the reclining lady. Other drawings in 1863 are ' Sibyl's Disappointment ', ' The Night before the Morrow ', and ' Cousin Phillis '. Gleeson White, I should add, is inclined to give him ' The First Meeting ', but personally I can detect in it no faintest trace of du Maurier's hand.

It is unnecessary to pursue my catalogue, because, from this on until 1883 du Maurier is never absent from the volumes of *The Cornhill*, though some years are lean, others prolific. The first serial he illustrates is Mrs. Gaskell's *Wives and Daughters*, which was begun in 1864, and these beautiful designs he never surpassed, never again indeed, to my thinking, equalled. For the later *Cornhill* novels—for Hardy's *Hand of Ethelberta*, Meredith's *Harry Richmond*, Mrs. Oliphant's *Rose in June*, Norris's *Mademoiselle de Mersac*, Black's *Three Feathers*, and the rest—he was content to supply his *Punch* work; or was it that he had become incapable by that time of departing from it? There are often charming things among these later illustrations, but as the years go by the charm diminishes. Charm, beauty, even adequate draughtsmanship, have all practically disappeared when we reach the drawings he made month by month for *Harper's Magazine*—drawings with their own legends attached to them, illustrating the society scenes one would have thought appeared with sufficient frequency in *Punch* to satisfy even the most insatiable admirer. It was in *Harper's* also, in the nineties, that he illustrated his own tales—*Peter Ibbotson, Trilby, The Martian*—and the fact that these illustrations, in which he must surely be giving us of his best, reveal the same incalculable inferiority to those executed a quarter of a century before for such feeble concoctions as *Hurlock Chase* and *The Notting Hill Mystery*, seems to prove that either over-production or some failure of eyesight is largely to blame for the collapse of a once brilliant talent.

Among the books illustrated by du Maurier I have found nothing earlier than Dalton's *Drawing Room Plays* [1861], for which he made a few unimportant drawings. In 1863 he supplied five illustrations for a one-volume edition of Mrs. Gaskell's *Sylvia's Lovers*—a frontispiece, a title page, and three illustrations in the text. Du Maurier is at his best in some of the drawings he made for Mrs. Gaskell, and, since these books were issued in a series, they may as well all be taken together. With the exceptions of *Sylvia's Lovers* and *Wives and Daughters* each has three full-page illustrations and an engraved title page. *Cranford* and *A Dark Night's Work* are dated 1864; *Lizzie Leigh, The Grey Woman*, and *Cousin Phillis* 1865. In the case of *The Grey Woman* and *Cousin Phillis* these are not only the first editions of the illustrations, but of the books themselves. *Wives and Daughters*, in its original two-volume form (1866), contained eighteen of the *Cornhill* designs: in the popular one-volume edition (where it found a place in 1867) the number of illustrations is reduced to five, including the vignette on the title page, which alone is new.

Luke Ashleigh (1864), a story of schoolboys in Holland, by Alfred Elwes, has half a dozen illustrations by du Maurier. In *English Sacred Poetry of the Olden Time* (1864) he has two drawings, and in *Our Life Illustrated by Pen and Pencil* [1865] he has one. In 1866 he contributed a couple of good designs (cut by Harral, unfortunately) to Adelaide Proctor's *Legends and Lyrics*, and one to Dr. Watts's *Divine and Moral Songs* (Nisbet). In this year he also made two illustrations I have only seen in proof, but which are said to be for a one-volume edition of *Lady Audley's Secret*; and four capital drawings for *The Ingoldsby Legends* (Bentley)—two for *The Leech of Folkestone* and two for *The Grey Dolphin*. To 1866 belongs Foxe's *Book of Martyrs*. Du Maurier has a large full page in the *Book of Martyrs*, but of the two vignettes which his biographer, Mr. T. Martin Wood,[1] says he also contributed to the work I can find no trace. The vignettes are one and all deplorable; none is in the least like a du Maurier; and since at this date his work is unmistakable I feel inclined to acquit him of the charge.

In 1867 du Maurier contributed to the rather dull *Savage Club Papers*, but in the same year we get a book of the first importance, Douglas Jerrold's *Story of a Feather* (Bradbury, Evans, 1867). This is one of du Maurier's masterpieces. Nothing could be daintier than the drawings he made for it: —initial letters, vignettes, full-page designs—all are in his happiest manner. The second masterpiece is *Esmond* (1868).[2] Fred Walker first had been called upon to make the drawings for *Esmond*, but a visit to Knowle not having produced the necessary inspiration, he threw up the task. A single drawing, as we have seen, he did make, but when the work was placed in du Maurier's hands this naturally was shelved. The choice of du Maurier as Walker's successor proved a fortunate one. An ardent admirer of Thack-

---

George du Maurier. By T. Martin Wood. (Chatto & Windus, 1913.)

[2] The 1868 edition is for some reason extremely rare. I have only come across a copy once, whereas the 1869 issue is constantly turning up.

G. Du Maurier: 'The Last of Beatrix'

[*Esmond*]

eray, he produced a set of drawings worthy of the book and ranking among his finest. He even, unwisely, returned to the work some years later to make a dozen additional designs (for the Standard Edition, 1884, Mr. John Murray tells me), but the new drawings are disappointing.[1]

Less uniformly excellent, but with many good things among them, are the fifteen designs he made for Shirley Brooks's *Sooner or Later* (1868), and the twenty-four for Owen Meredith's *Lucille* (1868). In 1870 we have the splendid drawing of ' Sophia Western ', contributed to *Pictures from English Literature*; in 1874 an unimportant frontispiece and vignette for Clement Scott's *Round About the Islands*, and eight illustrations for Florence Montgomery's *Misunderstood*.

The *Misunderstood* drawings have, I think, been over-praised. They are graceful, and several of them are brilliantly pretty, but the faults in the tale happen to be those which to du Maurier would appear as virtues and he has accented them. The small hero is supposed to be a scapegrace—a scapegrace as conceived by the tenderest of feminine imaginations, but still a boy who is constantly getting into scrapes of the kind that amuse grown-up readers. When du Maurier presents him in picture after picture always in immaculate velveteens and with never a curl out of place the last rag of verisimilitude is sacrificed. Writing to Lewis Carroll, he says, ' Miss Florence Montgomery is a very charming and sympathetic young lady, the daughter of the admiral of that ilk. I am, like you, a very great admirer of *Misunderstood*, and cried pints over it. When I was drawing the last picture I had to put a long white pipe in the little boy's mouth until it was finished, so as to get rid of the horrible pathos of the situation while I was executing the work. In reading the book a second time (knowing the sad end of the dear little boy), the funny parts made me cry almost as much as the pathetic ones.' This letter is in itself ominous, and we are hardly surprised to find that much of the sentimentality of the tale has passed into the drawings. *Misunderstood*, however, was a great success, became indeed something of a ' best-seller '. Not, however, as Mr. Martin Wood suggests, because of du Maurier's illustrations. That is to be quite unfair to the author, for the artist was only called in after the popularity of the story had been already firmly established and twelve thousand copies sold.

In 1875 du Maurier supplied a frontispiece to Mrs. Lynn Linton's *Patricia Kemball* and a few illustrations for a popular edition of Wilkie Collins's novels. For *Poor Miss Finch* he drew a very beautiful frontispiece, the remaining pictures being by Edward Hughes. The other Collins novels to which he contributed—always in collaboration with a second artist—are *The Moonstone*, with F. A. Fraser; *The New Magdalen*, with C. S. Reinhardt;

[1] The initial letters for this edition are by J. W. Atkinson.

and *The Frozen Deep*, with J. Mahoney. Just when he made the drawings for Thackeray's poems I do not know, but I put them in here. They will be found in *Ballads* (1879) and in vol. xxi of the *Works* (1879).

In 1876 he helped to illustrate Jemmett Browne's *Songs of Many Seasons*, and in 1877 supplied all the illustrations, with the exception of the tailpiece, to Cholmondeley Pennell's *Pegasus Re-Saddled*—drawings beginning to betray the inferiority of his last phase. From now on his work possesses little interest. He occasionally produces a good drawing, but none that equals the best of the early years, and even his few good things are swamped by the hack work he turned out with mechanical regularity. *Prudence: a Story of Aesthetic London*, by Lucy C. Lillie, in which the drawings have been much reduced in size, belongs to 1882; frontispieces to Mr. Anstey's *Black Poodle* and Grant Allen's *Strange Stories* to 1884. A large and singularly ugly édition-de-luxe of *As in a Looking Glass*, by F. C. Phillips, is dated 1889. The full-page drawings for this book, with the exception of the last design, show du Maurier at his very worst: they are things feeble in conception, and coarse and even vulgar in execution. The illustrations for his own novels have already been mentioned in connection with *Harper's Magazine*, and his collected *Punch* drawings in an earlier chapter.

CHAPTER X

ARTHUR BOYD HOUGHTON (1836-1875)

HOUGHTON,[1] like du Maurier, but to an even greater extent, was handicapped by the weakness of his eyes. From boyhood he had completely lost the sight of one of them, and in the other he suffered at times such great pain from inflammation that to attempt to draw was out of the question. Nevertheless he produced a vast number of designs, working at top speed, and drawing straight on to the wood without making preliminary studies. His method is naturalistic, but the realism of his work is modified by a temperament impatient of the obvious, which inclined him to seek the bizarre and fantastic even in ordinary life. The art of Houghton and Pinwell is more personal than that of any other of the younger men, and attracts or repels with proportionate strength. Houghton, however, possessed a technique far beyond that of Pinwell: as a draughtsman at times he approaches the virtuosity of Charles Keene. His earlier designs, in which he pursues and achieves a more decorative pattern, and pays greater attention to detail, are often akin to those of the idyllic group, but the later designs stand out in marked isolation, and both early and late have perhaps always been more appreciated by artists and critics than by the general public.

Houghton's early work for the magazines appeared chiefly in *Good Words* and *London Society*. The former periodical contains several drawings that are quite the finest examples of his first manner, not excepting those in *Home Thoughts and Home Scenes*. Indeed, the four illustrations belonging to 1862—'My Treasure' (a portrait of the artist's wife and children), 'On the Cliff', 'True or False', and 'About Toys', with the 'Childhood' of the following year—have, I should think, as drawings of children, never been surpassed. Certainly the charm of childhood could hardly be expressed with more understanding and less sophistication: the pouting lips, the modelling of the sturdy limbs, the lovely drawing of the hair—all are as true as they are beautiful. The two remaining drawings in *Good Words* for 1863 —'St. Elmo' and 'A Missionary Cheer'—are much less remarkable.

[1] Mr. Gilbert Dalziel, who knew him well, says that he would have been enraged by the modern fashion of calling him Boyd Houghton, as if he were in the habit of using a double-barrelled name.

Good Words for 1866 has ‘ The Voyage ’, and four admirable harvest scenes that nobody but Houghton could have drawn—‘ Reaping ’, ‘ Binding ’, ‘ Carrying ’, ‘ Gleaning ’. In these we see his style fully developed, completely individual, but with its individuality held in control, which was not always the case in his later work, where manner sometimes passes into mannerism. The ‘ Reaping ’ and the ‘ Gleaning ’ are particularly lovely things, of a perfect economy and delicacy.

In *Good Words* for 1867 Houghton has one of his Eastern drawings, and a design called ‘ Making Poetry ’, which marks a return, in his later manner, to the mood of the domestic and idyllic pictures. The ‘ Making Poetry ’, as I have already said, is a thing particularly typical of our period. It shows a room in the late afternoon light, with a young boy in the window-seat, stooping over his verses, while a lady sits with an open book in her lap, but not reading. The picture itself is poetry—it is like a window opening on to a world of half forgotten, half remembered enchantment. Neither of the figures is beautiful in a conventional sense; the beauty is one of atmosphere—is in the hour, the place, the spirit, the relation between the two figures, the feeling of profound tranquillity into which we sink deeper and deeper, till at last it seems to become a part of our own experience, actually to have happened, to be happening now. There are some verses by Fanny R. Havergal (better known as Frances Ridley Havergal) attached to the drawing.

Good Words for 1868 contains a large number of Houghton’s designs, the most interesting being a series of tiny vignettes for *A Russian Fabulist*. But among the remainder there are several first-rate things, including ‘ A Russian Farm-Yard ’, ‘ The Good Samaritan ’, ‘ The Victim ’—notable for the drawing of the naked child—and perhaps one might add the very Houghtonesque ‘ Dance My Children ’. In 1871 he has one drawing, while others will be found in *Good Cheer*, the Christmas Number, and in 1872 he has ‘ The Black Fast ’.

His contributions to *London Society* also began in 1862. ‘ Finding a Relic ’, in the second volume, is a typical example of his early work—an elaborate and beautiful composition, drawn in much detail, but with the strength and boldness of a master. The treatment of texture and of the hands is particularly worthy of study. The drawings in the volumes for 1866, 1867, and 1868 call for no special comment.

Among Houghton’s contributions to *Once a Week* (in vols. xii, xiii, and New Series i, ii, and iii), ‘ King Solyman ’ in vol. xiii, and ‘ A Hindoo Legend ’ in the New Series, vol. iii, are good specimens of his Eastern work, the latter being worthy to rank with the best of the *Arabian Nights* series.

From the beginning Houghton contributed to *The Sunday Magazine*,

A. B. Houghton: ' Childhood '

[*Good Words*, 1863]

A. B. Houghton: ' Reaping '

[*Good Words*, 1866]

though he has only one drawing in the first volume and none in the second. But in 1867 he illustrates the serial, *The Huguenot Family in the English Village*, and has a number of other designs—all in his later manner. In 1868, among several excellent things, ' George Herbert's Last Sunday ' must be mentioned. The boy and the cat offer a delightful example of the way the artist introduces character and actuality into his work by means of subsidiary incident: they are only minor figures in the group gathered round the old man's bed, but the abstracted fashion in which the boy is petting the cat, and the fixed determination of that animal to be caressed, strike a note that would be comedy were it not kept in such perfect subordination to the main intention of the picture. From this on, Houghton's contributions to *The Sunday Magazine* become more infrequent, but they maintain their quality to the end.

A bare list must suffice of those magazines in which he made only an occasional appearance. *Entertaining Things* (1861-1862); *The Churchman's Family Magazine* (1864)—a rather poor drawing; *The Quiver* (1866-1868) —containing perhaps a dozen drawings, among which the ' Golden Hours ' and the ' Sowing and Reaping ' of 1866 are particularly striking, while ' The Artist ' (1867) might be called ' Tribute to Pinwell '. In *The Argosy* (1866) ' The Vision of Sheik Hamil ' is good, but ' Knight-Errant of Arden ' (1867) has not quite come off; the first illustration for *Robert Falconer* (1867) also is Houghton's, the remainder being by William Small. Further drawings will be found in *Tinsley's Magazine* (1867-1868), *The Broadway, Golden Hours*[1] (1868), *Fun* (1866-1867). The drawings in *Fun* are nearly all political cartoons. Houghton, as *Fun* cartoonist, succeeded Paul Gray, who had succeeded F. W. Lawson. In *The Illustrated London News*, December 1865, he has a fine full page, ' Uncle John with the Young Folk '; and in the following December he again appears with ' The Children's Christmas Carol '. In *Every Boy's Magazine* (1866) Houghton illustrates the serial, *Barford Bridge*, with fascinating and highly characteristic drawings; in *Every Boy's Annual* of the same year he illustrates *The Pirate Island*. In *Good Words for the Young* particular mention must be made of the delightful drawing, ' Fibbing Bill ', for *The Boys of Axleford* (vol. i), and the masterly ' Don José's Mule ' (vol. iii), one of his happiest creations. There remains *The Graphic*, but the drawings for *The Graphic* demand a separate paragraph.

They are the most uncompromising Houghton ever made. The London scenes and the Paris scenes, brilliant as they are, may be left to speak for themselves; but the series of designs known as ' Graphic America ',[2]

---

[1] This engraving, ' The Oriental Bride ', does not suggest Houghton's technique. The drawing, 'after' one of his paintings, has probably been made by another hand.

[2] The blocks of ' Graphic America ' unfortunately have been destroyed.

which appeared from 1870 till 1872,[1] represents probably our artist's greatest achievement. Its reception was doubtful—except in the States. Houghton disliked America intensely, and the fact that he did so, though at the same time found it singularly stimulating, is apparent throughout these drawings. The qualities in ' the American scene.' that appeared to him the most salient were rawness, harshness, and intellectual and spiritual poverty, and they were the qualities he set himself to portray with all the virtuosity of an intensely personal style. In most cases the only beauty is the beauty of his own line, while the strangeness is the result of a slight exaggeration which turns reality to grotesque and yet somehow leaves it all the more real. As an example of this, take the drawing of the ' Barber's Saloon, New York ', where the immense height of the man standing up to be brushed produces the most fantastic effect. These designs are certainly not caricatures, but the accentuation of this or that element Houghton found significant does lend them an exotic appearance. America was indignant: America, conscious of possessing both sweetness and light, raised quite an outcry at this emphatic denial of her culture. The latent satire was regarded as an insult, the realism as a libel. Possibly this may be why the drawings were never reprinted, for there are sufficient to make a handsome folio, and as specimens of English black and white art they are in the first rank. Houghton, be it added, paid his tribute to beauty when he found it. In the design of ' The Ladies' Window at the New York Post-Office ' he does even more than justice to feminine charm. In the superb design of ' The Tombs ' it is strangeness that predominates. That stupendous white space of wall creates an indescribable impression. Beauty, again, is the note of ' A Boston Snow Plough '—black on white—the only beauty apparently he found in Boston. And then we come to the pictures of the Shakers, a peculiar people, who seem to have possessed a special fascination for Houghton, so large a place do they occupy in his presentation of this new world. The drawings of the Shakers are perhaps the most amazing of all. Here, in these masterpieces, if anywhere, we find the triumph of style over material. Out of surroundings devoid of beauty, out of figures which taken individually are devoid of every quality of grace and charm and even of intelligence, Houghton creates an effect that *is* of beauty. And how perfectly he expresses what he wants to express. What a sense of bleakness, spiritual and physical, is created by the massing of those whites in the drawing of the ' Shaker Settlement—Dinner Time '! One can feel the very coldness and thinness of the air, the clean and swept discomfort, the hardness and narrowness, the

[1] One or two of these designs appeared later. A superb drawing, with much of the quality of an etching, 'Pawnee Squaws', will, for instance, be found in the number for the 22nd of February 1873.

[192]

A. B. HOUGHTON: 'Coasting at Omaha'

[*The Graphic, 1871*]

A. B. HOUGHTON: 'Aladdin, in Despair, contemplates Suicide'
[*Dalziel's Arabian Nights*]

absence of all that mellows and enriches life.   Only the artist's love of children has led him to give a quaint charm to their stiff little figures.   Out in
the West he breathes more freely.   There is a marvellous design, ' Coasting
at Omaha ', an impression of snow and cloud, filled with the swirling lines he
loved, a thing of exquisitely balanced tones and rapid movement.   The
' Bartering with Indians ' gives him a chance to create one of his richest and
most decorative designs, and ' A Smoke with Friendlies ', ' Crossing a
Cañon ', ' On the Scout ' are equally good; while in ' Cornered ' and
' " Great Hawk " and Small Mormon ' we have examples of his humour,
almost the only examples in the series where it is untouched by irony.   But
Houghton liked the Indians and liked little boys.

I have called *Graphic America* his greatest achievement, and yet, when
I turn back to the *Arabian Nights* drawings which he made nearly ten years
earlier, from 1863 till 1865, it seems to me that they are, in their different
way, quite as good.   At all events, from the very first design for *The Three
Calenders*, they dwarf every other drawing in the book; and yet those others
were made by such artists as Millais, Tenniel, Watson, and Pinwell, while
T. Dalziel contributed more drawings than Houghton himself.   We regret
that the complete work was not placed in Houghton's hands—and also an
adequate text.   Even this very mediocre translation, 'revised and emendated'
by H. W. Dulcken—who was not qualified to do either the one or the other—
a translation which contrives to omit all the life, all the poetry, and all the
humour of the original—even this has mysteriously inspired him, so that life,
poetry and humour are restored in his drawings.   No artist, I think, in any
single book, has created such variety in beauty, in character, and in decoration—drawing after drawing bringing its little thrill of surprise.   Dalziel
repeats himself again and again in his designs; Houghton never.   His
invention seems inexhaustible; the animals are just as true as the humans;
look at the cat on page 69, the donkey on page 149, the rats on page 605,
and above all the kite on page 673.

I have taken *The Arabian Nights* out of its proper place, for the first
book on my list is Wilkie Collins's *After Dark* (1862), which was illustrated
by Houghton, though Walter Crane drew the engraved title page that was
for some reason omitted from later editions.   In A. B. Thompson's *Victorian
History of England* (Routledge, 1865) Houghton has a frontispiece of ' King
John Signing Magna Charta ', and in *The Temple Anecdotes*, by R. and C.
Temple (Groombridge, 1865—but published originally in monthly parts),
he has seven excellent designs.   *Stories Told to a Child* (1865) has, as well as
some capital John Lawsons, two beautiful drawings by Houghton: *Patient
Henry* (1865) has four, equally good.   The illustrations for Mrs. Eiloart's
Ernie Elton also belong to 1865, and four drawings for *Robinson Crusoe*.

But *the* book of 1865, not counting *The Arabian Nights*, is *Home Thoughts and Home Scenes* (Routledge), which was re-issued in 1868, and re-issued again with the title altered to *Happy Day Stories*.

Though few of them show Houghton quite at his best, there is something most attractive about the thirty-five elaborately printed designs of *Home Thoughts*, all early work, judging by the style and by the monogram which would place them prior even to the first of the *Arabian Nights* illustrations. The drawing of ' The Enemy on the Wall ' is typical of the care Houghton took at this period to achieve a decorative pattern. The composition of this picture is like the composition of a Pinwell, though nothing else in it resembles that artist. Houghton is said to have taken more pains over these particular drawings than over any others. His style in them is as far removed as possible from his later impressionism, therefore the book is essential to a collection of his work—more so than any of those we have still to chronicle, because it represents a distinct period in the development of his art, a period which will not be found represented elsewhere, except in his very earliest drawings for the magazines.

After the *Arabian Nights*, the hundred illustrations for *Don Quixote* (Warne, 1866) prove disappointing. In them we find no such creative richness of imagination. Better fifty full-page designs than a hundred small and frequently scrappy sketches. There are, of course, lovely things in the *Don Quixote*—one or two portraits of Rozinante especially are in the artist's best manner—but the standard set by *The Arabian Nights* was a high one, and it cannot, to my thinking, be claimed that the *Don Quixote* comes anywhere near it. Taken as a specimen of book making it is unattractive: there was far too much text to be crowded into a single volume, with the consequence that the blending of picture and text is ill contrived, and the whole has a stodgy appearance. The scarcity of *Don Quixote*, however, places it among the more expensive works on the collector's list.

The Arabian Nights (Warne, 1866), with eight full-page illustrations by Houghton, and eight by T. Dalziel, must not be confused with the more famous edition: the drawings are not reprints, but new designs. The same year also saw the seventeen characteristic if not particularly noteworthy drawings for *A Round of Days*; three or four full-page designs for Foxe's *Martyrs*, including an excellent picture of ' Bunyan in Bedford Gaol '; drawings for *The Spirit of Praise* and *Ballad Stories of the Affections*; a drawing for *Studies for Stories*, and others for a couple of boys' books—*Balderscourt*, by the Rev. H. C. Adams, with seven illustrations, and *The Boy Pilgrims*, by Anne Bowman, with eight.

In 1866, too, we have ' Ernie at School '. What, I wonder, did youngsters make of these curiously mannered *Ernie Elton* sketches? I read the

A. B. Houghton: ' Reach hither thy Hand '
[*Dalziel's Don Quixote*]

book myself when I was a very small boy, and when I came across it again a few years ago the pictures were still quite fresh in my memory though not an incident of the story remained. Yet I had liked the story and had not cared for the pictures. What is more, I distinctly remember finding them *strange*, which shows that even in those early years one is more sensitive to such things than is usually supposed.

In 1867 we find contributions to *The Savage Club Papers, Cassell's Illustrated Readings*, the *Longfellow*[1] in Warne's Chandos Poets, *Jean Ingelow's Poems*, and *Golden Thoughts from Golden Fountains*. Failing more accurate information, one may as well put in here the illustrations for Mrs. Lankester's *Marian and Her Pupils*. The first edition of this book, published by Routledge in 1864, is illustrated by Fred Walker and J. D. Watson— the Walker being a reprint of one of ' The Twins and Their Stepmother ' pictures: but later editions are illustrated by Houghton.

In *Old Friends and New Friends*, by H. W. Dulcken [1867], though the proofs of all the engravings were pulled in 1866, we find examples of Houghton's earlier and later styles. The admirable drawing of ' The Snow Man ' anticipates his *Graphic America* manner, while another picture, showing two delightful babies, one being bathed and the other having his hair combed, might have been made for *Home Thoughts and Home Scenes*. Both babies are so entirely in Houghton's first manner that they must have been drawn before 1865.

Books belonging to 1868 are Mrs. Eiloart's *Boys of Beechwood* (for which he made eight illustrations), *Christian Lyrics*, and Buchanan's *North Coast and Other Poems*. For *North Coast* he made thirteen designs, all good, while two—those on pages 109 and 169—are in his most mysteriously fascinating vein. The drawing on page 109 of a group of people gathered round the fire on Hallowe'en is a masterpiece of suggestiveness. ' Magic ', as the poem says, ' is in the air ', and the uneasy atmosphere of magic, of the super-normal, is conveyed principally by the face of the boy sitting there so quietly, with the firelight shining on his white profile—the retreating chin, the long nose, the smooth hair—so strangely like and yet unlike his granny, who is telling eerie tales of a world he knows at first hand.

In 1869 Houghton made half a dozen headpieces for *The Nobility of Life*, and illustrated *Krilof and His Fables* (Strahan) with a series of perfectly delightful vignettes, two or three of which were originally published in

---

[1] I am very doubtful about the date of this book. In the only copy I have seen the publisher's preface—referring to the 'new illustrations'—is dated 1879, which looks as if it were the first edition. On the other hand, the proofs of the engravings were pulled in 1866. Why should they have been held over for thirteen years?

Good Words. Gleeson White dates the *Krilof* 1867, but this is wrong: the proofs were not pulled till 1868, and the book is dated 1869.

The date of the first edition of Sarah Tytler's *Citoyenne Jacqueline* with Houghton's illustrations I have not succeeded in verifying, nor am I at all certain of the ' Chandos ' *Byron*. Prolonged search has failed to bring to light either of these books, but Gleeson White says the *Byron* contains ' a few excellent designs ' by Houghton.

To 1870 belongs that little gem, ' Tom, the Piper's Son ', made for Novello's *National Nursery Rhymes*.

Note.—For a cheap edition of *Hard Times and Pictures from Italy* (1866) Houghton drew a frontispiece. I discovered this book only in time to insert the present note, and it is possible there may be an edition dated 1865.

W. Q. ORCHARDSON: 'One in Every Circle'
[*Good Words*, 1860]

J. PETTIE: 'What Sent Me to Sea'
[*Good Words*, 1862]

J. PETTIE: 'The Country Surgeon'
[*Good Words*, 1862]

CHAPTER XI

SOME OCCASIONAL CONTRIBUTORS

ORCHARDSON, PETTIE, T. GRAHAM, ALBERT MOORE,
LEIGHTON, G. F. WATTS, SHIELDS

I. W. Q. ORCHARDSON (1835-1910)

ORCHARDSON'S few drawings on wood all appeared in *Good Words*, with the exception of one made for *The Sunday Magazine*. To the first volume of *Good Words* (1860) he supplied nine drawings, which one regrets were not engraved by Dalziel or Swain but by F. Borders, for the beauty of several of them is as striking as their originality. ' One in Every Circle ' is perhaps the finest; and like the rest is filled with soft silvery greys—grey upon grey, tone melting into tone, the only note of black being in the hair.

Good also, if not so good, are ' The Bells of Lorloches ', which he contributed to the next volume of *Good Words*, and ' Taken ', which appeared in *The Sunday Magazine* for 1872. Finally, in *Good Words* for 1878, we have an illustration for William Black's *Macleod of Dare*.

II. JOHN PETTIE (1839-1893)

The drawings of that fine illustrator John Pettie are more scattered, if hardly more numerous. In *Good Words* for 1861 he has two illustrations for *Cain's Brand*, a little hard perhaps, but admirably drawn. In 1862 he also has a couple (not ten, as Gleeson White says), ' The Country Surgeon ' and ' What Sent Me to Sea ', both beautiful designs; and in 1863 he has six, including ' The Passion Flower of Life ' and ' The Harlequin Boy '. To the volume for 1864 he contributes only an unimportant tailpiece, but in 1878 he gives us a full-page portrait of the hero of Black's *Macleod of Dare*.

In *The Sunday Magazine* for 1868 Pettie has an illustration for *The Occupations of a Retired Life* (J. Mahoney supplies the rest), and in the following year one for *Philip Clayton's First-Born*. A small drawing for *Hoity Toity* and a delightful tailpiece to *The Boys of Axleford*, both belonging to the first volume of *Good Words for the Young*, would appear to close the list of his contributions to magazines.

His illustrations for books are equally few. He helped to illustrate *The Postman's Bag* (1862) with charming drawings lithographed by A. Ritchie, Edinburgh; supplied half a dozen exquisite vignettes to *Wordsworth's Poems for the Young* (1863); and helped with *Pen and Pencil Pictures from the Poets* (1866).

III. THOMAS GRAHAM (1840-1906)

Outside the pages of *Good Words* I have not met with any drawings by Tom Graham, but the three designs he contributed in 1861 to that magazine are all excellent. The 'Honesty' of 1862 is also an attractive thing, and in 1863 he has five drawings, and in 1868 one, the not very important 'Christmas Day'. In 1878 he contributed the inevitable illustration to *Macleod of Dare*, that extraordinary serial (from a pictorial point of view), each instalment of which has a picture by a 'star' artist. What precisely was the object in calling in so many collaborators remains obscure, but doubtless the array of famous names made an imposing advertisement at the beginning of the year. It was a stupid idea for all that, fatal to any consistency in the presentation of character and scene, and bears witness to this once admirable magazine's sad lapse from grace.

IV. ALBERT MOORE (1841-1893)

It is really only his eminence as a painter that gives their interest to the three designs on wood made by Albert Moore for Milton's *Hymn on Christ's Nativity* (Warne [1867]), for though these outlined classical figures are characteristic in grouping and type, they are too slight, too empty of content, to be of much intrinsic importance. They are not in the least in the tradition of the sixties; in fact, they can hardly be called illustrations at all. They are decorations, to be classed with some of Walter Crane's work, though below his best.

V. FREDERICK LEIGHTON (1830-1896)

All Leighton's wood engravings were made for *The Cornhill Magazine* and *Dalziel's Bible Gallery*, and all the *Cornhill* drawings, with the exceptions of ' Drifting ', ' An Evening in a French Country House ',[1] and ' The Great

---

[1] Both 'Drifting' and 'An Evening in a French Country House' are given by Gleeson White to Fred Walker. They are by Leighton, however, and I have seen the original studies for them, now, like so many other things, in the possession of Mr. Harold Hartley.

T. GRAHAM: 'The Emigrant's Daughter'
[*Good Words*, 1861]

God Pan ', were made for George Eliot's *Romola*. For *Romola* he supplied twenty-four full-page illustrations, as well as a set of initial letters. That the *Romola* drawings are the work of a highly trained draughtsman is clear, that several have a kind of cold, formal dignity is also clear, but that they are sympathetic drawings will hardly be proposed. On the other hand, having seen photographs of the original designs, I must add that Swain and Linton have let the artist down badly. The subjects, and Leighton's technique, I should have thought, present fewer difficulties than usual, nevertheless the cutting is below the average, and in several cases the entire character of a drawing has been altered. Far better, though similar in kind—better as drawings and infinitely better as specimens of wood engraving—are the nine designs for the *Bible Gallery*. Here we have again a cold and academic line, but the drawings are really powerful and Dalziel has done wonders. The 'Cain and Abel ', the 'Escape of the Spies ', the 'Samson ' drawings—above all 'Samson Carrying the Gates '—show Leighton at his best. In this last design the bold simplicity and originality of the pattern is a delight to the eye: it is, I think, the finest of all the Leighton wood blocks, marred only by the serrated tops of the walls which strike a fussy and staccato note, breaking the long, bold, satisfying sweep.

VI. G. F. WATTS (1817-1904)

It is also in *Dalziel's Bible Gallery* that we find the three drawings on wood made by G. F. Watts. Remembering his paintings, we may be disappointed in them, yet the 'Esau Meeting Jacob ' is a noble design. Into the plan for an Illustrated Bible Watts had at first entered warmly enough; it was only when he actually began to make the drawings that his enthusiasm waned. He found the medium baffling, and after several attempts was inclined to withdraw from what now seemed to him a thankless task. There is a distinct acerbity in his reply to a criticism passed by the Dalziels on one of his wood blocks. 'Gentlemen, I am always ready to receive and act upon criticism, and have therefore added a little to the size of the head of Noah, according to your suggestion; but my object is not to represent the phrenological characteristics of a mechanical genius, but the might and style of the inspired Patriarch. . . . I made drawing my principal study for a great many years, and consider myself at liberty to depart from mere correctness if necessary for my purpose; especially if the incorrectness resulting be more apparent than real. . . . If I do anything for you, or anybody else, I must carry out my own sentiment.' [1]

[1] *The Brothers Dalziel: A Record of Fifty Years' Work*, p. 246. (Methuen, 1901.)

F. J. Shields made a few drawings for magazines. In *Once a Week*, vol. iv, ' An Hour with the Dead ' is his; in vol. v ' The Robber Saint ', and in vol. x ' Turberville ': ' Hide a Stick ', which appeared as an extra illustration in vol. iii of the New Series, is an engraving after one of his paintings. To *The Sunday Magazine* for 1865 he contributed ' Even as Thou Wilt ', and for *Punch* he made two or three drawings, the largest of which appeared on the 11th of December 1875. In *The Illustrated London News* (December 1859) he has ' Christmas Eve ', and in *The Graphic* (December 1870) an excellent drawing, ' Old Clothes Market: Camp Field, Manchester '—sometimes referred to as ' Knott Mill Fair '. In *The London Home Monthly* (March 1895) he has a process drawing, ' The Old Frenchman of the Strand '.

I must confess that the work of Shields does not seem to me to justify the very high estimation in which it is generally held. Mr. Joseph Pennell describes his engravings for Defoe's *History of the Plague of London* as ' Rembrandt-like ', and Gleeson White is equally appreciative. They are grim designs, revealing considerable power of imagination, but I should not be prepared to give an extravagant price for the book. As it happens, it is by far the rarest on our list. The British Museum does not possess it, and Mr. Harold Hartley told me he advertised offering ten pounds for a copy without result. Later, by good luck, he did acquire one, and at a much lower price, but I have never heard of anybody else who did. In fact, it is the kind of book more likely to turn up among the rubbish in a ' fourpenny box ' than to be discovered in a catalogue. *The History of the Plague of London* appeared in Laurie's ' Shilling Entertainment Library ', and was published at two prices—nine pence in paper wrappers and a shilling bound in cloth. In the *English Catalogue of Books* it is entered as published by Longman in September 1863; but the title page of Mr. Hartley's copy bears the imprint of John Marshall & Co., Simpkin & Co., Hamilton, Adams & Co., and H. S. King & Co. It is undated.

Shields's *Illustrations for Bunyan's Pilgrim's Progress* (Simpkin, 1864) consists of a series of designs and initial letters finely printed, with illustrative passages of text. The drawings, though interesting, are less interesting than those for *The Plague of London*, and probably were made earlier than the date of publication, for he received the commission in 1860. A small paper-covered book (also, I expect, extremely rare, but with nothing else to recommend it) is entitled *Th' Greyt Eggshibishun* (Manchester: John Heywood). This has a cover design and some very early and valueless illustrations by Shields, engraved on wood by Langton. The preface is dated 1851.

FREDERICK LEIGHTON: 'Samson Carrying the Gates'
[Dalziel's Bible Gallery]

T. Morten: 'Macdhonuil's Coronach'

[*Once a Week*, 1865]

CHAPTER XII

T. MORTEN AND WILLIAM SMALL

I. THOMAS MORTEN (1836-1866)

MORTEN'S work has not received the recognition it deserves. It is true that it is uneven, but at its best it is brilliant and highly decorative, with frequently a fantastic element both original and attractive. His first drawing in *Once a Week* (vol. iv, 1861), 'Swift and the Mohawks', is not a good example, though the figure of the drunken man on the ground foreshadows something of the quality of his later designs. 'The Father of the Regiment' (vol. v, 1861) is better, and 'Wish Not', in vol. x (1864), which also contains the 'Coast Guardsman', is characteristic of that side of his talent which found its happiest expression in the illustrations for *Gulliver's Travels*. Volume xi (1864) has two designs, including the powerful, if not entirely successful 'Cumaean Sibyl', and vol. xii (1865) has the lovely 'Macdhonuil's Coronach', the first drawing in *Once a Week* in which we see Morten quite at his best. 'The Dying Viking' in vol. i of the New Series (1866) is a fine thing, but more derivative, showing the influence of the Pre-Raphaelites, and particularly of Sandys; the 'King Erick' in the same volume is less interesting. In 'The Curse of the Gudmunds' (vol. ii, New Series, 1866) he is again at his best. This beautiful and completely individual drawing achieves—principally through the treatment of the dark branches of the cedar-tree, and the flowing line of the woman's hair—a peculiar elfin quality; but 'On the Cliffs', his second design in this volume, a graceful study of a woman in profile, is ruined by the extremely poor drawing of the man behind her.

Morten's first drawing in *Good Words*, 'The Waker, Dreamer, and Sleeper' (1861), is a strange composition of a group of men praying at night by the side of a breaking dyke. The printing is poor, and the solitary standing figure is not among the artist's more fortunate conceptions, but the design at once attracts attention. In the next volume he has three pictures, two at least up to his average, and the third, 'The Carrier Pigeon', a most decorative arrangement in lines. In 1863 'An Orphan's Family Christmas' is negligible, but 'Hester Durham' is good, while 'Cousin Winnie' and 'The Spirit of Eld' represent him at his best. After this, unfortunately,

[211]

he ceased to draw for *Good Words*, and we must look for his work in magazines where both printing and engraving are less reliable.

In *London Society* he is usually engraved by Harral, whose work is rarely so satisfactory as that of Dalziel and Swain. Nevertheless, the Christmas Number of 1862 contains a charming little drawing, 'The Ghost at Heatherbell Abbey'. In vol. iii (1863) he has three designs, including an excellent drawing for *Ruth Grey's Trial*; and in vol. iv, in which he illustrates the serial *The First Time I Saw Her*, he has nine. His last drawing for *London Society*, 'A Winter's Night', did not appear till December 1869, several years after his death; and this, and perhaps two or three others, though not equalling his best things in *Once a Week* and *Good Words*, fall only a little below them.

To the first volume of *The Churchman's Family Magazine* (1863) he contributes three drawings, and to the second the 'Peal of Hope', in which he has the advantage of Dalziel's engraving. It is a beautiful thing, yet not completely successful, the two subsidiary figures in the background being commonplace and out of tone. In vol. iii (1864) he has 'The Twilight Hour', another fine picture, with again Dalziel as the engraver.

Morten contributed to *Entertaining Things* (1861-1862), to *Every Boy's Magazine* (1862-1863), while some of his happiest illustrations appeared in *The Quiver* of 1865 and 1866, including the 'French Protestantism' of 1865, and the 'Hassan' and 'Isaac Walton' of 1866. Another drawing, 'One Summer Month', most inexplicably turns up in *Belgravia* (1871). He has an illustration for *The Lion in the Path* in *Cassell's Family Paper* (1866), and you will find contributions from him in *The Young Gentleman's Magazine* (1867); *Aunt Judy* (1866), to which he gave several excellent things; and the six shilling edition of *Beeton's Annual* (1866).[1]

Taking all these drawings into consideration—drawings so uneven in conception and execution—it becomes exceedingly difficult to place Morten. When he is good he is very good; on the other hand, just when he seems completely to have found himself, he will produce a design that looks like an imitation of so immature a draughtsman as Paul Gray. He had an excellent manner of his own, which makes it all the harder to understand why he should have troubled to show us that he can 'do' Sandys and other artists—some of whom require a great deal of 'doing'.

Turning to the books he illustrated, the first appears to be *The Laird's Return* [1861], which contains several charming designs. *Famous Boys* (Darton) is said by Gleeson White to have been illustrated by Morten, but

---

[1] Among the literary contents of the *Annual* is a school story, *Bob Trevor and I*, by Austin Dobson. One meets with not a few such surprises on turning over these ancient miscellanies.

T. Morten: 'Laputa—The People in the Street'
[*Gulliver's Travels*]

I could discover nothing in these very poor engravings at all resembling him. In *Tales of Life in Earnest*, by Miss Crompton (Darton & Hodge, 1862), the four drawings are signed with initials that look like T.M., but whether they are Morten's or not matters little, since they are quite unimportant and uncharacteristic.

Gulliver's Travels, illustrated by Morten, was originally issued in eleven parts, and in book form in October 1865. The first issue has the frontispiece in black and white: in a later issue—also in parts—it is coloured. In the first issue, too, the title page reads, 'illustrated by T. Morten'; in the subsequent issues it reads, 'illustrated by the late T. Morten'. *Gulliver's Travels* contains no drawing perhaps quite so remarkable as the cream of those I have mentioned among his contributions to *Once a Week* and *Good Words*, but, as a sustained work, it is by far the biggest thing Morten accomplished. Besides some eighty large designs, the book is decorated with many headpieces, tailpieces, and initial letters. It is a mingling of fantasy and grotesque, the finest drawings being the strange, half Japanese inventions for the Voyage to Laputa. Once or twice we find the artist at his old trick of imitation; the design on page 108, for example, in which Gulliver is giving an exhibition of fencing to the Brobdingnagians, is pure Gustave Doré (greater familiarity with the French artist would no doubt reveal the exact source of the drawing); but on the whole the illustrations are strikingly original, and the book must be placed among the collector's indispensable items. All the earlier issues are printed from the unaltered blocks, but in later issues some of the drawings have been slightly cut down. Though the book is undated, such later editions may easily be detected by an examination of the pictures, which will show in several cases a portion of the signature cut away. Some hint as to the date may also be found in the publisher's list at the end.

Three drawings in *Jingles and Jokes for Little Folks* [1865] show how amusingly Morten could have illustrated Grimm or any of the old nursery favourites. He has one illustration in *Dalziel's Arabian Nights*, one in *A Round of Days*, and one in Watts's *Divine and Moral Songs* (Nisbet's edition). This last drawing, 'Against Pride of Clothes', at first gives us an odd little shock. For, surprising as it may appear, the lady descending the steps, with her elaborate coiffure and elaborately embroidered robes, irresistibly suggests Beardsley's later work in *The Savoy*. The impression is superficial, I admit, and will not survive a close comparison, but at least it proves Morten's delight in experimentation.

For the verses, *What is Life, Father?* in Adelaide Proctor's *Legends and Lyrics* (1866) he made an interesting design of a little boy questioning a knight in armour on this subject—interesting not only for the drawing of

[215]

the knight, but also because the elevating nature of the poem has not prevented Morten from cribbing his background from Millais's ' Parable of the Prodigal Son '. Of his five drawings in Foxe's *Book of Martyrs*, that on page 164—' He was dragged, like a wild beast, to the cloister '—is an even more flagrant plagiarism. The chief figure—to say nothing of some of the subsidiary ones, and the horse, which has been turned artfully the other way—is copied from a design by J. D. Watson, ' The Curate of Suverdsio ', which appeared in *Good Words* in 1863. This is no case of a chance resemblance, nor of one of those vagrant influences to which Morten was so susceptible: a mirror could hardly produce a more faithful likeness. He has not troubled to alter the pose—the lowered head, the downcast eyes; nor the long black cloak, the flat cloth hat. The drawing is not signed, though Morten nearly invariably signs his work, but the printers have placed his name beneath it, together with that of W. L. Thomas, the engraver. The Watson drawing was engraved by Dalziel, as Morten knew, which decreased the risk of the theft being detected, and as a matter of fact it never was.

To Thornbury's *Two Centuries of Song* (1867) Morten gives a couple of passable things, but he is well represented in *Cassell's History of England*, his designs in the first volume—' Hereward ' and ' The Death of Harold '—being singularly powerful and decorative, worthy of comparison with William Small's drawings in the same book. *Woman's Strategy* also belongs to 1867. The only copy of this book I have seen bears the following imprint on the title page: ' New York: Carleton & Co. London: Hogg. 1867 '. The letterpress was printed in America on a thick common white paper; the drawings, engraved by Dalziel, are printed on a smooth paper of a pale brown tint; the effect of the combination being extremely ugly.

II. WILLIAM SMALL (1843-   )

William Small began his career as a pupil in the art department of Messrs. Nelson, the Edinburgh publishers, and he illustrated a number of their books before coming to work in London. Though his earlier drawings are line drawings and in the tradition of the sixties, he was one of the first to break away from that tradition, and among the younger men it was his influence that prevailed. In the pages of *Good Words*, *The Sunday Magazine*, and other periodicals, we see the new manner beginning; in *The Graphic* it is definitely established. Apart altogether from the substitution of ' wash ' for ' line '—in itself a sufficiently disastrous innovation—the old ideal has disappeared: art is turning to journalism, beauty to prettiness, sentiment to sentimentality, the work is planned from the beginning to appeal to a larger and less cultured public. In these changing times Charles Keene seems like a giant working alone, indifferent to passing fashions; but it was much easier and more profitable to imitate William Small than Charles Keene.

Yet Small is a brilliant and powerful draughtsman, a master in his own manner, though by far his most interesting work belongs to his first period, when he was still making line drawings in accordance with the older convention. His later drawings in wash, actually painted in body colour on the wood, and leaving the whole creation of the texture to the engraver, brilliant though they may be, coincide with the beginning of the decadence, for it was on these later drawings that the new school was founded, bringing our period of illustration to an end.

I have not found any magazine drawings by Small prior to 1864, when we get two or three—already completely characteristic—in *The Quiver*, including a very delicate and charming design called 'Milly's Doves'. And it might perhaps be as well before going further to clear up what is misleading in Gleeson White's account of this important magazine, so that the collector may not pass over the early volumes under the impression that they contain nothing. Gleeson White tells us that *The Quiver* was started in 1864 as a non-illustrated magazine, and implies that it did not begin to be illustrated till 1866. We have seen, however, that it contained drawings as early as 1864, and from that date on there are excellent things by M.E.E., Morten, John Lawson, and Small—the plates printed on a special, toned paper. In the volume for 1865, among other good drawings by Small, are the particularly attractive 'Little Boy on Crutches', and 'Rosanna endeavouring to convince Mrs. Shooldice'. 1866 has several masterly designs. Indeed, for decorative beauty of composition, I doubt if he ever surpassed 'Between the Cliffs', with its wonderful rocks and sky, and the dead woman's hair twined among the ferns. Further fine things appear in later volumes of *The Quiver*, in which we watch him altering his technique; but it would be a huge task to attempt an iconography of the illustrations of an artist like Small—one so prolific, and who, moreover, continued to draw far beyond the limits of our period, so that we actually find him contributing in 1915 to the first number of *The Gipsy*, collaborating with men who were not even born at the time he was producing his finest black and white work. Here, at all events, there is no room to do more than indicate broadly where his later work may be looked for by those who wish to follow it through the seventies, eighties, and nineties.

In *Cassell's Family Paper* (1865), the precursor of *Cassell's Magazine*, he illustrates the serial, *Bound to the Wheel*. These large bold drawings vary considerably in merit, but some of the best are amazing. A drawing like 'Gets in your eyes, indeed!' (the titles, I dare say, seem absurd) reveals unmistakably that a new master has arisen. Taken as an illustration—a

[217]

mere illustration if you like—for expressiveness, dramatic power, truth to nature and character, it is improbable that such work has ever been, or ever will be, surpassed. And there are others equally good. Note the expression on the faces—particularly on the dog's face—in ' There was Gibbs ! ' In this same magazine Small illustrates a few chapters of *The Secret Sign*. Despite the roughness of the printing, and the wretched quality of a paper through which the letterpress on the back is visible, what breadth and beauty there is in the design, ' Home, Nero ! ' This is great work, if of the earth earthy. Yet it is leading us away—far, far away from our ancient track. In the *Christmas Annual* for this year he has a drawing for *Poisoned Arrows*, and, still keeping to *Cassell's*, now *Cassell's Magazine*, in 1870 we get the thirty-seven illustrations for Wilkie Collins's unpleasant novel, *Man and Wife*. These are much smaller, and personally I find them much less attractive, than the best of the earlier drawings. No doubt they admirably fulfil their purpose, as an echo of the text, but as pictures one is hardly likely to linger over them. To which I hasten to add that Gleeson White *does* linger over them, and since he so seldom departs from his method of bare recording he must have found in them a particular excellence.

To me they seem infinitely less striking than the illustrations for Charles Reade's *Griffith Gaunt*, which ran through *The Argosy* during 1866. The *Griffith Gaunt* pictures are not better than the best of the *Bound to the Wheel* pictures, but they have the immense advantage of superior engraving and paper. They have, too, an exceptional richness and softness of tone—that lovely tone which, as in Watson's ' Aspen ', *may* be due to a happy accident —and several of them possess the beautiful decorative pattern Small at this period still at times sought and found. And what speed of galloping horses in the drawing of ' Griffith Gaunt and Paul Carrick ' ! In this and in the design of ' Miss Peyton ' Small beats the hunting-field artists on their own ground.

George MacDonald's *Robert Falconer* is the serial in *The Argosy* for 1867. Houghton made the first illustration, the drawing of the woman with the candle (the signature in the right-hand corner comes out more clearly in the proof), but the remainder are by Small, and Small at his best. He never got a finer effect of atmosphere than in the drawing of the man standing on the cliff's edge ; while the ' flying kite ' design is a little gem of which any artist might be proud.

The Boys' Own Volume (1866) contains a number of powerful and virile designs for *Ralph de Walden*, made in Small's earliest and best manner, but apparently so little known as to have escaped the attention of even his warmest admirers. Besides these twelve full-page plates, engraved by Thomas, there are a number of initial letters, each of which is in itself a tiny illustra-

WILLIAM SMALL: 'Lilies'

[*Good Words*, 1866]

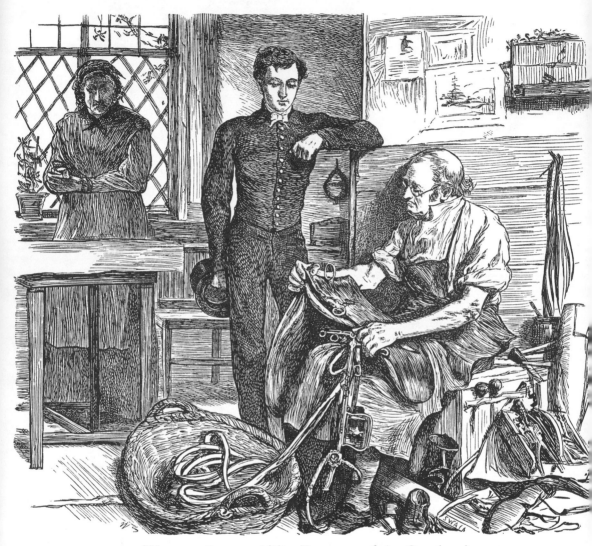

WILLIAM SMALL: 'The Fortunes of the Granbys'
[*Sunday at Home*, 1866]

tion. The early English costume here gives Small an opportunity for draw-ing those muscular limbs and strong athletic bodies he loved, and in which the individuality of his line is most marked.

We also in this year, 1866, get the admirable designs for *The Fortunes of the Granbys* in *The Sunday at Home*, and a good drawing, ' Lost on the Fells ', in *The Shilling Magazine* (vol. iii). The drawings in *Fun* I have not traced, but such as there are probably belong to the seventies, the only one I have seen, a picture of three drunken Scotchmen, being obviously in his second manner.

His first contribution to *Once a Week* appears in the Christmas Number of 1865; and in the following year (vol. i, New Series) he has six drawings. It is strange, yet perhaps really not so strange after all, how for every artist there is one face he returns to repeatedly, and the face of the sick boy in ' Billy Blake's Best Coffin ' is the face that haunted Small. In this particular example, it is true, the engraver has not been entirely successful with its enigmatic beauty; but we shall meet it again and again, altered—now masculine, now feminine—yet still the same. The superb drawing of ' The Stag-Hound ' on page 295—poorly printed, unfortunately—is equally characteristic of our artist, of his sense of dramatic action, which has never, I think, been excelled. The illusion of life, of speed, of ferocity, of strength, could hardly be more vividly conveyed than it is in this drawing of a dog tearing out the throat of his enemy. In vol. ii of the New Series of *Once a Week* there are seven designs, and one in the Christmas Number. Of these, ' Eldorado ' is a further example of Small's profound knowledge of anatomy, of his power to create flesh and muscle and sinew, and also of what perhaps sprang out of that power, a predilection for somewhat strained and distorted attitudes in which muscular exertion is brought prominently into play. No, certainly he was not a Greek: but what wind and weather, what move-ment and life in ' Dorette '! what strong, almost harsh beauty in ' The Gift of Clunnog Vawr '! In the third volume of the New Series we find only two drawings; in the fourth only one.

Small was not among the first contributors to *London Society*. From 1866 on, however, we meet with designs from his hand. In 1867 he illustrated *Playing for High Stakes*, and in 1868 he has a landscape—' You Did not Come '—drawn with all the minute detail of a Birket Foster. It is an excellent drawing, but were it not for the signature we should never give it to Small. Compare it with the drawing of the two fishermen on the bridge in ' Up and Down Moel Vammer ' (vol. xix, 1871), every line of which is characteristic. In the Christmas Number for 1873 he has ' The Model Theatre '.

In October 1865 Johnstone and Hunter, the Edinburgh publishers, started a juvenile magazine called *The Children's Hour*, with Small as principal illustrator. It was a quaint little magazine, unusual and rather charming in format, the page no bigger than that of the ordinary octavo book; and the price of each number was threepence. Small illustrated the first three serials, *Miss Matty*, *Horace Hazelwood*, and *Found Afloat*, with capital drawings in his early manner. In 1868 he dropped out, R. W. Macbeth taking his place, and he made only one more appearance in its pages, in 1870.

In *Good Words* Small has many drawings. He appears first in 1866, with four designs, two of which, ' Deliverance ' and ' Lilies ', rank among his happiest decorative inventions. In 1867 he supplies five illustrations for *The Starling*, and a couple of other drawings—all first rate—not to mention those in the Christmas Number. In 1868 he has thirty-seven designs, thirty-five of them illustrating *The Woman's Kingdom*. This number includes some initial letters, but the initial letters are always admirable little drawings—vignettes of figure or landscape possessing a definite relation to the story. *Good Words* for 1869 being practically given over to F. A. Fraser, who illustrates both the serials, Small has in it only one design. He has two or three in the Christmas Number, but *Good Cheer* was issued separately and is usually missing from the bound volumes. In 1870 his drawings are entirely confined to *Good Cheer*, in which he illustrates a longish story, *Gideon's Rock*: and then, in 1871, he comes back again, with twenty-one designs, twenty belonging to the serial, *The High Mills*.

To *Good Words for the Young* he seems to have contributed only that single fine drawing which appears on page 295 of the third volume.

Small's first drawing in *The Sunday Magazine* (1866), ' Hebe Dunbar ', is most interesting, because, though it is ' from a photograph ', it presents all the characteristics of his first manner, even the face being of the type I have alluded to as his. Not a trace of its photographic origin remains; it is in every line an original drawing. Following it we have ' A Sunday Afternoon in a London Court ', an exquisite composition, and three perhaps even more beautiful designs for *Annals of a Quiet Neighbourhood*. We have only to set any of these beside his later work to fall more deeply in love with our period than ever, and with its predominant idea of naturalism expressed in terms of beauty. In 1867 we get two more of Small's most attractive drawings, but 1868 gives us only the ' Sunday Morning '. After this there occurs a break, and when he returns in 1871 his second manner has been evolved. Nevertheless, these illustrations of 1871, made for *The Story of a Mine*, appeal irresistibly to the imagination: one or two of them, so sombre is their power, might have been made for Zola's *Germinal*.

In *The People's Magazine* (1867) Small illustrates the second serial,

Up and Down the Ladder; and in *The Day of Rest* (1878) he illustrates
' Be-Be, the Nailmaker's Daughter '.

We have not space, however, to follow our artist through the seventies,
eighties, and nineties, when he illustrated the novels of James Payn, William
Black, and others in *The Cornhill* and *The Graphic*, to say nothing of his
contributions to minor periodicals. Of the *Cornhill* drawings it must suffice
to say that they will be found in the volumes of the late seventies and early
eighties: those in *The Graphic* are more important. The large page *The
Graphic* placed at his disposal happened particularly to suit Small, and in
1871 he made a most interesting series of sketches of life in Connemara.
These records of a tour through the West of Ireland may not, and in fact
do not, rival Houghton's famous *Graphic America* designs, but they do show
the work of a great draughtsman on holiday, as it were—picking his own
subjects, drawing to please himself. And in the illustrations of the *Graphic*
fiction he is sometimes amazingly powerful, as in the magnificent full-page
drawing of ' Radoub ', made for Hugo's *Ninety-Three* (which *The Graphic*
serialized in 1874), or the so different yet equally wonderful drawing of the
wicked chambermaid dressing the heroine's hair, made in the same year
for Wilkie Collins's *The Law and the Lady*. The later designs—for *Under
One Roof* and other novels and tales—interesting and charming though
they are, must here be left unrecorded.

Faced with the book illustrations, we find a less voluminous but still
unwieldy mass of material, and the list that follows is certainly incomplete.
The obscurity of many of the works illustrated with wood engravings is
abysmal. I have before me now a tale, published in small quarto and entitled
Jack the Conqueror, or Difficulties Overcome. I had never heard of it till I
picked it up the other day, yet it contains many excellent full-page designs
by Robert Barnes, whose name, as so frequently happens, is omitted from
the title page. *Jack the Conqueror* [1868] is dateless, but this copy was
presented to Herbert Carnegie Knox, with Uncle Henry and Aunt Emma's
love, on the 28th of February 1870, and appended to it is Messrs. Partridge's
list. It is a list that opens up unknown possibilities. Who has ever heard of
these authors? Who knows anything about Nelsie Brook, or Old Humphrey
(who appears mysteriously to have been two persons—G. Mogridge and
Ephraim Holding), about Mrs. Balfour and the rest? Their ' seconds ' are
probably as rare as their ' firsts '. But all their works are illustrated with
wood engravings, and the point is that some, or all, or none, may contain
masterpieces.

Small made a series of admirable Eastern drawings for A. L. O. E.'s
Exiles in Babylon (Nelson, 1864). These were printed in a brown tint,
apparently by some kind of lithographic process. A later edition (1869)

contains a number of extra drawings (not by Small) illustrating the English scenes of the story, and in this edition all the designs are printed in the customary black and white. Three other juvenile tales published by Nelson in 1864—*Words for the Wise*, by T. S. Arthur, *Miracles of Heavenly Love*, and *Marion's Sundays*—are illustrated by Small. In 1865 he helped to illustrate *Wordsworth's Poems* (Nimmo); in 1866 *Studies for Stories*, *The Spirit of Praise, Ballad Stories of the Affections, The Book of Martyrs*, and *Pen and Pencil Pictures from the Poets*. *Home Sunshine*, by C. D. Bell (Warne, 1866), and *Sketches of Scripture Characters* (1866), are also illustrated by him.

Small has thirty-one delicate little drawings in Dr. Watts's *Divine and Moral Songs* (Sampson Low, 1866), and it is the Doctor's fault if their charm at times is not unmingled with an unconscious humour. The author of *How Doth the Little Busy Bee* was devoted to children, but it was on the whole a gloomy affection, so that he appears to have pictured hell as very like a large kindergarten. The peculiar trend of his imagination gives the artist a rather difficult task. It is not easy, for instance, to picture a schoolboy 'meditating by night on the excellency of the Bible'. Small (possibly remembering that the Scotch are a theological people) gives us a boy in knickerbockers and a tam-o'-shanter, leaning over a balustrade above a starlit garden. Dr. Watts might have liked this drawing: there is no reason in the world why he shouldn't: but I don't think he would have approved of some of the others. He would have agreed that in 'Against Evil Company' it was dangerous to make the wicked boys appear to be having such a good time, to make them look so jolly and so pleasant. In comparison, the good boy is depressing. Even the thought that ' never shall one cooling drop to quench their burning tongues be given ', has failed to cheer him. It is plain that the others regard him as a hopeless little squirt, and we cannot help sharing their opinion. The good boy, according to Small, is invariably alone, except when he is accompanied by papa, who is bald and has a beard. The ' evil companions ' always have a dog or two. There is a delightful drawing where four of them are lying on a bank under the summer trees. One has a pipe, another is ' defiling his tongue ' with a ' wanton song ', a third is simply lying on his back in the sun with his hands in his pockets (very nearly a sin, however), the fourth is pointing, it is to be feared in derision, at the good boy on his way to school burdened with surely an unnecessary load of books. Their own few books are scattered on the grass; their terrier has his head in a rabbit-hole; moreover, whether it is the charm of the spot they have chosen between the hayfields and the wooded hillside, or whether it is the fault of Nature, who has given them too fair an exterior, in spite of the pipe, in spite of the wanton song, in spite of hands in pockets,

WILLIAM SMALL: 'Griffith Gaunt'

[*The Argosy*, 1866]

WILLIAM SMALL:
'In Dismal Dance about the Furnace Blue'
[Milton's *Hymn on Christ's Nativity*]

hell seems far away. As for the good boy who 'shuns' them, he has the appearance of bottling up the whole graceless scene to bring it out at the first opportunity to his schoolmaster or papa. 'My God!' he says (which sounds naughty, but, from him, isn't)—'My God, I hate to dwell with sinful children here.'

Little Lays for Little Folks (1867) contains more of Small's charming drawings for children. Gilbert's *The Washerwoman's Foundling* (1867) is illustrated by him; and he contributed three designs to the Chandos *Longfellow* (including a beautiful drawing of a boy, ' " I saw the moon behind the islands fade " '). Other works to which he contributed in 1867 are *Heber's Hymns*; *The Illustrated Book of Sacred Poems*; *Golden Thoughts from Golden Fountains* (which has, among other designs, on page 233 one of his most exquisite landscapes); *Two Centuries of Song* (containing 'Colin and Phœbe', a masterpiece); *Cassell's Illustrated Readings*; *Jean Ingelow's Poems*; Milton's *Hymn on Christ's Nativity*; and *Cassell's History of England* —for the first volume of which he made three designs in his finest style.

A couple of drawings for Buchanan's *North Coast* belong to 1868, and a frontispiece and vignette for Charles Reade's *Christie Johnstone* to the same year. In 1870 we have the admirable and highly characteristic 'John Gilpin', contributed to *Pictures from English Literature*, and two minor drawings for Novello's *National Nursery Rhymes*.

For the sumptuous edition of *The Pilgrim's Progress* published by Strahan in 1880 at five guineas and illustrated chiefly by Fred Barnard, who is responsible for sixty-six out of its hundred designs, Small made two drawings, 'The Slough of Despond' and 'At the Gate'. The entire series of these *Pilgrim's Progress* illustrations appeared in *The Day of Rest* during 1878 and 1879, but in the book the larger plates are printed on India paper.

Small's two designs for *Dalziel's Bible Gallery* were made in 1876— wash drawings and average examples of his *Graphic* style, but here singularly out of place, looking, for all their slickness and dash—perhaps indeed on account of it—slightly common in comparison with the line drawings of most of his collaborators. It is the method that triumphs; the old method; for some of the men who executed these line drawings were markedly Small's inferiors in talent.

Among the later books to which he contributed are *Illustrated British Ballads* (1881); *Fielding's Works* (1882), in which he illustrated the novels, the other volumes having no pictures; Blackmore's *Lorna Doone* (1883); and Bret Harte's *A Protégée of Jack Hamlin's* (1894). But these works are merely picked out at random: they have little interest even for the most omnivorous collector; for they contain nothing that recalls either the manner or the spirit of the sixties.

CHAPTER XIII

A MISCELLANEOUS GROUP

J. LAWSON, WALTER CRANE, LUKE FILDES, LINLEY SAMBOURNE

I. JOHN LAWSON

JOHN LAWSON (unrelated to the brothers Wilfrid and Cecil, who will be mentioned later) is not among the greater artists of our period, but his work is often good, and at its best is distinguished by a purity of line and a pleasing use of rich solid blacks. The Christmas Number of *Once a Week* (1865) contains a few drawings by him, and five others, more interesting, will be found in vol. i of the New Series (1866). In the second volume for 1866 there are three, two of which, ' Ariadne ' and ' The Mulberry Tree ', show him at his best. To the Christmas Number he contributes ' The Birth of the Rose '; and three more designs in vol. iii (1867) conclude his work for *Once a Week*. It is, as I say, good work, though one can hardly call it first rate. With the closing of our period nothing is more obvious than that a new standard of taste has arisen, and Lawson's taste is not always impeccable. This is perhaps more noticeable in his imaginative designs. In them we occasionally find that confusion between the ornate and the decorative which E. G. Dalziel will carry several steps further, bringing the end definitely in sight.

Lawson has many illustrations in *The Sunday Magazine, Cassell's Magazine*, and *The Quiver*. In the last named he has a particularly good drawing in July 1865. Other excellent designs will be found in *The British Workman* for August 1866; *The Argosy*, 1866 ('The Earl o' Quarterdeck'); and *The Shilling Magazine*, vol. iii, 1866 (' Incident in the Year 1809 '). The three illustrations for *Grace's Fortune* in *Good Words* (1867) I am inclined to give to John Lawson, though Gleeson White gives them to Wilfrid —that is to say, F.W.—and the index, as if in doubt, to an ambiguous J.W. In the following year ' A Letter ' is signed J. Lawson in full. He also contributed to *The Children's Hour* (1865), and I dare say to one or two other periodicals I have not noted.

A list of the books in which his work will be found includes: *Stories Told to a Child* (1865); *Pen and Pencil Pictures from the Poets* (1866)—one

J. LAWSON: 'The Earl o' Quarterdeck'
[*The Argosy*, 1866]

excellent drawing; Buchanan's *Ballad Stories* (1866); *Golden Thoughts from Golden Fountains* [1867]; *Roses and Holly* (1867), containing a fine drawing, ' Vanity Fair '; *Ballads: Scottish and English* [1867], with several good things, among them the admirable ' Edom o' Gordon '; *Nursery Time* (1867) with the plates in colour; Marryat's *Early Start in Life* (1867); and *The Children of Blessing* (1867). Both these last are excellent, especially *The Children of Blessing*. In it will be found the charming ' Bernard discovers Edward Foster in the Ditch ', a drawing which, under new titles, was re-printed again and again in later books. Lawson's best design in *The Golden Gift* [1868] is for Charles Lamb's *Dream Children*; in *Original Poems* (1868) he has several beautiful vignettes. He has also good drawings in Hutton's *Tales of the White Cockade* (1870) and *The Runaway* (1872), but *The Children's Garland* (Macmillan, 1873), an anthology compiled by Coventry Patmore, where we should have expected him to be particularly successful, is dis-appointing. Hutton's *The Fiery Cross* belongs to 1875; E. Lynn Linton's *The World Well Lost* to 1877, and *Clever Hans* to 1883. The last is a delightful toy book published by de la Rue, with the pictures most deli-cately printed in colour; but Lawson's later colour books, Mrs. Wilde's *There Was Once* [1888], and *Childhood Valley* [1889], are negligible, the wash drawings, crudely lithographed, being indistinguishable from scores of others turned out at this time.

II. WALTER CRANE (1845-1915)

No artist of the sixties of equal eminence has so narrowly limited a talent as Walter Crane. Most of the attempts he made at a naturalistic representation of life are feeble in the extreme; those in *London Society* have even an inexplicable commonness, which places them on a level with the work of Adelaide and Florence Claxton and other third-rate illustrators. Yet Crane had a remarkable gift for decorative design, and did so much through his toy books to raise the standard of nursery illustration that we need not grudge him the praise he has received, even if, in comparison with that doled out to several of his fellow-artists, it strikes us as excessive. After all, when he is on his own ground, it is impossible to compare him with them. He is doing something quite different, and in his really characteristic drawings the use of the human figure is purely conventional, the drawings themselves possessing no more emotional content than the cool pleasant pattern of a wall-paper. That is why in the end they tend to weary us, for all art that is divorced from nature in the end tends to weary us. The num-ber of books Crane illustrated is enormous, but when we have looked through *Flora's Feast*, say, and turn to the next, we find our admiration diminishing,

[231]

till at last it is only the very finest of his decorative schemes that arouse our interest.

He himself has given an account of the books which, with Edmund Evans, the colour printer and engraver, he produced for the nursery. 'The books for babies, current at that time—about 1865 to 1870—of the cheaper sort called toy books were not very inspiriting. These were generally careless and unimaginative woodcuts, very casually coloured by hand, dabs of pink and emerald green being laid on across faces and frocks with a somewhat reckless aim. There was practically no choice between such as these and cheap German highly coloured lithographs. The only attempt at decoration I remember was a set of coloured designs to nursery rhymes by Mr. H. S. Marks, which had been originally intended for cabinet panels. Bold outlines and flat tints were used. . . . It was, however, the influence of some Japanese printed pictures given to me by a lieutenant in the navy, who had brought them home from there as curiosities, which I believe, though I drew inspiration from many sources, gave the real impulse to that treatment in strong outlines and flat tints and solid blacks, which I adopted with variations in books of this kind from that time onwards.'

Walter Crane was born in Liverpool, his father being the secretary and treasurer of the Liverpool Academy. He was apprenticed for three years to W. J. Linton, not as an engraver but to learn to be a draughtsman on wood. His first published drawing, 'A Man in the Coils of a Serpent', appeared in 1861 in *Entertaining Things*, and about the same time he supplied illustrations for certain tracts by the Rev. H. B. Power. Two drawings appeared in *Once a Week*, one in December 1863 and the other in December 1865; and in *Good Words* (1863) appeared a solitary design, 'Treasure Trove'. Of the drawings for *London Society* the less said the better.

On the 21st of July 1866 appeared Walter Crane's only contribution to *Punch*, a half page entitled 'Great Show of Chignons'. In Routledge's *Every Boy's Magazine* (1867) he illustrated Mrs. Henry Wood's serial, *Orville College*, with a set of drawings, the best of which look like Arthur Hugheses that have not quite come off, and in *The Argosy* (1868) he illustrated the same author's *Anne Hereford* equally unsuccessfully. Further drawings for modern fiction will be found in *The Churchman's Shilling Magazine* (1869), but frankly they are not worth looking up. In *The People's Magazine*, however, he gives us a surprise. Here, amid smaller unimportant drawings, are his illustrations for the serial novel *Esther*, and though they will not for a moment stand the comparison—which they inevitably suggest—with Charles Keene's illustrations for *A Good Fight*, they are distinctly interesting, especially that on page 257, 'The Flight of Esther', in which the white horse, the two fugitives, and the black forest,

[232]

make a really effective composition. In the same magazine for 1869 he continues the drawings for *Esther*, and in addition illustrates a short serial called *Hubert and Ida*. In *The Graphic* he has two or three coloured supplements (November 1874 and February 1875).

Although the vast bulk of Crane's work belongs to the seventies and later, from 1862 on he illustrated and helped to illustrate many books. The first on our list is *Stories of Old; or Bible Narratives* (1862), in two series, and in the same year he designed a title page for Wilkie Collins's *After Dark* and illustrated Hadley's *Children's Sayings*, while the illustrations for A. J. Symington's *Pen and Pencil Sketches of Faroe and Iceland* are described as 'finished' by Walter Crane. *The New Forest*, by J. R. Wise (1863), contains a lot of landscapes quite unlike the Crane we are familiar with, and other early books are de Haviland's *Stories from Memel* [1863], in which his decorative manner is still undeveloped; Holme Lee's *True Pathetic History of Poor Match* (1863); *Goody Platts and Her Two Cats* (1864); *Broken to Harness*, by Edmund Yates (1865); Hawthorne's *Transformation* (1865); *The Perils of Greatness* (Nimmo, 1865); *Sandford and Merton* [1] (1866?); *Evenings at Home* (1866?); Mark Lemon's *Wait for the End* (1866); a frontispiece and title page for Trollope's *Miss McKenzie* (1866); J. S. Roberts's *Legendary Ballads of England and Scotland* (1868); *King Gab's Story Bag*—a good book this—[1869]; Mayhew's *Magic of Kindness* [1869]; *Stories of the Olden Time* (1870); and *Labour Stands on Golden Feet*, a tale by Zschokke [1870], containing a charming frontispiece and one other good illustration.

The toy books present a difficulty. I myself have never collected them, and neither at the British Museum nor at South Kensington do they possess original sets of the early books. The best I can do is to give a list of titles, with approximate dates, of those supposed to have appeared between 1865 and 1870—a list I take from Gertrude Massé's *Bibliography of Walter Crane*,[2] published in 1923. *Sing a Song of Sixpence* (1865), *One, Two, Buckle my Shoe* (1867), *Multiplication in Verse* (1867-68), *Annie and Jack in London* (1867-68), *The Fairy Ship* (1869), *This Little Pig* (1869), *The Adventures of Puffy* (1869), *King Luckieboy's Party* (1870), *Valentine and Orson* (1870), *The House that Jack Built* (1870), *Cock Robin* (1870), and *Dame Trot* (1870).

---

[1] I have seen only the proofs of the engravings for *Sandford and Merton*, the book itself I was unable to find, nor have I traced the first edition of *Evenings at Home*. My choice of 1866 as a probable date is based on the fact that the Dalziels' proofs of the engravings for both works were pulled in 1865.

[2] *Bibliography of First Editions of Books illustrated by Walter Crane.* By Gertrude Massé. With a preface by Heywood Sumner. (1923.)

I cannot vouch for the accuracy of this list. The *Bibliography*, for instance, places *King Gab* (1870) and *The Merrie Heart* (1870) among the toy books; but *King Gab* is not a toy book nor is its date 1870, and *The Merrie Heart*—which was not issued till September 1871—looks to me like a collection of plates from early toy books reduced in size.

In the seventies and eighties—which I do not propose to chronicle— the list becomes much longer, and, with a few exceptions, all the books belong to nursery literature: in the nineties and later the works illustrated are miscellaneous in character. For all alike I must refer the reader to Gertrude Massé's bibliography. It contains some hundred-and-fifty items, yet it is expressly stated that a complete set of the toy books has not been examined. Nor, as a matter of fact, have I found the bibliography exhaustive even where ordinary books, books that are not toy books, are concerned. Of the twenty-one volumes mentioned in my list—bringing us up to 1870— thirteen have escaped Gertrude Massé's notice. It should be added that I have examined only the entries of the sixties, and since from 1870 on Crane's work is much more fully catalogued in the British Museum and elsewhere omissions during these later years are less likely to have occurred.

The illustrations vary greatly in quality. The best of all the Crane books I have seen is *Grimm's Household Stories* (Macmillan, 1882). This is really a fine book, worthy of a distinguished place in any collection. But for average examples of his work in black and white the whole series of Mrs. Molesworth's tales, commencing with *Tell Me a Story* (1875), may be consulted.

Crane is one of the artists who are reputed to have designed pictorial covers for 'yellow-backs'. It is a subject upon which I can offer no opinion. I have found, however, that the pictures on such covers are by no means always original designs: they are frequently only reprints in colour of an illustration that had appeared earlier elsewhere in black and white.

III. S. L. FILDES (1843-   )

Luke Fildes came too late perhaps to be among those men of the sixties whose work is likely to arouse the collector's ardent enthusiasm. Turning over my prints, I find nothing by him earlier than 'The Goldsmith's Apprentice'; nothing much better, either, than this drawing, which appeared in *Once a Week* for June 1867. The second volume for 1867 also contains three good drawings, including the 'Cassandra', an extra illustration. Though all are characteristic, the variety in these designs—the decorative quality of 'The Child-Queen', the tenderness of 'Feuilles d'Automne', the power of 'Cassandra'—arouse our highest hopes, for

LUKE FILDES: 'Feuilles d'Automne'
[*Once a Week*, 1867]

here certainly we seem once more to have a first-rate illustrator. If subsequently those hopes are not fulfilled, it must be remembered that the golden days are drawing to an end, that artists no longer have the opportunities with which publishers, editors, and engravers provided the earlier men. Less and less are the drawings counted as in themselves of the first importance; more and more they have become limited to the secondary purpose of accompanying and advertising serial novels. What gave the artist his best chance was the custom of illustrating in both books and magazines brief pieces in prose and verse, and that custom has now practically ceased.

In *Once a Week* for the first half of 1868 Fildes has only one drawing, 'The Orchard'. It is not indexed, but it will be found on page 396—a none too happy example of Swain's engraving so far as the very subsidiary human figures are concerned. In the second half he has three designs, and in the Christmas Number a capital drawing of 'The Gallery in Drury Lane Theatre on Boxing Night'. But by 1869 *Once a Week* was rapidly approaching its inglorious end. In the first volume Fildes has five drawings, two of which, 'The Duet' and 'Basking', are graceful and accomplished studies.

His few drawings in *Good Words*, the first of which is dated August 1867, do not call for special notice. Other designs appear in *The Sunday Magazine*, *The Quiver*, *Cassell's Magazine*, *The Sunday at Home*—competent work, if not of outstanding interest. In *The Cornhill* he makes his first appearance in 1870, supplying from then on until 1872 a large number of illustrations for Charles Lever's interminable *Lord Kilgobbin*. In 1873 he illustrates *The Willows*; but it is in *The Graphic* that we must now look for his best work.

In the first volume of *The Graphic*, in the very first number in fact, will be found that magnificent design, 'Houseless and Hungry'—one of the genuine masterpieces of wood engraving. From this drawing Fildes afterwards painted a picture exhibited at the Royal Academy in 1874, and it was this drawing which so struck Charles Dickens that he engaged the artist to illustrate *The Mystery of Edwin Drood*. Fine also are the illustrations for Wilkie Collins's *Miss or Mrs.?*, which appeared in *The Graphic* in 1871; for *The Wandering Heir* (Christmas Number 1872), for *The Law and the Lady* (1874), and other designs; but 'Houseless and Hungry' remains Luke Fildes's best *Graphic* drawing.

Fildes contributed to *Cassell's Illustrated Readings*, to Foxe's *Book of Martyrs*, to *Pictures from English Literature*. He illustrated Charles Reade's *Peg Woffington* (1868): and then, in 1870, we get the powerful drawings for *Edwin Drood*—drawings used later on in the 'Household' edition. For Victor Hugo's *By Order of the King* (1870) he made twenty excellent designs, engraved by Swain; in 1875 he illustrated Trollope's *The Way We Live Now*; and for Thackeray's *Men's Wives* (1879) he made half a dozen illustrations which, if less dramatic than the *Edwin Drood* pictures, are more delicate and distinguished.

IV.   LINLEY SAMBOURNE (1845-1910)

A fortnight during which he drew at a life school is said to comprise the whole of Linley Sambourne's artistic training—unless we count what he received in the draughtsman's office of an engineering firm, for it was originally intended that he should become an engineer.   His own inclinations eventually led him to show a few sketches to Mark Lemon, then editor of *Punch*.   This was in 1867, and from that date Sambourne became a regular contributor to the great comic journal, though at first only in a very modest capacity, as befitted an amateur.   It was agreed that his style of drawing, acquired in his daily business, did not lend itself to the representation of modern life—the artist himself recognized this—and instead of attempting ' socials ' in the manner of Charles Keene or du Maurier, he struck out on a path of his own.   In the beginning he merely invented initial letters, which he submitted to the editor, and those that were accepted he re-drew on wood: his first large drawings are the half-page headpiece and tailpiece to the preface of volume fifty-three.

But Sambourne's technique developed rapidly—became infinitely more flexible and expressive.   He himself said that he formed his style on that of Albert Dürer—deliberately making it as simple as possible however; giving the engraver little or no cross-hatching to do, and relying for effects on single lines of varying thickness.   The beauty he achieved was largely a beauty of decoration and silhouette, but he learned to draw the human body with a wonderful purity of line and grace of modelling.   Up till the end of 1888 all his drawings were made direct on the wood and were therefore destroyed in the cutting, but after that he drew for ' process ', modifying his style and, incidentally, losing much of his quality.   In the ' process ' drawings the gradation of tone tends to disappear, the figures lose their solidity, while he sacrifices the fine rich blacks that were so beautifully effective in his earlier designs.   But nothing can deprive him of his inventiveness: in imaginative grotesque he is without a rival.   Sambourne revelled in quaint ornament; he was the Cosimo Tura of the sixties; during his best period those marvellous initial letters that go twirling and twining over three-quarters of a page, with their innumerable birds and beasts, boys and girls, sprites and gnomes, reveal a fantastic genius that makes his *Punch* drawings unique.

[238]

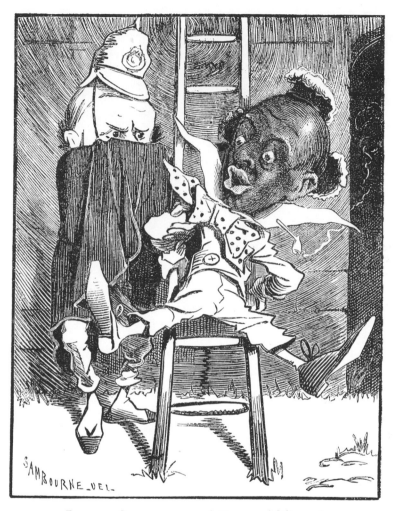

LINLEY SAMBOURNE: ' One-and-Three '

[*Punch*, 1874]

He drew principally from photographs. Of these he had a collection of over ten thousand—mostly taken by himself—all carefully classified, labelled, and arranged in cabinets. He had photographs of birds, beasts, and insects, photographs of human beings, draped and nude—human beings of all ages and professions, of all sorts and conditions, from little boys to bishops. He was particularly interested in costumes and uniforms, and very careful to get them right: when he drew Gladstone as the Duke of Wellington he borrowed the clothes Wellington had actually worn.

Sambourne drew animals with a delightful truth and humour, and could draw them so that they became human without losing their individuality. In 1877 he has a picture of an Irish monkey (its nationality is obvious) trying to pull away the flag upon which a bulldog lies. It is, of course, a political allegory—with the Home Rule Bill sticking out of the monkey's pocket—but what matters is not the allegory, it is the superb drawing of the bulldog, a portrait absolutely living in its power and truth and beauty. He was particularly good at bulldogs: there is a vignette on page 5 of *The Water Babies* presenting a family group of them that is unsurpassable.

More than he found anybody else, Sambourne seems to have found Disraeli suitable for animal caricature. Sometimes, as in the racehorse of 1878, the alteration of feature has been so slight that it is only at a second glance one sees there has been any alteration at all. With Gladstone he was not so successful, the metamorphoses are less subtle; but he has drawn Disraeli as a camel, as a bat, as a kangaroo, as a blackbird, as a seagull, as a cock, as a tortoise, as a fox—this last a masterpiece in its beautiful realization of the texture of the fur.

The humour of these animal drawings is charming, and never perhaps is it happier than in the 'evolutionary procession' of 1881, with its absurd likeness between all the impudent intermediate types and Mr. Charles Darwin, who sits rapt in meditation in their midst.

If Mr. Punch hampered some of his artists, to Sambourne he gave exactly the opportunity he required. In no other paper would he have found so free a field to express his inventiveness and love of the fantastic. He has a few drawings elsewhere—in *London Society*, *The Graphic*, *The Sketch* (for which he designed the cover), but all his most powerful and beautiful designs were given to *Punch*, not excepting even the book illustrations.

It may be said that Sambourne's work has really no more claim to be considered here than that of Randolph Caldecott and several other artists whom I have omitted as belonging to a later period; and indeed we just manage to squeeze him in on account of the first *Punch* drawings, and one in the Christmas Number of *London Society* (1868). He reappears in this magazine (now past its prime) in vols. xvii, xix, xx (the unindexed ' King Toby ' on page 489), xxi, xxii, and xxiv, which brings us as far as the Christmas of 1873.

The majority of Sambourne's book illustrations were made for works by F. C. Burnand, but though the first volume of the Collected Edition of Burnand's *Punch* writings was not published till 1890, both drawings and writings had originally appeared a great deal earlier. This first Burnand volume is entitled *Very Much Abroad* (Bradbury, Agnew, 1890), and is a handsomely printed and produced book. In it Sambourne's illustrations are confined to *The Boompje Papers*. *Rather at Sea* (1890) and *Quite at Home* (1890) contain perhaps a greater number of his drawings, and in the *Happy Thoughts* volume, though *Happy Thoughts* itself is cleverly illustrated in silhouette by Harry Furniss, he supplies practically all the drawings for its sequel. His best work, however, is in the fifth and last volume, *Some Old Friends* (1892). Here we have the matchless illustrations for Burnand's burlesque novels—parodies of Ouida, Anthony Trollope, and Victor Hugo. The parodies are good, but they are not so good as Sambourne's designs. All the early Ouida is in the portrait of Strapmore on page 20. Things like this, or the drawing of the coachman and the little groom on page 14, are in the very first rank of comic design.

The New History of Sandford and Merton, by F. C. Burnand, with a cover design and seventy-six illustrations by Linley Sambourne (Bradbury, Evans, 1872), represents the artist's most sustained achievement in book illustration. Unlike those for the works just mentioned, the drawings here appear for the first time. Among illustrated books, it seems to me that *The New Sandford and Merton* ranks with Tenniel's *Alices*. The artist in both cases has found a text that suits him as perfectly as if he had invented it, and in both cases he has risen to his opportunity. Tenniel, of course, was the more fortunate, in that he was illustrating a tale destined to become a classic; nevertheless, the adventures of the sanctimonious Mr. Barlow with the odiously knowing little Harry Sandford and the ingenuous and much abused Tommy Merton are irresistibly funny, while the drawings for the mock-edifying tales and poems with which the tutor improves the minds and morals of his pupils are in the finest spirit of farcical grotesque. To the same year belong the unimportant illustrations for E. D. Fenton's *Military Men I Have Met*.

Our Autumn Holiday on French Rivers, by J. L. Molloy (1874), contains a capital title page and a large number of sketches. *Our Holiday in the Scottish Highlands*, by Arthur A'Beckett (1876), is less interesting, because there are fewer figure pieces, the illustrations consisting chiefly of landscapes drawn in charcoal and reproduced by photo-lithography. To these may be

LINLEY SAMBOURNE: 'The Dragon-fly'
[*The Water Babies*]

added, out of its place, *Venice, from Lord Byron's Childe Harold* (1878), a huge unwieldy folio published at five guineas and containing thirty-one landscapes, the majority printed on a bilious yellow, or equally bilious green paper. The drawings themselves—with one or two exceptions, such as 'Moonlight on the Grand Canal'—are merely accurate and dull, and since the paper they are printed on is of a quite incredible ugliness this most expensive experiment must be regarded as a failure. It is strange how in these charcoal drawings Sambourne seems to lose all his quality, and even his identity: it is still stranger how he could have tolerated, much less chosen, those impossible greens and yellows. The whole book is a mystery that is better forgotten.

The Modern Arabian Nights, by Arthur A'Beckett and Linley Sambourne (Bradbury, Agnew [1877]), was issued in four parts, with some of the plates coloured by hand. For the edition de luxe of *Thackeray's Works*, vol. xiii, 1879, Sambourne supplied two or three illustrations to *The English Humourists*. To 1880 belong *A Caricature by E. Linley Sambourne of W. E. Gladstone on the Occasion of the Parliamentary Election for Mid Lothian*, 1880, and *The Royal Umbrella*, a children's book, containing four illustrations. In the following year he made a superb drawing of 'The Raven', which appears as a frontispiece to Andrew Lang's edition of *Poe's Poems* (Kegan Paul, 1881). *Society Novelettes* (1883) contains a few unimportant illustrations by Sambourne for *Kites and Pigeons* and *The Rose without a Thorn*, but these had appeared previously in *London Society*. *The Water Babies* (1885) contains a hundred illustrations, and this book we may set beside *The New Sandford and Merton*, or perhaps just a little below it, because, though many of them are of his best, there are some failures among *The Water Babies* drawings. *Buz*, by Maurice Noel [1885], contains a frontispiece by Sambourne, and possibly the headpiece on page 35 is his. *Friends and Foes from Fairy Land*, with a cover design and 'numerous illustrations' by Linley Sambourne (1886), proves disappointing, largely because the illustrations are *not* numerous, or at any rate not nearly numerous enough for a book of this size. For Mr. Anstey's *Burglar Bill* [1888] Sambourne designed the paper wrapper, which is reprinted as an illustration, in addition to the *Punch* illustrations now first collected, in an enlarged edition published under the title of *Mr. Punch's Young Reciter*. *The Green above the Red*, by C. L. Graves (1889), contains two full-page political cartoons and a cover design by Sambourne, and he has two or three *Punch* drawings in Mr. Anstey's delightful *Model Music-Hall Songs and Dramas* (1892), though most of the illustrations in this volume are by E. T. Reed. F. C. Burnand's *The Real Adventures of Robinson Crusoe* (Bradbury, Agnew, 1893) has fifty-six illustrations in the broadly farcical vein of the *Sandford and Merton* drawings, but their technique, which is that of the later Sambourne, makes them much less pleasing than the earlier designs.

Like Phil May, it is possible that Sambourne made a few drawings for advertisements. At all events, in the Victoria and Albert Museum I came across the proof of one such drawing—and a good one—' The Last Drop ', advertising somebody's Lime Juice Cordial. Several of the proofs in this collection are particularly interesting, because of the marginal instructions to the engraver. One such admonition I have copied: the drawing is a ' Girton Girl ', for *Punch,* and on the margin Sambourne has written, 'Damn it, you've put a white space outside the figure after all I said before. I'm sick of it.'

CHAPTER XIV

THE RANK AND FILE: WITH SOME NEW RECRUITS

HARRISON WEIR, GEORGE THOMAS, F. R. PICKERSGILL,
T. D. DALZIEL, EDWARD DALZIEL, E.V.B., NOEL PATON,
H. S. MARKS, J. MAHONEY, R. BARNES, CHARLES GREEN,
M.E.E., PAUL GRAY, BASIL BRADLEY, MARCUS STONE,
F. A. FRASER, F. W. LAWSON, CECIL LAWSON, E. G. DALZIEL,
J. D. LINTON, H. HERKOMER, ARTHUR HOPKINS, FRANK
DICKSEE

1. HARRISON WEIR (1824-1906)

QUITE a number of illustrators remain to be mentioned, as well as several new recruits who, like Linley Sambourne, come in just at the tail end of our period, or—in the case of the last two—do not come in at all. To none of these can I afford to give much space, though the collector, following his own choice, may perhaps rank one or two of them higher than several whose work has been chronicled more fully. Others again—such as C. H. Bennett, Townley Green, J. Wolf, Edward Hughes, Gordon Thomson, R. B. Wallace, E. F. Brewtnall—must be omitted altogether.

Among the earliest of those to be treated in so summary a fashion are Harrison Weir, George Thomas, and F. R. Pickersgill. Weir, at his best, is the finest black and white artist of the three. He is known principally, if not entirely, as a drawer of animals, and these frequently beautiful drawings do in fact form much his most important work; nevertheless, to the earlier books of the period he contributed several landscapes which have a genuine distinction. In the Catalogue of the British Museum the list of books associated with Harrison Weir's name fills no less than five columns, though of course a lot of these books contain only reprints. He has many drawings in *The Illustrated London News* during the fifties and later, and some particularly good ones in *The British Workman* and *The Band of Hope Review.*

II. GEORGE THOMAS (1824-1868)

George Thomas crowded a great many activities into his short life of forty-five years, working in England, in Paris, in New York, and then again in London, and always successfully. For a time he devoted his attention to the engraving of banknotes, and we find him in 1848 undertaking a special expedition to Italy, while in 1854 a drawing in *The Illustrated London News* led Queen Victoria to employ him to paint a series of pictures depicting the principal events of her reign—a rather chilling commission, but one which would not daunt Thomas. His illustrations are numerous, and were made chiefly for such well-tried favourites as *Robinson Crusoe*, *The Pilgrim's Progress*, *The Vicar of Wakefield*, etc.—books of which every publisher wanted his own illustrated edition.

Two more important efforts were the twenty designs for Wilkie Collins's *Armadale* (1866) and the thirty-two for Trollope's *Last Chronicle of Barset* (1867). The former tale had appeared first serially in *The Cornhill Magazine*, the latter in thirty-two sixpenny parts. These illustrations are conscientious work, by no means devoid of merit, though they rarely attain beauty, and are not free from a certain coarseness of touch. According to the Dalziels, Thomas was one of the first, if not indeed the very first, to draw direct from life on to the wood. The most charming drawing by him that I recollect appeared in the Christmas Number of *London Society* (1866). This is a picture of a little girl playing the fiddle, and has a delicacy and distinction he rarely achieved.

III. F. R. PICKERSGILL (1820-1900)

Pickersgill, like Harrison Weir, is to be found not only in the earliest books of the sixties, but in those of the fifties also, where his drawings reveal a greater breadth of handling than was common at that time. They lack variety, but their silvery greys and delicately pencilled effect are often very pleasing. The Dalziels, who thought highly of Pickersgill's work, placed their first venture in his hands, an *Illustrated Life of Christ*, to be published in parts at a shilling each, and each part to contain six large engravings printed in a flat tint. The experiment failed, and only two parts ever appeared. Some proofs, however, of what I take to be the designs for this *Life of Christ* will be found in the Dalziel collection in the British Museum. Subjects that I noted are ' The Wise Men's Offering ', ' Christ Blessing the Children ', ' The Woman Taken in Adultery ', ' Mary Anointing the Feet of Christ ', ' The Entry into Jerusalem ', and ' The Entombment '. These pulls belong to 1850, but no particulars are given. The designs are very

T. DALZIEL: 'The Genie Brings the Hatchet and Cord'

[*Dalziel's Arabian Nights*]

much akin to those he made for *The Lord's Prayer*, a large thin quarto published by Longmans in 1870, but probably commissioned earlier. The engravings in *The Lord's Prayer* are printed on a yellowish paper, and like these for *The Life of Christ* seem strangely static and two-dimensional. Their chief merit, perhaps, is that they express a sincere religious feeling. But Pickersgill's work is always that of an artist, never the careless journalism which some more brilliant draughtsmen were content to produce.

IV. THOMAS DALZIEL (1823-1906)

In 1839 the celebrated firm of Dalziel Brothers was founded by George and Edward Dalziel. In 1852 they were joined by John Dalziel, and in 1860 by a fourth brother, Thomas. Both Thomas and Edward were accomplished draughtsmen, the former, especially, making many original designs. By far the greater number of these were illustrations for books, although he contributed occasionally to *The Churchman's Family Magazine*, *The Sunday Magazine*, *Good Words*, and *Good Words for the Young*. In 1857 he has ten little drawings in Barry Cornwall's *Dramatic Scenes*, all more or less influenced by John Gilbert, and in the same year he contributed some designs to *Bryant's Poems*, and to Willmott's *Poets of the Nineteenth Century*. His best thing in this last work is the delicate little vignette, ' Taste ', on page 39, a marvel of minute workmanship. For *Gertrude of Wyoming* (also 1857) he made nineteen drawings, mostly of figures however, and his figure pieces are usually less interesting than his landscapes. In 1858 he contributed to *Home Affections*, and supplied to *Lays of the Holy Land* a series of landscapes which he never surpassed. Apart from their excellence as designs, such things as ' Akeldama ' and ' The Wailing Place of the Jews ' are masterpieces of engraving and printing—on this account alone being worthy of study. An edition of *The Pilgrim's Progress*, with a hundred illustrations by Thomas Dalziel, belongs to 1863. In *The Golden Harp* we get a further series of admirable vignettes; and in *Dalziel's Arabian Nights* a large number of figure pieces, in which he has shaken off the cramping influence of the school of Harvey and Gilbert. In Warne's edition of *The Arabian Nights* he collaborates with Houghton, and in *A Round of Days* we find him once more turning to landscape with marked success, even though he has here such an artist as J. W. North to compete with. In Buchanan's *Ballad Stories*, among others, he has a really charming design for *The Children in the Moon*. I shall not particularize further drawings, with the exception of the ' Seven Times Seven ' in *Jean Ingelow's Poems*, which, as a rendering of moonlight on rock and sea and cloud, could hardly be bettered. It is a beautiful thing, full of atmosphere, and achieving in a half-page drawing an effect of vastness, loneliness, and mystery.

Besides those alluded to, Thomas Dalziel helped to illustrate the following books: *Golden Thoughts from Golden Fountains, The Spirit of Praise, North Coast,* Novello's *National Nursery Rhymes,* and the same publisher's *Christmas Carols.* In *Dalziel's Bible Gallery* he has fourteen designs, of which the most remarkable are two for *The Deluge* and two for *The Destruction of Sodom.* In these he gets striking atmospheric effects of light and darkness, cloud, water, and mist. He has three further drawings in *Art Pictures from the Old Testament.*

I have mentioned only a tithe of the books for which T. Dalziel made illustrations. On my list are some forty others, unimportant children's tales for the most part—*Susan and Her Doll, Little Paul,* etc.—each illustrated with three or four pictures, competently executed, but belonging nevertheless to what one might call high-class journeyman work, so that a fuller catalogue seems unnecessary.

v.　edward dalziel (1817-1905)

Edward Dalziel was a much less prolific artist than Thomas. He made few if any designs for periodicals, and, though he contributed to a fair number of books, his contributions were as a rule limited to a drawing or two, and not all of these were signed. He was by no means a great draughtsman, yet some of his drawings, especially his drawings of children, have a charm which the more conventional figure work of his brother lacks. Rarely is anything he does, I dare say, quite so accomplished as Thomas's best work in landscape, but both had the great advantage of knowing exactly what the craft of the engraver could and could not reproduce. To the uninitiated it would seem as if many of Thomas Dalziel's landscapes would be almost impossible to cut, yet that the difficulties were always those which either his own hand or that of another could surmount the prints themselves are there to prove.

With more practice Edward would, I think, have been the best of the three Dalziels. Even as it is, he is the most interesting. He contributed several illustrations to *Bryant's Poems,* among them a pleasing design for ' The Battlefield ', which, in spite of its title, is a pastoral drawing of two little girls and a shepherd boy decking a sturdy young lamb with a necklace of cowslips. Its Wordsworthian naturalism, and its sentiment, so charmingly free from mawkishness, mark it as emphatically of our period: if it betrays any artistic influence it is that of such things as Mulready's ' Sleeping Child '.

EDWARD DALZIEL: 'The Battle-Field'
[*Bryant's Poems*]

'The Evening Song', which he gives to Barry Cornwall's *Dramatic Scenes*, is not nearly so good, but the 'Threnody' in *Home Affections*, another drawing of children, is delightful. The two designs he made for *Poets of the Nineteenth Century* are modestly attributed in the index to D. Edwards, and are not particularly striking; some drawings, however, in *Dalziel's Arabian Nights* are well worthy of their place in that work; and in *A Round of Days* he has two lovely vignettes for *The Silent Pool*, and a third, less pleasing design. His drawings in *The Spirit of Praise* may be passed over; but one of those in *Golden Thoughts from Golden Fountains*—'What Though My Bed be now My Grave?'—which shows an old Jew praying, with the lamplight shining on his face, is really effective in its simplicity. His work in *Jean Ingelow's Poems* is also of his best; the landscape on page 56, with its long row of dark slender poplars by the water's edge, is excellent, and excellent too that so different scene on page 63, a thing filled with summer sunlight. Further drawings, all up to his average, will be found in Buchanan's *Ballad Stories* and *North Coast*, and in *National Nursery Rhymes*.

VI. E.V.B. (THE HON. MRS. RICHARD BOYLE)

If I mention here the work of E.V.B., it is not with the purpose of denying its slightness and amateurishness, but because, at its best, it possesses a naïve charm which has a distinct value of its own. Such drawings as the frontispiece to the one-volume edition of Richard Jefferies's *Wood Magic*, and several of the designs for *The Magic Valley* (Macmillan, 1877), are really lovely things in their own unpretentious fashion. The coloured illustrations, of which there are many, are far less pleasing, and seem crude in the extreme when compared with the colour prints of Kate Greenaway or Randolph Caldecott. In addition to the books named, one might mention *Child's Play* [1852]; *A Child's Summer* (1853), with the drawings—charming things—etched on steel; *The May Queen* (1861); *Favourite English Poems* (1859); *Waifs and Strays* (second edition, 1862). The very delicate drawings in this last book are dated from 1859 to 1861: it is really only a sketch-book, but it contains a most interesting and varied collection. *The Story Without an End* (1868) is in colour, and so are Andersen's *Danish Fairy Legends* (1872) and *Beauty and the Beast* [1875], though the latter has some pleasant little drawings in black and white as well. In *A Dream Book* (1870) the drawings are reproduced in phototype; in *The New Child's Play* (1877)—one of the most delightful of all E.V.B.'s books—they are reproduced by 'heliotype' process.

[253]

Noel Paton, from whose correct and careful designs I have never been able to derive much pleasure, contributed hardly at all to the magazines, but his illustrations for Aytoun's *Lays of the Scottish Cavaliers* (Blackwood, 1863) have been much admired. In this year he supplied two or three drawings for Kingsley's *Water Babies*, which were reprinted till Linley Sambourne's designs supplanted them. Lewis Carroll—who unfortunately for himself 'missed' Sambourne, giving *Sylvie and Bruno* to Harry Furniss —had a great admiration for Paton's work. He considered his drawings of children to be more successful than those of any other artist (Walter Crane's he puts next!) and was most anxious that he should illustrate *Through the Looking Glass*. It is to Paton's credit that he refused the task, adding, ' Tenniel is the man '.

Further examples of Paton's work will be found in *Gems of Literature* (1866), the new and enlarged edition of *Puck on Pegasus*, and *The Princess of Silverland* (1874), to which he contributed a frontispiece. One should perhaps mention also, though such things are quite out of touch with the spirit of the sixties, his designs for Shelley's *Prometheus* (1844), *The Ancient Mariner* (1863), and *The Tempest* (1877).

VIII. H. STACY MARKS (1829-1898)

Stacy Marks was also an infrequent contributor to magazines. In *Once a Week* there are only two drawings by him, both extra illustrations, ' The Servants' Hall ' in vol. i of the New Series, and the charming ' Fetching the Doctor ' in vol. iv. In the first volume of *The Churchman's Family Magazine* (1863) he has a couple of less interesting designs, and he has three (one in colour) in the Christmas Number of *London Society* (1870). Besides these he has a drawing in *The Quiver* (1873), and a few things here and there in *The Graphic* and *Punch*.

Among the books illustrated by him the earliest seems to be Thornbury's *Songs of Cavaliers and Roundheads* (1857), a very unattractive volume. *Lyra Germanica* (1861) contains four of his drawings; Willmott's *English Sacred Poetry* (1862) seven, much better. But his work is singularly uneven. The illustrations for *Half-Hours with Our Sacred Poets* [1863] are mediocre; *Two Centuries of Song* (1867), on the other hand, contains a capital design in his quasi-medieval manner. He has some crudely coloured pictures in *Ridiculous Rhymes* [1869], and three headpieces in Novello's *National Nursery Rhymes* [1870]. The illustrations for Dickens's *Child's History of England* (1873) are again good, while Stuart's *The Good Old Days* (1876) is another coloured and unimportant book.

Of the designs alluded to by Walter Crane I have no note, unless they belong to *Nursery Rhymes* and *Nursery Songs*, which are the titles of two toy books issued by Routledge in 1866. It is possible, therefore, that the *Ridiculous Rhymes* of 1869 may be a reprint of these: not having seen the early toy books I cannot tell.

IX.   J. MAHONEY

Since his name does not appear in dictionaries and books of reference, a confusion is liable to arise between Mahoney the illustrator, and a slightly earlier Irish artist of the same name.   From Mr. Harold Hartley, who had them from Edward Whymper, I learn a few facts concerning *our* man. Mahoney, it appears, was practically uneducated, and indeed had received little early training of any kind.   He began work as an errand boy in the employment of Vincent, Son and Brooks, a firm of lithographic printers, one of his duties being to carry proofs to and from Whymper's office. While waiting, he would scribble drawings on the blotting-pad, but nobody thought anything of this till Whymper himself happened to catch him at it. Struck by something in the drawing, he asked the boy where he had been taught, and was told he had taught himself.   He was also told that Vincent, Son and Brooks did not approve of his efforts, and had even gone to the length of insisting that his pockets should be sewn up so that he could not carry a pencil.   Whymper offered him a pound a week if he would give up his job of errand boy and come to them to learn drawing, and at a month's end he had made so much progress that they were able to place small and unimportant illustrations in his hands.

Such a beginning seems promising, but unfortunately this is the brightest period in Mahoney's troubled career.   Though he was soon earning plenty of money, he developed at the same time habits that faced the Whympers with a second problem—namely, how to get rid of him.   The Dalziels, too, found him impossible.   It was not only that he was usually drunk, but that he was singularly unpleasant when he *was* drunk—quarrelsome, aggressive, reckless.   One day, in the Dalziels' office, he assaulted an inoffensive person who, in addressing him, had stressed the second syllable of his name, a peculiarity to which the English are prone, but which Mahoney would only tolerate when accompanied by a commission for drawings.   And such incidents were frequent.   His life seems to have been a passionate and disreputable one, haunted no doubt by visions of an utterly different kind, but of which we can know nothing.   It ended sordidly in a public latrine.

His work is as wayward as his life, and probably reflects its violent reactions.   The most distinguished design he ever produced, I think, is

'The Doctor's Boy', a very beautiful and sympathetic drawing which, printed in tints rather than colours, appeared in *The Sunday at Home* (1866). This drawing is first rate, and it is impossible to compare it with the bulk of Mahoney's work without feeling conscious of the waste of a genuine gift. He made a few beautiful drawings, a good many average drawings, and, alas! principally for *Judy*, a great many so crude and clumsy that we might take them for the work of an untrained amateur devoid not only of talent, but of taste. A dreadful suspicion is aroused that bad drawing and debased faces were regarded by Mahoney as amusing, and that a sense of ugliness indeed represents his entire equipment as a comic draughtsman. But perhaps one should ignore these pictures, evidently designed to appeal to an unintelligent public.

Mahoney drew more for periodicals than for books. He has a host of things in *The Leisure Hour*, and a good many in *The People's Magazine*, these latter belonging chiefly to 1867. In *The People's Magazine*, on page 169 of the volume for 1867, appeared one of his most spirited designs, 'The Battle of Hohenlinden'. He is also represented in *The Day of Rest*, *Cassell's Magazine*, *The Argosy*, *The Quiver*, and *Fun*; but most of his best work was given to *The Sunday Magazine* and *Good Words*. In the former, among other things, he illustrated the serial, *Occupations of a Retired Life* (1867), and in the latter another serial, *At His Gates* (1872). He also made some excellent drawings for *Good Words for the Young*, and we even find him, in the seventies, contributing to *Little Folks*.

Those who desire to look up his book illustrations may be referred to a charming frontispiece and vignette made for a one-volume edition of Trollope's *Three Clerks* (Bentley), to *Cassell's Illustrated Readings*, *The Nobility of Life*, Whymper's *Scrambles amongst the Alps*, *National Nursery Rhymes*, Jean Ingelow's *Little Wonder-Horn* (1872), and, in the 'Household' Dickens, *Oliver Twist* (1871), *Little Dorrit*, and *Our Mutual Friend*. A curious tendency to dwarf his figures is carried, one might fancy, into the very shape of many of Mahoney's designs, and into the square squat monogram with which they are signed.

X.   ROBERT BARNES

If ever human beings sprang straight from English soil they are the men and women, the boys and girls, drawn by Robert Barnes. But these men and women and boys and girls are so limited in type that they might nearly all be members of a single family—a family of the well-to-do farming class, healthy, sturdy, producing no disquieting variations from the sound yeoman stock that has reached back from generation to generation. Barnes

J. MAHONEY: 'Occupations of a Retired Life'
[*Sunday Magazine*, 1868]

would have been the right man to illustrate George Eliot's earlier novels; he would have been the wrong man to illustrate the novels of Mr. Hardy. As it is, we find him supplying capital drawings for the semi-bucolic serials in *Good Words* and *The Sunday Magazine—Alfred Haggart's Household, Annals of a Quiet Neighbourhood, Kate the Grandmother.* Once only do we see him faced with the problem of dramatic creation, and that is when the editor of *The Cornhill Magazine* placed the illustration of a novel by Charles Reade in his hands. He acquitted himself of the task well. The illustrations for *Put Yourself in His Place*, a labour problem novel (*Cornhill*, 1869), are good. Still, it is in such family groups, such domestic scenes, as 'The Children's Good-Night' (*Quiver*, 1871) that we get the essential Barnes. He contributed to all the important magazines of the period, and to one or two that might appear not at all important[1]—*The British Workman*, for example, and *The Band of Hope Review*, the unusually large size of the engravings in these particular journals lending them an interesting novelty. The drawings of Barnes are bold, strong, and very much alive, but here as elsewhere they exhibit the narrow limitations of his subject matter.

His book illustrations show him in no new light; there is the same absence of imagination, the same preference for a somewhat bovine type of beauty. Barnes must have been particularly fond of boys and girls, he draws so many of them; but, one and all, they are the most unmitigated little animals conceivable. They have never had a day's illness in their lives, but neither will they ever be moved by any spiritual or intellectual enthusiasm. Barnes made many drawings for such books as *Little Lays for Little Folks* and Watts's *Divine and Moral Songs* (the Sampson Low edition), some of his vignettes in these works being extremely dainty, and all the drawings admirably fresh and natural. He also illustrated several of Partridge and Co.'s 'juveniles'—pious tales of an indescribable dreariness, the young heroes of which are as untrue to nature as his portraits of them are true. *Sybil and Her Live Snowball* (1866) and *Jack the Conqueror* [1868], each containing twelve full-page designs by him, are typical. Most important of all, however, and a book the collector really cannot ignore, is *Pictures of English Life* (Sampson Low, 1865). This thin folio consists of ten large wood engravings, eight of which are by Barnes, while the remaining two are by E. M. Wimperis. Barnes's subjects, as usual, are drawn from English working-class and rural life, and are treated, as usual, in an idyllic spirit. That is to say, they set forth all the joys that may be conceived to arise from the possession of a growing family of remarkably well-fed youngsters, each perfectly qualified to secure a prize at any agricultural show which should

[1] There are some particularly good Barneses in *Golden Hours* for 1868.

include the human species among its exhibits. It is Barnes's conception of the idyllic, and to realize it one had at least to be able to draw.

I append a list of other books illustrated either wholly or in part by him. *Romantic Passages in English History* [1863]. Marriott, the engraver, may be given all the credit for the illustrations in this volume, since there is not a trace of Barnes, nor indeed of anybody else, in them. Barbauld's *Hymns in Prose* (1864); *The Months* [1864]; *Our Life* [1865]; *Studies for Stories* (1866); Foxe's *Book of Martyrs* (1866); *Christian Lyrics* (1868); *Original Poems* (1868); Gray's *Elegy* (1868), in colour; Cowper's *Table Talk* [1868]—an uninteresting volume, illustrated by Barnes and Tenniel, but one at least of the Tenniels is a cliché from *The Mirage of Life*, and the best thing in the book is Barnes's drawing on page 155 of a fight between two schoolboys; *Prince Ubbely Bubble* [1870]—hardly worth mentioning, as it contains only one Barnes and that not a good one; *Pictures from English Literature* [1870]; *Ben's Boyhood* [1873]; *Thoughtful Joe* [1880]; *In Prison and Out* (1880); *Children of the Village* (1880).

XI. CHARLES GREEN (1840-1898)

Had Charles Green given us many such designs as his ' Christmas Eve ' in *Cassell's Christmas Annual* (1865), or his ' Amateur Performance ' in *The Graphic* (1871), we should feel inclined to place him among the greater illustrators of the sixties, for such work falls little below the best. But these are exceptional things, though at the same time it is but fair to remember that—until he began to draw for *The Graphic*, where his work is nearly always excellent—Green was not fortunate in the commissions he received. In spite of wretched paper and indifferent engraving and printing, enough remains to show us how good the drawings he made for *Anne Judge, Spinster* (*Cassell's Magazine*, 1867) must have been; and the drawing of ' Dick Dowlas ', in *Pictures from English Literature*, is among the best that book contains. A novel such as *Barry Lyndon* would have suited him to perfection (he is very successful with his Irish types), but, instead, we have to look for him in works like *English Sacred Poetry of the Olden Time*, Cumming's *Life and Lessons of Our Lord*, Watts's *Divine and Moral Songs* (Nisbet), *The Book of Martyrs*, *The Pleasures of Memory*, *The Nobility of Life*. It is true, he does not always make the most of a chance when he gets one. His illustrations for Mark Lemon's *Tinykins' Transformation* (1869), in which he has a free hand and the advantage of good paper and printing, might have been better; and the illustrations for *The Old Curiosity Shop* in the Household Edition of Dickens also prove disappointing, even after we have made allowance for the fact that their setting,

R. Barnes: 'Alfred Hagart's Household'

[*Good Words*, 1865]

[Showing the Artist's instructions to the Engraver]

CHARLES GREEN: 'Thinking and Wishing'

[*The Churchman's Family Magazine*, 1864]

in the middle of a large page printed in double columns, is far from ideal. Other books in which his work will be found are Craik's *Playroom Stories* (1863)—in colour; Tillotson's *Our Untitled Nobility* [1863]; *Cassell's Illustrated Readings*; *Episodes of Fiction* (1870), and a small paper-covered book by Burnand and A'Beckett, *The Doom of St. Querec* [1875], beyond which date we need not follow him.

XII.   M. E. E(DWARDS)

M. Ellen Edwards, better known as M.E.E., would occupy a higher position among our illustrators had she not repeated herself so monotonously. But whether she is picturing one of the lugubrious scenes in Foxe's *Book of Martyrs*, or a mildly sentimental scene from some innocent love tale, she gives us always precisely the same pretty maiden.   Yet she had, in her own small way, a genuine talent, and her work in the beginning was interesting.   I should think the drawings in *The Churchman's Family Magazine* for 1863 must be the very earliest she published, and there is little or nothing in the later drawings that cannot be found in these first efforts: the type she was never to abandon is already completely realized, and the grace—that was later to become mannered and mechanical—is there too.   Certainly, by the time we reach the attractive drawings for *Ruth Thornbury* (*Good Words*, 1866) her style is entirely mature.   She never surpassed these drawings; indeed, rarely again equalled them.   In the same year we find her illustrating Miss Braddon's *Birds of Prey* in *Belgravia*, but here the designs, possibly because they have not had the advantage of Swain's engraving, are distinctly inferior in charm.   The illustrations for *The Claverings* in the *Cornhill* (1866-1867) again show her at her best, and she followed up these in succeeding years and in the same magazine with illustrations for *The Bramleighs of Bishop's Folly* and *That Boy of Norcott's*—all maintaining, but none I think adding to, her reputation.   From this on, her work decreases in interest—not because it ceases to exhibit the qualities that made it so popular, but because the constant repetition of a single note inevitably begins to pall, and in the end produces an effect of weakness.   M.E.E. contributed to many of the illustrated books of the day.   Among those illustrated entirely by her may be mentioned *Family Fairy Tales* (1864); but her work appears throughout the sixties, seventies, and eighties in innumerable story-books and magazines for children, and in nearly all the magazines for older readers from *The Quiver* to *The Graphic*.

Though Paul Gray made a few delicate and charming drawings, I cannot help thinking their importance has been exaggerated. The work of this unfortunate youth, who died of consumption at the age of twenty, is really too immature for us to judge from it of what he might have become. Besides the illustrations for *Hereward the Wake*, which ran through *Good Words* during 1865, he produced a considerable number of designs, some of the best being remarkable for a boy of his age, but none, to my mind, proving that he had more in him than the makings of a thoroughly competent draughtsman. The majority of his designs are poor; only the 'Cousin Lucy' of *The Quiver* (1866) having a really outstanding distinction, and it we might take for a Morten. On the whole, the work of M.E.E. at the same age shows a more sustained level of accomplishment, and yet the talent of M.E.E., as we have seen, never developed. It is pleasant, at any rate, to find the artist receiving ample encouragement during his short career. We meet with him in several of the most important magazines; he was even tried for *Punch*, three of his drawings appearing in that paper in December 1864 and two more in the following January. He contributed a few designs to *Jingles and Jokes, A Round of Days, The Spirit of Praise*, and *The Savage Club Papers* (1867). His name appears on the title page of *Ghosts' Wives*, a shilling Christmas Annual published in 1867. Most of the illustrations in this very mediocre production are by Phiz and C. H. Ross, but ' Raymond ', ' You Only ', and ' Silencing a Spy ' are probably Paul Gray's. He has a drawing in the Chandos *Longfellow*, but the only books I have discovered that are illustrated entirely by him are *The Medwyns of Wykeham* (Routledge, 1867), which contains four drawings, the frontispiece being among his best things; and *Kenneth and Hugh*, by C. D. Bell (Warne, 1866), which contains five. Both these works were unknown to Gleeson White, a Paul Gray enthusiast, who tells us he has mentioned ' all Gray's illustrations which it has been possible to identify ' (he does not, as a matter of fact, mention the *Longfellow* either, or *Ghosts' Wives*; and there may well be others). One finds such things by chance, for the British Museum Catalogue is a poor guide to our period, the artists in most cases being ignored. Gray's name is not mentioned on the title page of *The Medwyns*, so that here neither the fullest cataloguing nor the study of contemporary advertisements would have helped us. It probably does not appear on the title page of *Kenneth and Hugh* either, the drawings for which I discovered among the Dalziel proofs in the Print Room of the Museum, though the book itself is not in the library.

M. E. Edwards: 'That Boy of Norcott's'

[*The Cornhill Magazine*, 1868]

XIV. BASIL BRADLEY (1842-1904)

Among our illustrators Basil Bradley has been unjustly ignored. He is not among the bigger men, of course, but his Sussex pastorals are in the true spirit of the sixties. Such things as ' Evening ' and ' Another Day's Work Done '—in *Once a Week* for 1866 and 1868—are refreshing in their simple naturalism, their suggestion of a kind of poetry of the soil. Cattle, horses, dogs, and sheep occupy so prominent a place in Bradley's landscapes that he might very nearly be classed among the animal artists, were it not that he did a lot of figure work as well. How admirably he could draw dogs will be seen in ' The Herdsman's Repose ' (*Once a Week*, 1866) and ' The Fox-hounds ' (*Once a Week*, 1868). His figure subjects are less striking. In spite of such a fine drawing as ' " What's here? " exclaimed Tabitha ', in *Cassell's Illustrated Readings*, illustrations for fiction were not in his line, and most of those he made have neither more nor less interest than the average pot-boiler of the average professional draughtsman.

XV. MARCUS STONE (1840-1921)

Marcus Stone contributed to *The Cornhill, Good Words*, and other magazines, but his principal achievements in illustration are the drawings for *Our Mutual Friend* (1865), and those (probably the best he ever made) for Trollope's *He Knew He was Right*, two vols. (Strahan, 1869). He made a few designs for other works by Dickens and Trollope—*American Notes and Pictures from Italy* (1862), *Great Expectations* (1863), and a frontispiece for *Tales of All Countries* (1864). His drawings for *The Sacristan's Household* (1869) appeared first in *St. Paul's Magazine*; he has an illustration in *Pictures from English Literature* [1870], and his six illustrations for Eastwood's *Calumny* [1877] are admirably reproduced by a ' New Typographic Process '.

XVI. F. A. FRASER AND F. W. LAWSON

With F. A. Fraser and F. W. Lawson, both prolific and popular illustrators whose work crops up at every turn, we reach the decadence. Occasionally they will surprise us by a really excellent design, but more frequently they do not surprise us—Fraser, in particular, as a rule being content to supply the journalism of art. In a single volume of *Good Words*, that for 1869, he has no fewer than seventy-five illustrations. One wonders what Rossetti, during the period of his interest in wood engraving, would have thought of this activity; but probably Rossetti would not have admitted that Fraser was an artist at all. As good examples of his work as any will be found in the illustrations for *The Vicar's Daughter* in *The Sunday Magazine* for 1872.

Wilfrid Lawson was a more careful artist. His illustrations for *Stone Edge*, *Avonhoe*, and *Lettice Lisle*, in *The Cornhill* for 1867, 1868, and 1869, are typical; and, in a different vein, several of the designs he made for Foxe's *Book of Martyrs* hold their own with anything else in that curious work.

XVII.   CECIL LAWSON (1849-1882)

Cecil Lawson, younger brother of F. W., but three years older than he is usually stated to be, had a gift for decorative landscape which he reveals in a number of pleasant designs that for the most part appeared in *The Quiver*, *Good Words*, and *The Sunday Magazine*. He has a good drawing, 'Spring', in *Dark Blue*, which is worth looking up, since his drawings are far from numerous.

XVIII.   E. G. DALZIEL (1849-1888)

E. G. Dalziel was the son of Edward. His work is associated with the sixties, but belongs really to the early seventies, and is inferior to that of both his father and uncle. One of his best if least characteristic designs, 'A Frosty Day', appeared in *Good Words* in 1871, and was reprinted with two or three others in *Picture Posies* (Routledge, 1874), a book containing a large collection of fine work, though it has not been described here, because its designs are not first impressions, having all appeared in earlier books and magazines.

As well as to *Good Words* E. G. Dalziel contributed to *Good Words for the Young*, *The Sunday Magazine*, *Fun* (a great many drawings), *Judy*, *The People's Magazine*, *The Day of Rest*, *The Graphic*, and possibly other periodicals. He helped to illustrate Novello's *National Nursery Rhymes* and the same publisher's *Christmas Carols*, and for the 'Household' Dickens he illustrated *The Uncommercial Traveller*, *Christmas Stories*, and *Reprinted Pieces*. But even more than F. A. Fraser and Wilfrid Lawson he represents the decadence, and his solitary design in *Dalziel's Bible Gallery*, 'The Five Kings Hiding in the Cave', shows how completely out of touch he was with the whole spirit of the sixties. He has half a dozen drawings in Fred Barnard's *Pilgrim's Progress*, where they are more in place.

XIX.   J. D. LINTON (1840-1916)

A far more powerful artist is **J. D. Linton**, whose work is chiefly associated with *The Graphic*. His designs contributed to the Barnard *Pilgrim's Progress* are, with William Small's, the best that book contains.

F. A. FRASER: 'Wilfrid Cumbermede'

[*Saint Paul's Magazine*, 1871]

XX. HUBERT HERKOMER (1849-1914)

Like Linton, Herkomer belongs less to the ending of the old school than the beginning of the new. His work is distinctly individual, though he has been influenced by Pinwell and Houghton. For his most powerful drawings we must turn to the pages of *The Graphic*, but excellent things are to be found in *The Quiver*, *The Sunday Magazine*, *Good Words*, *Good Words for the Young*, and *The Cornhill*, in the volumes belonging to the early seventies.

XXI. ARTHUR HOPKINS (1848-)

With that accomplished illustrator Arthur Hopkins, who was influenced by William Small and perhaps, in the beginning, slightly by du Maurier, the new generation has definitely arrived. Hopkins is a good draughtsman, with a strong dramatic sense, to which is added a sense of character, as his drawings for *The Prescotts of Pamphillon* (*Good Words*, 1873), and still more his drawings for *Whiteladies* (*Good Words*, 1875) and *The Atonement of Leam Dundas* (*Cornhill*, 1875) show. Besides contributing to our usual periodicals, he was one of the mainstays of Miss Braddon's magazine, *Belgravia*, in which he illustrated many serial novels, including James Payn's *By Proxy* (1877), Wilkie Collins's *Haunted Hotel* (1878), Hardy's *Return of the Native* (1878), Payn's *Confidential Agent* (1879), Charles Gibbon's *Queen of the Meadow* (1879), and Justin McCarthy's *Donna Quixote* (1879). And all these illustrations are competent, those for *The Return of the Native*, as was inevitable, being the least satisfying, missing the superbly poetic quality of that great novel.

XXII. FRANK DICKSEE (1853-)

With Hopkins I have overstepped the line where I had intended to break off, and I seize on this feeblest of excuses to mention one more name, or rather one more series of drawings, in *The Cornhill Magazine* of 1879. In that year we get the masterly designs Frank Dicksee made for Mrs. Oliphant's *Within the Precincts*—designs which would have held their own even in the great decade.

And here I close this chronicle. The last two sections have carried it well into the days of Randolph Caldecott and Kate Greenaway, artists who have little or nothing to do with the sixties, though Caldecott, as early as 1874, was illustrating one of the serials, *Lost for Love*, in *Belgravia*.

[269]

APPENDIX

A LIST OF FIRST EDITIONS OF BOOKS ILLUSTRATED BY ARTISTS OF THE SIXTIES

WHILE I have taken every care in compiling the following list, I should be surprised if it were free from errors. Where a book is undated I have given between square brackets the year in which it was issued; where the title page is dated, I have, of course, given that date, though often the book itself actually was issued in the October, November, or December of the previous year. But, quite apart from the ordinary dangers of transcription, in several instances I have been obliged to rely on the evidence of catalogues, etc., and I should be grateful to the reader if he would point out to me any mistake he may discover.

With a few exceptions, I have not included those books which made their first appearance in magazines. It is unlikely that the collector will want duplicates of the engravings, and the titles of the stories published serially will be found in the general index, their dates in the text.

Accidents of Childhood. Routledge. 1861. *J. D. Watson.*
Adèle. By Julia Kavanagh. 'Standard Library.' Hurst and Blackett. [1862.] *John Gilbert.*
Adventures of Alfan. By J. H. Burrow. Smith, Elder. 1863. *J. D. Watson.*
Aesop's Fables. Murray. 1848. *Tenniel.*
After Dark. By Wilkie Collins. Smith, Elder. 1862. *Houghton and Crane.*
Alice's Adventures in Wonderland. By Lewis Carroll. Macmillan. 1865. *Tenniel.*
    The first edition was printed in Oxford: all later editions by Richard Clay in London.
American Notes and Pictures from Italy. By Charles Dickens. 'Library Edition', vol. xvii. Chapman and Hall. 1862. *Marcus Stone.*
The Ancient Mariner. By Coleridge. Art Union of London. 1863. *Noel Paton.*
Andersen's Danish Fairy Legends. Sampson Low. 1872. *E.V.B.*
Arabian Nights (Dalziel's). Ward and Lock. 1865. 2 vols. *Houghton, etc.*
    First published in parts.
Arabian Nights. Warne. 1866. *Houghton and T. Dalziel.*
Armadale. By Wilkie Collins. Smith, Elder. 1866. 2 vols. *George Thomas.*
Art Pictures from the Old Testament. S.P.C.K. 1894. *Various Artists.*
As in a Looking Glass. By F. C. Phillips. Ward and Downey. 1889. *Du Maurier.*
At the Back of the North Wind. By George MacDonald. Strahan. 1871. *Arthur Hughes.*

Babies' Classics. Longmans. 1904. *Arthur Hughes.*
Balderscourt. By Rev. H. C. Adams. Routledge. 1866. *Houghton.*

Ballad Stories of the Affections. By Robert Buchanan. Routledge. [1866.] *Pinwell, Houghton, Small, etc.*

Ballads. By W. M. Thackeray. Smith, Elder. 1879. *Du Maurier, etc.*
    Also in the 'Works', vol. xxi.

Ballads and Songs of Brittany. By Tom Taylor. Macmillan. 1865. *Keene, Millais.*

Barbara's History. By Amelia B. Edwards. 'Standard Library.' Hurst and Blackett. [1864.] *J. D. Watson.*

Barry Lyndon. By W. M. Thackeray. Smith, Elder. 1879. *Millais.*

Beauties of English Landscape. By Birket Foster. Routledge. 1873.

Beauty and the Beast. Sampson Low. 1875. *E.V.B.*

Ben's Boyhood. By C. E. Bowen. Partridge. 1873. *R. Barnes.*

Bennett's Poems. Routledge. 1862. *J. D. Watson.*

The Black Poodle. By F. Anstey. Longmans. 1884. *Du Maurier.*

Book of British Ballads. Edited by S. C. Hall. Jeremiah How. 1842. *Tenniel, etc.*

Book of Drawing Room Plays. By H. Dalton. Hogg. [1861.] *Du Maurier.*

Book of German Songs. Translated by W. H. Dulcken. Ward and Lock. 1856. *Keene.*

The Boy Pilgrims. By Anne Bowman. Routledge. 1866. *Houghton.*

The Boy Tar. By Mayne Reid. Kent. 1860. *Keene.*

The Boys of Beechwood. By Mrs. Eiloart. Routledge. 1868. *Houghton.*

Broken to Harness. By Edmund Yates. Maxwell. 1865. *Crane.*

Bryant's Poems. New York : Appleton. 1857. *E. Dalziel, T. Dalziel, etc.*

Burglar Bill. By F. Anstey. Bradbury, Agnew. [1888.] *Sambourne.*

Buz. By Maurice Noel. Arrowsmith. [1885.] *Sambourne.*

By Order of the King. By Victor Hugo. Bradbury, Evans. 1870. 3 vols. *Luke Fildes.*

Calumny. By F. Eastwood. Blackwood. [1877.] *Marcus Stone.*
    First published in parts.

The Cambridge Grisette. By Herbert Vaughan. Tinsley. 1862. *Keene.*

A Caricature by E. Linley Sambourne of W. E. Gladstone on the Occasion of the Parliamentary Election for Mid Lothian 1880. Blackwood.

Cassell's History of England. 1867 ?. *Small, etc.*

Cassell's 'Illustrated Readings'. 1867. *Small, Basil Bradley, Watson, etc.*

Catalogue of a Collection of Drawings by the late Charles Keene exhibited at the Fine Art Society's Galleries. 1891.

Chamber Dramas. By Mrs. George MacDonald. Strahan. 1870. *Arthur Hughes.*

A Child's History of England. By Charles Dickens. Chapman and Hall. 1873. *Stacy Marks.*

Child's Play. By E.V.B. Addey and Co. [1852.]

A Child's Summer. By E.V.B. Addey and Co. 1853.

Childe Harold. Thirty Illustrations. Art-Union of London. 1855. *Tenniel, etc.*

Childhood Valley. Nister. [1889.] *J. Lawson.*

The Children of Blessing. Routledge. 1867. *J. Lawson.*

Children of the Village. By Miss Mitford. Routledge. 1880. *R. Barnes.*

The Children's Garland. Selected by Coventry Patmore. Macmillan. 1873. *J. Lawson.*

Children's Sayings. By C. Hadley. Smith, Elder. 1862. *Crane.*

Christian Lyrics. Sampson Low. 1868. *Houghton, etc.*

Christian's Mistake. By Miss Muloch. 'Standard Library.' Hurst and Blackett. [1866.] *Sandys.*

Christie Johnstone. By Charles Reade. Bradbury, Evans. 1868. *Small.*

Christmas Books. By Charles Dickens. Chapman and Hall. 1869. *Tenniel.*

Christmas Carols. Novello, Ewer. [1871.] *Hughes, etc.*

Christmas Stories. By Charles Dickens. 'Household Edition.' Chapman and Hall. (Published in parts from 1871 on.) *E. G. Dalziel.*

Citoyenne Jacqueline. By Sarah Tytler. Strahan. 1866 ?. *Houghton.*
> There are no illustrations in the original edition in 3 vols. The first one-volume edition was published by Strahan in 1866. This may contain the Houghton drawings, but I have not succeeded in finding a copy.

Clever Hans. De la Rue. [1883.] *J. Lawson.*

Eliza Cook's Poems. Routledge. 1861. *Armstead, Watson, etc.*

The Cornhill Gallery. Smith, Elder. 1864. *Leighton, Millais, Walker, etc.*

The Course of Time. By R. Pollok. Blackwood. 1857. *Tenniel, etc.*

Cousin Phillis. By Mrs. Gaskell. Smith, Elder. 1865. *Du Maurier.*

Cowper's Table Talk. Religious Tract Society. 1868. *R. Barnes, etc.*

Crane's Toy Books : printed by Edmund Evans and published by Routledge.
> Sing a Song of Sixpence. 1865.
> One, Two, Buckle My Shoe. 1867.
> Multiplication in Verse. 1867-1868.
> Annie and Jack in London. 1867-1868.
> The Fairy Ship. 1869.
> This Little Pig. 1869.
> The Adventures of Puffy. 1869.
> King Luckieboy's Party. 1870.
> Valentine and Orson. 1870.
> The House that Jack Built. 1870.
> Cock Robin. 1870.
> Dame Trot. 1870.
> All these dates doubtful. See chapter on Crane.

Cranford. By Mrs. Gaskell. Smith, Elder. 1864. *Du Maurier.*

The Brothers Dalziel. A Record of Fifty Years' Work. Methuen. 1901.

Dalziel's Bible Gallery. Routledge. 1881. *Various Artists.*

A Dark Night's Work. By Mrs. Gaskell. Smith, Elder. 1864. *Du Maurier.*

A Daughter of Heth. By William Black. Sampson Low. 1872. *Walker.*

The De Cliffords. By Mrs. Sherwood. Darton. 1847. *Keene.*

Dealings with the Fairies. By George MacDonald. Strahan. 1867. *Arthur Hughes.*

Dick Boldhero. By Peter Parley. Darton. 1842?. *Keene.*
> See note in chapter on Keene.

Divine and Moral Songs. By Isaac Watts. Nisbet. [1867.] *Du Maurier, Green, Morten, Watson, etc.*

Divine and Moral Songs. By Isaac Watts. Sampson Low. 1866. *Barnes, Small, etc.*

Don Quixote. Warne. 1866. *Houghton.*

The Doom of St. Querec. By F. C. Burnand and A. A'Beckett. Bradbury, Agnew. [1875.] *Charles Green.*

Double Marriage. By Charles Reade. Bradbury, Evans. 1868. *Keene.*

Dramas in Miniature. By Mathilde Blind. Chatto and Windus. 1891. *Ford Madox Brown.*

Dramatic Scenes. By Barry Cornwall. Chapman and Hall. 1857. *Tenniel, etc.*

A Dream Book. By E.V.B. Sampson Low. 1870.

The Early Start in Life. By E. Marryat Norris. Griffith and Farren. 1867. *J. Lawson.*

Egmont. Translated from Goethe by A. D. Coleridge. Chapman and Hall. 1868. *Millais.*

Eildon Manor : a tale for girls. Routledge. 1861. *J. D. Watson.*
Elegy written in a Country Churchyard. By Gray. Sampson Low. 1868. *R. Barnes.*
England's Antiphon. By George MacDonald. 'Sunday Library.' Macmillan. [1868.] *Arthur Hughes.*
           Originally published in 3 parts.
English Humourists. By Thackeray. 'Works, vol. xiii.' Smith, Elder. 1879. *Sambourne, Walker.*
English Illustration : 'The Sixties'. By Gleeson White. Constable. 1897.
English Rustic Pictures. By F. Walker and G. J. Pinwell. Routledge. [1882.]
English Sacred Poetry. Edited by Willmott. Routledge. 1862. *Armstead, Hunt, Keene, Sandys, etc.*
English Sacred Poetry of the Olden Time. Religious Tract Society. 1864. *Du Maurier, Green, Walker, Watson, etc.*
English Society at Home. By George du Maurier. Bradbury, Agnew. 1880.
Enoch Arden. By Tennyson. Moxon. 1866. *Arthur Hughes.*
Episodes of Fiction. Edinburgh : Nimmo. London : Simpkin. 1870. *Charles Green, etc.*
Ernie at School. By Mrs. Eiloart. Routledge. 1866. *Houghton.*
Ernie Elton, the Lazy Boy. By Mrs. Eiloart. Routledge. 1865. *Houghton.*
Esmond. By W. M. Thackeray. Smith, Elder. 1868. *Du Maurier.*
Exiles in Babylon. By A.L.O.E. Nelson. 1864. *Small.*
Eyebright, a tale from Fairy Land. Basingstoke : C. J. Jacob. 1862. *Keene.*

The Fairy Family. Longman. 1857. *Burne-Jones.*
Family Fairy Tales. Hotten. 1864. *M. E. Edwards.*
Favourite English Poems. Sampson Low. 1859. *Foster, Thomas, Weir, E.V.B., etc.*
           This book was frequently reprinted with alterations and additions. There are editions belonging to 1862, 1863, and 1870. The 1863 edition is in two volumes, that of 1870 contains a drawing by Keene.
Fielding's Works. Smith, Elder. 1882. *Small.*
The Fiery Cross. By Barbara Hutton. Griffith and Farren. 1875. *J. Lawson.*
Five Days' Entertainment at Wentworth Grange. By F. T. Palgrave. Macmillan. 1868. *Arthur Hughes.*
Flower of Christian Chivalry. By Mrs. W. R. Lloyd. Hogg. [1863.] *J. D. Watson.*
Flower Pieces. By William Allingham. Reeves and Turner. 1888. *Rossetti.*
The Four Georges. By Thackeray. 'Works, vol. xiii.' Smith, Elder. 1879. *Frank Dicksee.*
Foxe's Book of Martyrs. Cassell, Petter and Galpin. [1866.] *Houghton, du Maurier, Fildes, F. W. Lawson, Morten, Small, etc.*
           First published in parts from 1865 on.
Framley Parsonage. By Anthony Trollope. Smith, Elder. 1861. 3 vols. *Millais.*
Friends and Foes from Fairyland. By Lord Brabourne. Longmans. 1886. *Sambourne.*
The Frozen Deep. By Wilkie Collins. Chatto and Windus. 1875. *Du Maurier and Mahoney.*

Gems of Literature. Nimmo. 1866. *Noel Paton.*
Gertrude of Wyoming. By Campbell. Routledge. 1857. *Foster, T. Dalziel, Weir, etc.*
Ghosts' Wives. Dean. 1867. *Paul Gray, etc.*
The Giants of Patagonia. Captain Bourne's Account of his Captivity. Ingram, Cooke. 1853. *Keene.*
Gil Blas. By Le Sage. Routledge. 1866. *Pinwell.*

Goblin Market. By Christina Rossetti. Macmillan. 1862. *Rossetti.*
The Gold Thread. By Norman Macleod. Strahan. 1861. *J. D. Watson and MacWhirter.*
The Golden Gift. Edinburgh : Nimmo. London : Simpkin. [1868.] *J. Lawson, etc.*
The Golden Harp. By H. W. Dulcken. Routledge. [1864.] *J. D. Watson.*
Golden Thoughts from Golden Fountains. Warne. [1867.] *Pinwell, Houghton, Small, etc.*
Goldsmith (Dalziel's Illustrated). Ward and Lock. 1865. *Pinwell.*
       First published in parts.
A Good Fight. By Charles Reade. Frowde. 1910. *Keene.*
The Good Old Days. By Esmé Stuart. Marcus Ward. 1876. *Stacy Marks.*
Goody Platts and Her Two Cats. By Thomas Miller. Sampson Low. 1864. *Crane.*
The Gordian Knot. By Shirley Brooks. Bentley. 1860. *Tenniel.*
Grandmother's Money. By F. W. Robinson. 'Standard Library.' Hurst and Blackett.
   [1862.] *Tenniel.*
The Graphic Portfolio. Graphic Office. 1876. *Various Artists.*
Grass of Parnassus from the Bents o' Buchan. Peterhead : David Scott. 1887. *Keene.*
The Grave. By Blair. A. and C. Black. 1858. *Tenniel, etc.*
Great Expectations. By Charles Dickens. 'Library Edition', vol. xxiv. Chapman and Hall.
   1863. *Marcus Stone.*
The Green Above the Red. By C. L. Graves. Swan, Sonnenschein. 1889. *Sambourne.*
Green's Nursery Annual. Darton and Clark. 1847. *Keene.*
The Grey Woman. By Mrs. Gaskell. Smith, Elder. 1865. *Du Maurier.*
The Greyt Eggshibishun. Manchester : John Heywood. n.d. *Shields.*
Grimm's Household Stories. By Lucy Crane. Macmillan. 1882. *Crane.*
Gulliver's Travels. By Swift. Cassell, Petter and Galpin. [1865.] *Morten.*
       First published in parts.
Gutta Percha Willie. By George MacDonald. King. 1873. *Arthur Hughes.*

Hacco the Dwarf. By H. Lushington. Griffith and Farren. 1865. *Pinwell.*
Half-Hours with Our Sacred Poets. By A. H. Grant. Hogg. [1863.] *Stacy Marks.*
The Happy Home. By H. Lushington. Griffith and Farren. 1864. *Pinwell.*
Happy Thoughts. By F. C. Burnand. 'Illustrated Collected Edition.' Bradbury, Agnew.
   [1890.] *Sambourne.*
Hard Times. By Charles Dickens. Chapman and Hall. 1862. Published with Barnaby
   Rudge. *Walker.*
Hard Times and Pictures from Italy. By Charles Dickens. Chapman and Hall. 1866.
   Houghton.
He Knew He was Right. By Anthony Trollope. Strahan. 1869. 2 vols. *Marcus Stone.*
       First published in parts.
Heber's Hymns. Sampson Low. 1867. *Small, etc.*
History of the Plague of London. By Defoe. 'Lawrie's Shilling Entertainment Library.'
   John Marshall and Co., Simpkin and Co., Hamilton, Adams and Co., H. S. King and Co.
   [1863.] *Shields.*
Home Affections. Routledge. 1858. *Millais, Tenniel, Weir, etc.*
Home Sunshine. By C. D. Bell. Warne. 1866. *Small.*
Home Thoughts and Home Scenes. Routledge. 1865. *Houghton.*
The Hunting of the Snark. By Lewis Carroll. Macmillan. 1876. *Henry Holiday.*
Hurlock Chase. By G. E. Sargent. Religious Tract Society. [1876.] *Du Maurier.*
Hymn on Christ's Nativity. By Milton. Warne. [1867.] *Albert Moore, Small.*
Hymns in Prose. By Mrs. Barbauld. Murray. 1864. *Barnes, etc.*

Idyllic Pictures. Cassell, Petter and Galpin. 1867. *Various Artists.*

Illustrated Book of Sacred Poems. Edited by R. H. Baynes. Cassell, Petter and Galpin. [1867.] *Edwards, Small, Watson, etc.*
    First published in parts.
Illustrated British Ballads. Cassell. 1881. 2 vols. *Small, etc.*
Imprisoned in a Spanish Convent. By E. C. Grenville-Murray. Vizetelly. 1886. *Keene.*
In Prison and Out. By Hesba Stretton. Isbister. 1880. *R. Barnes.*
Jean Ingelow's Poems. Longmans. 1867. *Pinwell, Houghton, North, etc.*
The Ingoldsby Legends. Bentley. 1864. *Tenniel, Leech, etc.*
The Ingoldsby Legends. Bentley. 1866. 2 vols. *Tenniel, du Maurier, Leech, Walker, etc.*
It is Never too Late to Mend. By Charles Reade. Bradbury, Evans. 1868. *Pinwell.*

Jack and Jill. By Greville MacDonald. Dent. 1913. *Arthur Hughes.*
Jack Buntline. By W. H. Kingston. Sampson Low. 1861. *Keene.*
Jack the Conqueror. By C. E. Bowen. Partridge. [1868.] *R. Barnes.*
The Jest Book. By Mark Lemon. 'Golden Treasury Series.' Macmillan. 1864. *Keene.*
Jingles and Jokes for Little Folks. By Tom Hood. Cassell, Petter and Galpin. [1865.] *Paul Gray, Morten, etc.*
John Halifax, Gentleman. By Miss Muloch. 'Standard Library.' Hurst and Blackett. n.d. *Millais.*
Juvenile Verse and Picture Book. Burns. 1848. *Tenniel, etc.*

Charles Keene (The Work of). By Joseph Pennell. T. Fisher Unwin. Bradbury, Agnew. 1897.
Charles Keene (Life and Letters of). By George Somes Layard. Sampson Low. 1892.
Kenneth and Hugh. By C. D. Bell. Warne. 1866. *Paul Gray.*
King Gab's Story Bag. By Heraclitus Grey. Cassell, Petter and Galpin. [1869.] *Crane.*
King James' Wedding. By J. Sands. Arbroath : T. Buncle. 1888. *Keene.*
Krilof and His Fables. By W. R. S. Ralston. Strahan. 1869. *Houghton.*

Labour Stands on Golden Feet. By Heinrich Zschokke. Cassell, Petter and Galpin. [1870.] *Crane.*
The Laird's Return. By Geraldine Stewart. Hogg. 1861. *Morten.*
Lalla Rookh. By Thomas Moore. Longman. 1861. *Tenniel.*
The Last Chronicle of Barset. By Anthony Trollope. Smith, Elder. 1867. 2 vols. *George Thomas.*
    First published in parts.
Lays of the Holy Land. Nisbet. [1858.] *T. Dalziel, Millais, etc.*
Lays of the Scottish Cavaliers. By W. E. Aytoun. Blackwood. 1863. *Noel Paton.*
A Legend of Camelot. By George du Maurier. Bradbury, Agnew. 1898.
Historical and Legendary Ballads. By Walter Thornbury. Chatto and Windus. 1876. *Various Artists.*
Legendary Ballads of England and Scotland. Edited by J. S. Roberts. Warne. 1868. *Crane, etc.*
Legends and Lyrics. By Adelaide Anne Proctor. Bell and Daldy. 1866. *Keene, du Maurier, Morten, etc.*
Legends of Number Nip. By Mark Lemon. Macmillan. 1864. *Keene.*
Leslie's Musical Annual. Cassell. 1870. *Pinwell, etc.*
Leslie's Songs for Little Folk. Cramer and Co. n.d. *Millais.*
Life and Lessons of Our Lord Unfolded. By John Cumming. J. F. Shaw. 1864. *Charles Green.*

Lilliput Levée. By Matthew Browne. Strahan. 1864. *Pinwell, Millais.*
Little Dorrit. By Charles Dickens. 'Household Edition.' Chapman and Hall. (Published in parts from 1871 on.) *Mahoney.*
Little Lays for Little Folk. Selected by J. G. Watts. Routledge. 1867. *Small, etc.*
Little Songs for Me to Sing. Cassell, Petter and Galpin. [1865.] *Millais.*
Little Wonder-Horn. By Jean Ingelow. King. 1872. *Mahoney, etc.*
Lizzie Leigh. By Mrs. Gaskell. Smith, Elder. 1865. *Du Maurier.*
Longfellow's Poems. Routledge. 1856. *John Gilbert.*
Longfellow's Poems. 'Chandos Poets.' Warne. n.d. 1879-1880 ? *Houghton, etc.*
    I am quite uncertain of the date. See note to Houghton.
The Lord's Prayer. By F. R. Pickersgill and Dean Alford. Longmans. 1870.
Lorna Doone. By R. D. Blackmore. Sampson Low. 1883. *Small.*
Lucille. By Owen Meredith. Chapman and Hall. 1868. *Du Maurier.*
Luke Ashleigh. By Alfred Elwes. Griffith and Farren. 1864. *Du Maurier.*
Lyra Germanica. Longman. 1861. *Keene, Lawless, etc.*
Lyra Germanica. Longmans. 1868. *Ford Madox Brown, etc.*

The Magic Crook. By Greville MacDonald. Fifield. 1911. *Arthur Hughes.*
The Magic of Kindness. By Mayhew Brothers. Cassell. [1869.] *Crane.*
The Magic Valley. By F. Keary. Macmillan. 1877. *E.V.B.*
Marie Louise. By Emilie Carlen. Ingram, Cooke. 1853. *Keene.*
Marion's Sundays. Nelson. 1864. *Small.*
The May Queen. By Tennyson. Sampson Low. 1861. *E.V.B.*
The Maze of Life. Routledge. 1861. *J. D. Watson.*
The Medwins of Wykeham. By C. Lankester. Routledge. 1867. *Paul Gray.*
Men's Wives. By W. M. Thackeray. Smith, Elder. 1879. *Luke Fildes.*
Military Men I Have Met. By E. D. Fenton. Tinsley. 1872. *Sambourne.*
Millais's Illustrations. Strahan. 1866.
Miracles of Heavenly Love. By A. L. O. E. Nelson. 1864. *Small.*
The Mirage of Life. Religious Tract Society. [1867.] *Tenniel.*
Les Miserables. By Victor Hugo. 'Standard Library.' Hurst and Blackett. [1864.] *Millais.*
Miss Mackenzie. By Anthony Trollope. Chapman and Hall. 1866. *Crane.*
Misunderstood. By Florence Montgomery. Bentley. 1874. *Du Maurier.*
Modern Arabian Nights. By Arthur A'Beckett and Linley Sambourne. Bradbury, Agnew. [1877.] *Sambourne.*
Mokeanna ! By F. C. Burnand. Bradbury, Agnew. 1873. *Millais and Du Maurier.*
James Montgomery's Poems. Routledge. 1860. *Foster, Gilbert, etc.*
The Months: Illustrated by Pen and Pencil. Religious Tract Society. [1864.] *Barnes, North, etc.*
The Moonstone. By Wilkie Collins. Chatto and Windus. 1875. *Du Maurier and F. A. Fraser.*
Mr. Punch's Model Music-Hall Songs and Dramas. By F. Anstey. Bradbury, Agnew. 1892. *Sambourne.*
Mrs. Caudle's Curtain Lectures. By Douglas Jerrold. Bradbury, Evans. 1866. *Keene.*
The Music Master. By William Allingham. Routledge. 1855. *Rossetti, Hughes, Millais.*
My Beautiful Lady. By Thomas Woolner. Macmillan. 1863. *Arthur Hughes.*
The Mystery of Edwin Drood. By Charles Dickens. Chapman and Hall. 1870. *Luke Fildes.*
    First published in parts.

A Narrative of the Indian Revolt. By Sir Colin Campbell. Vickers. 1858. *Keene.*
    Issued in 37 parts.
National Nursery Rhymes. Novello, Ewer. [1870.] *Pinwell, Houghton, Hughes, etc.*
The New Child's Play. By E.V.B. Sampson Low. 1877.
The New Forest. By J. R. Wise. Smith, Elder. 1863. *Crane.*
New History of Sandford and Merton. By F. C. Burnand. Bradbury, Evans. 1872. *Sambourne.*
The New Magdalen. By Wilkie Collins. Chatto and Windus. 1875. *Du Maurier and C. S. Reinhardt.*
No Church. By F. W. Robinson. 'Standard Library.' Hurst and Blackett. [1862.] *Tenniel.*
No Name. By Wilkie Collins. Sampson Low. 1863. *Millais.*
Nobility of Life. By R. Valentine. Warne. 1869. *Houghton, Poynter, etc.*
A Noble Life. By Miss Muloch. 'Standard Library.' Hurst and Blackett. [1869.] *Tenniel.*
North Coast and Other Poems. By Robert Buchanan. Routledge. 1868. *Pinwell, Houghton, Small, etc.*
Nothing New. By Miss Muloch. 'Standard Library.' Hurst and Blackett. [1861.] *Millais.*

The Old Curiosity Shop. By Charles Dickens. 'Household Edition.' Chapman and Hall. (Published in parts from 1871 on). *Charles Green.*
Old Friends and New Friends. By H. W. Dulcken. Warne. [1867.] *Houghton, Watson, etc.*
Oliver Twist. By Charles Dickens. 'Household Edition.' Chapman and Hall. (Published in parts from 1871 on.) *J. Mahoney.*
Original Poems. Routledge. 1868. *J. Lawson, etc.*
Orley Farm. By Anthony Trollope. Chapman and Hall. 1862. 2 vols. *Millais.*
    First published in parts.
Our Autumn Holiday on French Rivers. By J. L. Molloy. Bradbury, Agnew. 1874. *Sambourne.*
Our Holiday in the Scottish Highlands. By Arthur A'Beckett. Bradbury, Agnew. 1876. *Sambourne.*
Our Life Illustrated by Pen and Pencil. Religious Tract Society. [1865.] *Pinwell, North, du Maurier, Barnes, etc.*
Our Mutual Friend. By Charles Dickens. Chapman and Hall. 1865. 2 vols. *Marcus Stone.*
    First published in parts.
Our Mutual Friend. By Charles Dickens. 'Household Edition.' Chapman and Hall. (Published in parts from 1871 on.) *J. Mahoney.*
Our People. By Charles Keene. Bradbury, Agnew. 1881.
Our Untitled Nobility. By J. Tillotson. Hogg. 1863. *Charles Green.*

Papers for Thoughtful Girls. By Sarah Tytler. Strahan. 1862. *Millais.*
    This is the third edition, but the first in which Millais's illustrations appear.
Parables and Tales. By T. Gordon Hake. Chapman and Hall. 1872. *Arthur Hughes.*
Parables from Nature. By Mrs. Gatty. Bell and Daldy. 1861. *Holman Hunt, etc.*
Parables from Nature. By Mrs. Gatty. Bell and Daldy. 1867. *Keene, Burne-Jones, etc.*
Parables of Our Lord. By J. E. Millais. Routledge. 1864.
Passages from Modern English Poets, illustrated by the Junior Etching Club. Day and Son [1862.] *Keene, Lawless, Millais, Whistler, etc.*

Passages from the Poems of Thomas Hood, illustrated by the Junior Etching Club. Gambart. 1858. *Keene, Millais, etc.*

Patient Henry. Warne. 1865. *Houghton.*

Patricia Kemball. By E. Lynn Linton. Chatto and Windus. 1875. *Du Maurier.*

Paul Duncan's Little by Little. Edited by Frank Freeman. Sampson Low. 1862. *Keene.*

Peg Woffington. By Charles Reade. Bradbury, Evans. 1868. *Luke Fildes.*

Pegasus Re-saddled. H. C. Pennell. King. 1877. *Du Maurier.*

Pen and Pencil Pictures from the Poets. Edinburgh: Nimmo. London: Simpkin. 1866. *J. Lawson, Small, etc.*

Pen and Pencil Sketches of Faroe and Iceland. By A. J. Symington. Longman. 1862. *Crane.*

The Perils of Greatness. Nimmo. 1865. *Crane.*

Phantastes. By George MacDonald. Fifield. 1905. *Arthur Hughes.*

Phineas Finn. By Anthony Trollope. Virtue. 1869. 2 vols. *Millais.*

Pictorial Bible and Church History Stories. By H. Formby. Longman. [1862.] *Lawless.*

Pictures from English Literature. Cassell, Petter and Galpin. [1870.] *Du Maurier, Green, Fildes, Small, etc.*

Pictures of English Landscape. By Birket Foster and Tom Taylor. Routledge. 1863.

Pictures of English Landscape. By Birket Foster. (India Proof Edition.) Routledge. 1881.

Pictures of English Life. Sampson Low. 1865. *Barnes and Wimperis.*

Pictures of Society. Sampson Low. 1866. *Various Artists.*

Pilgrim's Progress. By Bunyan. Nisbet. 1857. *George Thomas.*

Pilgrim's Progress. By Bunyan. Routledge. 1861. *J. D. Watson.*

Pilgrim's Progress. By Bunyan. Ward and Lock. [1863.] *T. Dalziel.*

Pilgrim's Progress. By Bunyan. Strahan. 1880. *Fred Barnard, Small, etc.*

Playroom Stories. By G. M. Craik. Griffith and Farren. 1863. *Charles Green.*

Pleasures of Memory. By Rogers. Sampson Low. [1865.] *Watson, Green, etc.*

Poe's Poems. Sampson Low. 1858. *Tenniel, etc.*

Poe's Poems. Edited by A. Lang. Kegan Paul. 1881. *Sambourne.*

Poems and Pictures. Burns. 1846. *Tenniel.*

Poets of the Nineteenth Century. Edited by Willmott. Routledge. 1857. *Millais, Madox Brown, Hughes, etc.*

Poor Miss Finch. By Wilkie Collins. Chatto and Windus. 1875. *Du Maurier and Edward Hughes.*

The Postman's Bag. By John de Liefde. Strahan. 1862. *Pettie.*

Prince Ubbely Bubble. By J. T. Lucas. Hotten. 1870. *Barnes, etc.*

The Princess. By Tennyson. Moxon. 1860. *Maclise.*

Princess Althea. By F. M. Peard. Bell. 1883. *R. Barnes.*

Princess of Silverland. By E. Strivelyne. Macmillan. 1874. *Noel Paton.*

Prometheus, Compositions from Shelley's. By J. Noel Paton. Holloway. 1844.

A Protégée of Jack Hamlin's. By Bret Harte. Chatto and Windus. 1894. *Small.*

Proverbial Philosophy. By Tupper. Hatchard. 1854. *Foster, Gilbert, Pickersgill, etc.*

Prudence. By J. C. Lillie. Sampson Low. 1882. *Du Maurier.*

Puck on Pegasus. By H. C. Pennell. Hotten. 1861. *Tenniel, Leech, etc.*

Punch's Pocket Books. Bradbury, Evans. From 1865 to 1881 inclusive. 17 vols. *Keene, Sambourne, du Maurier.*

     These are all the Pocket Books for which Charles Keene made drawings. In the earlier numbers the etched frontispieces are by Leech.

Quite at Home. By F. C. Burnand. Bradbury, Agnew. 1890. *Sambourne.*

Rachel Ray. By Anthony Trollope. Chapman and Hall. 1864. *Millais.*
Rather at Sea. By F. C. Burnand. Bradbury, Agnew. 1890. *Sambourne.*
Real Adventures of Robinson Crusoe. By F. C. Burnand. Bradbury, Agnew. 1893. *Sambourne.*
Reminiscences of the late Thomas Assheton Smith, Esq. By Sir J. E. Eardley Wilmot. Routledge. 1860. *Walker.*
Reprinted Pieces. By Charles Dickens. Chapman and Hall. 1861. *Walker.*
    Published with The Old Curiosity Shop.
Reproductions of Woodcuts by F. Sandys. Carl Hentschel. n.d.
Rhyme? and Reason? By Lewis Carroll. Macmillan. 1883. *A. B. Frost and Henry Holiday.*
Ridiculous Rhymes. By H. S. Marks. Routledge. [1869.]
Robert. Bradbury, Agnew. [1885.] *Keene.*
Robert. Bradbury, Agnew. [1888.] *Keene.*
Robinson Crusoe. By Defoe. 'Select Library Edition.' Burns. 1847. *Keene.*
Robinson Crusoe. By Defoe. Cassell. 1864. *George Thomas.*
Robinson Crusoe. By Defoe. Routledge. 1864. *J. D. Watson.*
Robinson Crusoe. By Defoe. Edited by J. W. Clark. 'Golden Treasury Series.' Macmillan. 1866. *Millais.*
Romantic Passages in English History. By M. Beverlay. Hogg. 1863. *R. Barnes.*
Roses and Holly. Nimmo. 1867. *J. Lawson, etc.*
Rossetti's Poems. Ellis and Elvey. 1904. 2 vols. *Rossetti.*
Round About the Islands. By Clement Scott. Tinsley. 1874. *Du Maurier.*
A Round of Days. Routledge. 1866. *Houghton, North, Walker, etc.*
Roundabout Papers. By W. M. Thackeray. 'Works, vol. xxii.' Smith, Elder. 1879. *Keene.*
The Royal Umbrella. By A. F. P. Harcourt. Griffith and Farren. 1880. *Sambourne.*
The Runaway. Macmillan. 1872. *J. Lawson.*

The Sacristan's Household. Virtue. 1869. 2 vols. *Marcus Stone.*
The Salamandrine. By Charles Mackay. Ingram, Cooke. 1853. *John Gilbert.*
The Savage Club Papers. Tinsley. 1867. *Houghton, du Maurier, Watson, Gray, etc.*
Scenes and Narratives from the Early History of the United States of America. S.P.C.K. [1862.] *Walker.*
Scrambles amongst the Alps. By Edward Whymper. Murray. 1870. *J. Mahoney.*
Sea Kings and Naval Heroes. By J. C. Edgar. Bell and Daldy. 1861. *Keene.*
Shakespeare's Works. Routledge. (Published in parts from 1856 to 1858.) *John Gilbert.*
The Shaving of Shagpat. By George Meredith. Chapman and Hall. 1865. *Sandys.*
Shipwrecks and Adventures at Sea. S.P.C.K. [1860.] *Walker.*
Sing-Song. By Christina Rossetti. Routledge. 1872. *Arthur Hughes.*
Sketches of Scripture Characters. By A. Thomson. Johnstone, Hunter. [1866.] *Small.*
The Small House at Allington. By Anthony Trollope. Smith, Elder. 1864. 2 vols. *Millais.*
Society Novelettes. Vizetelly. 1883. 2 vols. *Sambourne.*
Some Old Friends. By F. C. Burnand. Bradbury, Agnew. 1892. *Sambourne.*
Songs of Cavaliers and Roundheads. By Walter Thornbury. Hurst and Blackett. 1857. *Stacy Marks.*
Songs of Many Seasons. By Jemmet Browne. Simpkin. 1876. *Du Maurier.*
Songs of the North. Edited by Macleod and Boulton. Field and Tuer. [1885.] *Keene.*
Sooner or Later. By Shirley Brooks. Bradbury, Evans. 1868. 2 vols. *Du Maurier.*

Speaking Likenesses. By Christina Rossetti. Macmillan. 1874. *Arthur Hughes.*
The Spirit of Praise. Warne. [1866.] *Pinwell, Houghton, North, Small, etc.*
Stories from Memel. By Mrs. A. De Haviland. Hunt. [1863.] *Crane.*
Stories of Old : or Bible Narratives. By C. Hadley. Smith, Elder. 1862. 2 series. *Crane.*
Stories of the Olden Time. By M. Jones. Cassell, Petter and Galpin. 1870. *Crane.*
Stories Told to a Child. Strahan. 1865. *Houghton and J. Lawson.*
Story of a Feather. By Douglas Jerrold. Bradbury, Evans. 1867. *Du Maurier.*
Story of Elizabeth. Smith, Elder. 1867. *Walker.*
A Story with a Vengeance. By A. B. Reach and Shirley Brooks. Cooke. [1852.] *Keene, Leech, etc.*
Story Without an End. Sampson Low. 1868. *E.V.B.*
Strange Stories. By Grant Allen. Chatto and Windus. 1884. *Du Maurier.*
Studies for Stories. Strahan. 1866. *Millais, Houghton, Small, etc.*
Studies from Life. By Miss Muloch. 'Standard Library.' Hurst and Blackett. [1862.] *Holman Hunt.*
Sunlight of Song. Novello, Ewer. 1875. *Pinwell, etc.*
Sybil and Her Live Snowball. Seeley. 1866. *R. Barnes.*
Sylvia's Lovers. By Mrs. Gaskell. Smith, Elder. 1863. *Du Maurier.*

Tales of All Countries. By Anthony Trollope. Chapman and Hall. 1864. *Marcus Stone.*
Tales of the White Cockade. By Barbara Hutton. Griffith and Farren. 1870. *J. Lawson.*
Tell Me a Story. By Ennis Graham. Macmillan. 1875. *Crane.*
The Temple Anecdotes. By R. and C. Temple. Groombridge. 1864 and 1865. 2 series. *Houghton.*
The Tempest, Compositions from. By J. Noel Paton. Nimmo. 1877.
Tennyson's Poems. Moxon. 1857. *Rossetti, Millais, Hunt, etc.*
Miss Thackeray's Works. 'Uniform Edition.' Smith, Elder. 1875 on. *Arthur Hughes.*
    The first two volumes appeared in November and December 1875, commencing with 'Old Kensington'.
There Was Once. By Mrs. Wilde. Nister. 1888. *J. Lawson.*
Thoughtful Joe. By Ruth Lamb. Religious Tract Society. [1880.] *R. Barnes.*
The Three Clerks. By Anthony Trollope. Bentley. 1865. *J. Mahoney.*
Through the Looking Glass. By Lewis Carroll. Macmillan. 1871. *Tenniel.*
Tinykin's Transformations. By Mark Lemon. Bradbury, Evans. 1869. *Charles Green.*
Tom Brown's Schooldays. By Thomas Hughes. Macmillan. 1869. *Arthur Hughes.*
Tom Cringle's Log. By Michael Scott. Blackwood. 1861. *Walker.*
Touches of Nature. Strahan. 1867. *Various Artists.*
Tracks for Tourists. By F. C. Burnand. Bradbury, Evans. 1864. *Keene.*
Transformation. By Nathaniel Hawthorne. Smith, Elder. 1865. *Crane.*
The True, Pathetic History of Poor Match. By Holme Lee. Smith, Elder. 1863. *Crane.*
Trystie's Quest. By Greville MacDonald. Fifield. [1913.] *Arthur Hughes.*
The Twins and their Stepmother. Routledge. 1861. *Walker.*
Two Centuries of Song. Edited by Thornbury. Sampson Low. 1867. *Morten, Small, Marks, etc.*

The Uncommercial Traveller. By Charles Dickens. Chapman and Hall. 1868. *Pinwell*
The Uncommercial Traveller. By Charles Dickens. 'Household Edition.' Chapman and Hall. (Published in parts from 1871 on.) *E. G. Dalziel.*
Undine. By Fouqué. Burns. 1846. *Tenniel.*

The Valley of a Hundred Fires. 'Standard Library.' Hurst and Blackett. [1861.] *Millais*.

Venice, from Lord Byron's Childe Harold. By Linley Sambourne. Bradbury, Agnew. 1878. *Sambourne*.

Very Much Abroad. By F. C. Burnand. Bradbury, Agnew. 1890. *Sambourne*.

The Vicar of Wakefield. By Goldsmith. Sampson Low. 1857. *George Thomas*.

Victorian History of England. By A. B. Thompson. Routledge. 1865. *Houghton*.

Voyage of the Constance. By Mary Gillies. Sampson Low. 1860. *Keene*.

Wace, ses œuvres, sa patrie. Par John Sullivan of Jersey. Second edition. *Millais*.
> For particulars of this book see the chapter on Millais.

Waifs and Strays. By E.V.B. Cundall. 1856.
> This is the second edition—the earliest in the British Museum. 1856 is also the earliest date given in The English Catalogue of Books.

Wait for the End. By Mark Lemon. Bradbury, Evans. 1866. *Crane*.

The Washerwoman's Foundling. By William Gilbert. Strahan. 1867. *Small*.

Water Babies. By Charles Kingsley. Macmillan. 1863. *Noel Paton*.

Water Babies. By Charles Kingsley. Macmillan. 1885. *Sambourne*.

The Way We Live Now. By Anthony Trollope. Chapman and Hall. 1875. 2 vols. *Luke Fildes*.
> First published in parts.

Wayside Posies. Routledge. 1867. *Pinwell, North, Walker*.

What Men Have Said about Women. Edited by Henry Southgate. Routledge. 1865. *J. D. Watson*.

The White Slave. By R. Hildreth. Ingram, Cooke. 1852. *Keene*.

Wild-Cat Tower. By G. C. Davies. Warne. 1877. *J. D. Watson*.

Wives and Daughters. By Mrs. Gaskell. Smith, Elder. 1866. 2 vols. *Du Maurier*.

Wives and Daughters. By Mrs. Gaskell. Smith, Elder. 1867. *Du Maurier*.

Woman's Strategy. New York: Carleton and Co. London: Hogg. 1867. *Morten*.

The Wooden Walls of Old England. By Margaret Fraser Tytler. Hatchard. 1847. *Keene*.

The Word: the Star out of Jacob. Nisbet. 1868. *J. D. Watson*.

Words for the Wise. By T. S. Arthur. Nelson. 1864. *Small*.

Wordsworth's Poems. Nimmo. 1865. *Small, etc.*

Wordsworth's Poems for the Young. Strahan. 1863. *Pettie and MacWhirter*.

The World Well Lost. By E. Lynn Linton. Chatto and Windus. 1877. 2 vols. *J. Lawson*.

INDEX

Abbey, E. A., 23.
Accidents of Childhood, 169.
Adèle, 22.
Adventures of Alfan, 170.
Aesop's Fables, 6, 27.
After Dark, 195, 233.
Alfred Haggart's Household, 257.
Alice's Adventures in Wonderland, 6, 8, 23, 28, 29.
Allingham, William, 30, 31, 32, 33.
American Notes and Pictures from Italy, 265.
Ancient Mariner, The, 254.
Andersen's Danish Fairy Legends, 253.
Anglers of the Dove, The, 80.
Annals of a Quiet Neighbourhood, 222, 257.
Anne Hereford, 232.
Anne Judge, Spinster, 258.
Anstey, F., 245.
Arabian Nights, Dalziel's, 8, 28, 76, 161, 170, 195, 215, 251, 253.
Arabian Nights, Warne's, 196, 251.
Argosy, The, 8.
  Crane, 232.
  Houghton, 191.
  Lawson, J., 228.
  Mahoney, 256.
  Pinwell, 158.
  Sandys, 60.
  Small, 218.
Armadale, 248.
Armitage, E., 49.
Armstead, H. H., *104–107*.
L'Art,
  Du Maurier, 180, 183.
Art Pictures from the Old Testament, 49, 104, 252.
Artist's Son, The, 180.
As in a Looking Glass, 186.
' Aspen, The ', Watson's drawing of, 167.
At His Gates, 256.
At the Back of the North Wind, 23, 88, 89.

Atkinson, J. W., 185.
Atonement of Leam Dundas, The, 269.
Aunt Judy,
  Morten, 212.
Aunt Mavor's Alphabet, 171.
Aurora Leigh, 45.
Avonhoe, 266.
Awdries, The, 180.

Babies' Classics, 95.
Balderscourt, 196.
Ballad Stories of the Affections, 162, 170, 196, 224, 231, 251, 253.
Ballads, Thackeray's, 186.
Ballads and Songs of Brittany, 131.
Ballads, Scottish and English, 231.
Balston, T., 8.
Band of Hope Review,
  Barnes, 257.
  Watson, 168.
  Weir, 247.
Barbara's History, 170.
Barford Bridge, 191.
Barnard, Fred, 227.
Barnes, R., *256–258*.
Barry Lyndon, 79.
Bate, Percy, 56.
Beardsley, Aubrey, 39, 215.
Beauties of English Landscape, 24.
Beauty and the Beast, 253.
Be-Be, the Nailmaker's Daughter, 223.
Beeton's Annual,
  Morten, 212.
Belgravia,
  Caldecott, 269.
  Edwards, 261.
  Hopkins, 269.
  Morten, 212.
Bell, Malcolm, 33.
Ben's Boyhood, 258.
Bennett, C. H., 14, 247.